SPIRAL GUIDE

MUNICH

AA Publishing

Contents

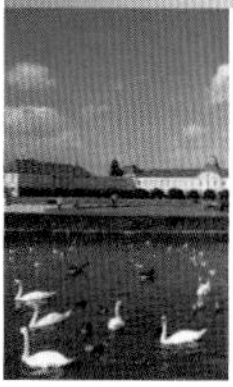

Written by Daniela Schetar and Friedrich Köthe
Copy edited by Katrin Wampula
Picture research by Gabriele Forst
Page layout by Cyclus – Visuelle Kommunikation
English version produced by Silva Editions Ltd
Translated by Sylvia Goulding
Copy edited by Marilynne Lanng and Jacquelne Fortey

ISBN-10: 0 7495 4539 9
ISBN-13: 978 0 7495 4539 0

Published by AA Publishing, a trading name of Automobile Association Developments Limited, whose registered office is Southwood East, Apollo Rise, Farnborough, Hampshire, GU14 0JW. Registered number 1878835.

Printed and bound in China by Leo Paper Products

A02225

the magazine

The Glyptothek sculpture museum at Konigsplatz

A typical resident of Munich, or *Munchner*, it is said, attaches a high value to honesty, but has a sneaking admiration for the lovable rogue. Certainly there is something of a "Let's wait and see" approach to life in this city, where traditional Bavarian values mix with cosmopolitan culture.

Munich

The city of Munich certainly has a lifestyle that is uniquely its own. Beer is only one of the many treats in store when you visit the Bavarian regional capital, with its splendid onion-dome skyline. Second only to Berlin in popularity as a tourist destination in Germany, this "village of millions" combines urban sophistication with provincial charm, artistic flair with common sense, high-tech industry with beer gardens and green spaces. Its high profile in the realm of sport has been assured by the stellar career of soccer legend "Kaiser" Franz Beckenbauer, who twice took West Germany to World Cup victory. The hallmarks of The Kaiser's style of play were elegance, determination and tactical skill. Munich is a city that respects these qualities and is known for its relaxed approach to life.

Page 5: Stachus and the towers of Frauenkirche

People-watching at the Café Munchner Freiheit.

Cultural Chic

Culturally, Munich looks to southern Europe. Italian-style cafés and restaurants abound and women, in particular, tend to use *tschau*, a Bavarian version of *ciao*.

Fabled *foehn*: the Alps look close enough to touch.

Lenbachhaus: Tuscany on the Isar River

Lifestyle

rather than *servus*, the standard greeting. This is accompanied by a kiss, or *bussi*, on both cheeks – the Munich in-crowd is described as a *bussi* society. Cool weather does nothing to diminish the pull of the café. The minute the first ray of sun filters through the clouds, the citizens of Munich wrap up warmly and sit outside to sip a *latte macchiato*, as if they were in a street café in Verona or Florence. The city's ultimate chic set, the *schickeria* or *schickimickis*, congregate in the clubs and cafés of the fashionable Schwabing district, around the University.

Italian Influence

There is nothing new about Munich's love affair with the South, and specifically with Italy. King Ludwig I of Bavaria, who ruled from 1825–48, set out to turn the town into a German version of Florence. His architect, Leo von Klenze, was allowed to give free reign to his passion for the Italian Renaissance in the Residenz (➤ 76) and the Alte Pinakothek gallery, along the Ludwigstrasse (➤ 110). This trend continued throughout the 19th century in the work of private builders, such as the painter Franz von Lenbach, who built himself a rustic Italianate villa on the Isar River. Lenbachhaus, as it is called, now houses the city art gallery. Behind it is another neo-classical building – the Propyläen – built by Gabriel von Seidl in 1887–91. By the end of the 19th century, art historian Heinrich Wölfflin was moved to describe

The Green Gallery in the Residenz

Lakes for bathing and mountains for skiing are just outside Munich

Munich as "the foremost Italian town in Germany". And in summer, it is the most northerly place in which to experience *la dolce vita*.

Southern Lights

A warm southerly wind – the *foehn* – blowing from the Alps, brings a special quality to the Munich sky. The air becomes crystal clear and the heavens turn a glorious blue, bathing the city in shimmering light. The down side to this particular weather pattern is *granteln* – a certain irritability which overcomes residents and visitors alike. If people seem to be rather gruff, don't take it too seriously: just blame it on the *foehn*. You can always escape to the extensive Englischer Garten (English Garden) (➤ 107), a vast park stretching north of Prinzregentstrasse, or visit the animals at Hellabrunn Zoo (➤ 10), or go on a cycle tour of the city.

The Outdoor Life

Southward too are the lakes and mountains, with facilities for recreation and leisure that are among the best in

Germany. It is less than 20 minutes by car from the city centre to one of the fabulous lakes around Munich, Starnberger See (➤ 60) – an extensive lake with much to offer sailors, surfers and swimmers, as well as walkers and cyclists. For the less active, there are steamship rides and attractive lakeside towns to explore, using the S-Bahn train, if you do not have a car.

In less than an hour, you can drive from Munich to the nearest ski slopes at Hausberg Brauneck (1,556m/5,105 feet) and some beautiful walking areas around Tegernsee. Busy times are best avoided, because at weekends everyone has the same idea and southbound motorways can get heavily congested. However, if you plan ahead, you can make full use of these leisure facilities within spitting distance of the vibrant city.

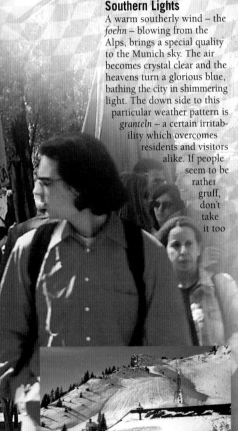

Highlights at a Glance

Long Nights

The city's seasonal calendar offers a series of lively late-opening events, so it's worth checking the dates when planning your trip (www.muenchen.de). During the *Lange Nacht der Museen* – the Long Night of Museums – in mid-October, museums and galleries stay open till 2 am, offering a wide range of entertainments. Shuttle buses are provided to take you from one event to another. A combined bus and admission ticket costs 15 euros. There's a Long Night of Music in mid-May, with music and dance in pubs, concert halls, even the opera, and tram and bus transport to ferry you to and from events. Other "Long Nights" include those of the media and books.

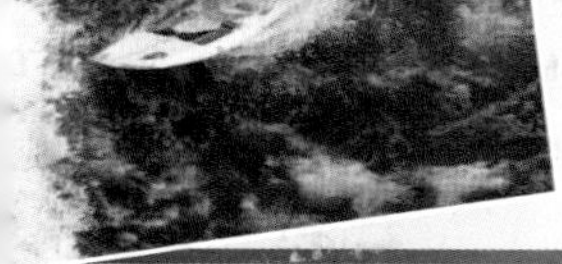

River Surfing

Believe it or not, there's surf to be had on the Eisbach River: a big wave is created by a man-made break in a tributary of the Isar. The most popular (and dangerous) surfing spot is by the Eisbach Bridge next to the Haus der Kunst, but beginners can try Flosslände farther up river. A crowd of onlookers regularly gathers to watch the intrepid surfers and canoeists who decide to brave the icy waters.

Munich on Ice

Before Christmas each year, an ice rink is set up, at either Marienhof or Stachus. What could be more enchanting than skating here at night to the sound of seasonal tunes, lit by the glow of electric candles? And of course there's hot mulled wine on hand to warm you from top to toe!

A Bird's-Eye View

To experience a ride on a paternoster lift, go to the Altes Technisches Rathaus (Old Technical Town Hall) Blumenstrasse 28b, and take the lift, which moves continuously. From the 10th floor of this 1929 skyscraper, a flight of stairs leads you up to a platform, at 40m (131 feet) height, which gives fabulous panoramic views over the city (Mon–Fri 9 am–5 pm).

The Flaucher Grill

For swimming and sunbathing on warm summer days, pick up a picnic and make your way to Flauchersteg – a popular local beauty spot on the gravel-bank beach of the Isar River (U-Bahn U3 Thalkirchen). As evening draws in, light a barbecue, spread out your rug, chill your beer in the river and get out the guitar. There'll be plenty of company, background music and dancing to add to the holiday atmosphere.

Munich Zoo

The Hellabrunn Zoo is an all-year-round attraction, with plenty to offer every age group. It prides itself on its natural habitats and endangered-species breeding programmes. Not to be missed are the new predator house, the large aviary with black storks and little egrets that fly freely around visitors, and the nurseries of gorillas and orang-utans in the ape house. Inside Villa Dracula you can watch light-sensitive bats in the glow of infrared lamps. A winter treat is the penguins' parade, while in summer a resident "dove whisperer" presents displays with stunt-flying doves. For up-to-date information see the zoo's home page. (Tierparkstrasse 30, tel: 089/62 50 80, Apr–Sep 8 am–6 pm, rest of year 9 am–5 pm; U-Bahn Thalkirchen; admission: expensive, www.zoo-muenchen.de).

THE BEER GARDEN

In 1539, the brewing of beer was forbidden between May and October, because it posed too much of a fire risk in the summer. This ban was to have a lasting influence on the quality of life and urban landscape of Munich.

Since much more beer is consumed in summer than in winter, the breweries had to start producing beer in advance and storing it in chilled rooms. Underground "beer cellars" were built to keep the beers chilled, and chestnut trees were planted on top. The brewery owners then had the excellent idea of selling their beer directly to the consumer, and they placed benches and tables under the trees. Thus, the beer garden was born. This caused a storm of protests from Munich pub landlords, who feared the competition. King Ludwig I eventually legalized beer gardens and, by around 1830, drinks, but no food, could be served in a beer garden. While the food ban has long since

"Brotzeit"

Brotzeit – literally time for bread – is the typical Munich snack or light supper. Essential ingredients are: a white radish, sausage salad, Swiss cheese, *leberkäse* (meat loaf), butter, and large pretzels, served in a basket and often set on a checked tablecloth. All washed down with a beer from the beer garden.

Weight-lifting Munich style

A beer beside the lake

Deer come up close to the tables in Hirschgarten

The local beer beer is enjoyed by all ages in Englischer Garten

disappeared, every genuine beer garden still has an area where customers are allowed to eat the food they have brought along, and many make use of the privilege. Some bring fine foods spread on tables lit with candlebras while other set out a simple picnic.

A Matter of Choice

Munich has more than 80 beer gardens, so there's something for every taste. Families with children like the Hirschgarten (► 157); which is next to a playing field and an enclosure where deer can be fed and stroked.

Students hang out at Chinesischer Turm (► 114) and more mature customers and visitors meet at the legendary Hofbräuhaus (► 85) beer garden. Some beer gardens follow fashion trends and you can find Prosecco and Thai food at the Mangostin (Maria-Einsiedl-Strasse 2, U-Bahn: Thalkirchen), and, unusually, you carry on drinking at the beer garden of the music pub Backstage (► 158). At any truly traditional beer garden, guests sit at wooden tables; the menu features *hendl* (roast chicken), *schweinsbrodn* (roast pork) and *steckerlfisch* (grilled fish); the beer is a local Munich brew; and at midnight, at the latest, or at 11 pm in

The Fifth Season

Although Lent is a period of fasting, the Paulaner monks of Munich were given special dispensation to brew a fortifying beer. A week-long celebration of this beer begins two weeks after Ash Wednesday. As the first barrel of Salvator is tapped at the Paulaner am Nockherberg (► 135), famous politicians come to be "derbleck'n" (made fun of).

The world's largest and most famous festival is not the only record-breaking event in Munich's entertainment calendar. Find out with a visit to Europe's longest party mile!

Oktoberfest and clubbing

The state of emergency, better known as Oktoberfest, begins in Munich in mid-September: on the Saturday next to the last weekend in September, to be precise. It lasts for a fortnight and is commonly referred to as "Wies'n" (meadows) by the locals. The collective booze-up begins with a ritual tapping of the first beer barrel by Munich's mayor. His cry "O'zapft is" (it's been tapped) is the official signal for the beer to be served. In the crammed Wies'n tents, hundreds of thousands of visitors are anticipating this moment, a moment for which Napoleon is indirectly to blame. The story of Oktoberfest begins with Ludwig, Crown Prince of Bavaria, who feared that Napoleon would force him into an arranged marriage. To pre-empt this, on 12 October 1810, he married Princess Therese von Sachsen-Hildburg-hausen. A week later a horse race was held to cele-brate the royal

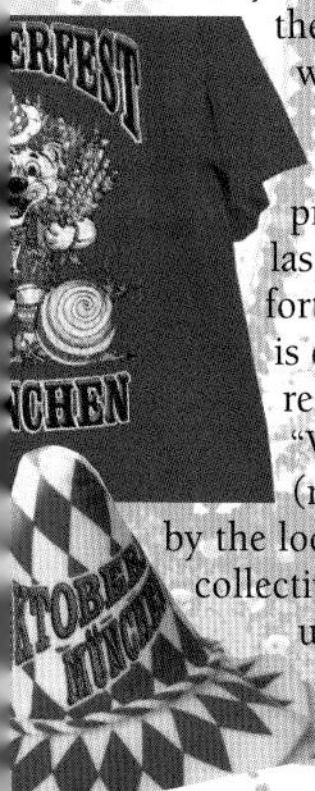

Wies'n-Kult

Let's go to Schichtl's: variety show and mock execution of a spectator
Flea Circus: probably the smallest performers at the Oktoberfest
Crinoline: merry-go-round with brass music
Toboggan: giant wooden slide – best experienced after a beer or three
Devil's Wheel: the person who stays on longest wins

The fun of the fair at Oktoberfest

Oktoberfest and clubbing

Oktoberfest Parades

For a snapshot of Bavarian customs, look out for the opening parades. Splendidly decorated dray horses pull along floats carrying landlord's families and beer waitresses, accompanied by brewery bands. Best costumes: the Oktoberfest Costume and Riflemen's Parade.

wedding, in a meadow on the outskirts of town. The year after, the race was repeated, and eventually the regular event was combined with an agricultural fair. The meadow was named Theresienwiese (Theresa's fields), after the Princess. In 1869, the Schichtl Family added a colourful dimension to the fair by opening their Theatre of Illusions. A visit to Schichtl's and the "execution on the open stage" are among the undisputed highlights of the fairground programme.

Other adrenaline-boosting events are "multiple looping" and "Eurostar". But the heart of the Wies'n beats in the beer tents, where young and old, conservative and liberal, Bavarian and Prussian, Japanese and Italian, fraternize while shouting "Oans, zwoa, gsuffa" (one, two, drink up!), and finally spring up to dance on benches and tables, with a conviviality fuelled by beer.

Showtime at Tollwood

"Tollwood" started life as a theatre freak show in the 1970s and has blossomed into the second most important event in the Munich calendar, after the Oktoberfest. Every year, in December and June, the tents on the Wies'n host a highly original multicultural programme of variety, circus shows and cabaret, over a period of several weeks. In addition, an alternative

Left to right: beer heaven in the tent; a thrilling fairground ride; winter Tollwood on Theresienwiese

funfair sells food from all over the world, didgeridoos and African drums, henna tattoos, batik dresses and incense (www.tollwood.de).

Dumpling Disco

Munich's reputation as the European capital of disco is due to Wolfgang Nöth and his Kunstpark-Ost. Bars, discos and clubs are based in a former dumpling factory. The name and music style changed once a month and eventually the halls of the factory grew into a giant party zone. The Kunstpark, now known as Kultfabrik (► 137), has been earmarked for redevelopment. But, don't be too downcast – Wolfgang Nöth will be opening Kunstpark-Nord next to the new Allianz-Arena (► 17).

Clubbers are wondering whether he'll be able to make the new venue as wonderful as the old dumpling factory, with its huge variety of clubs.

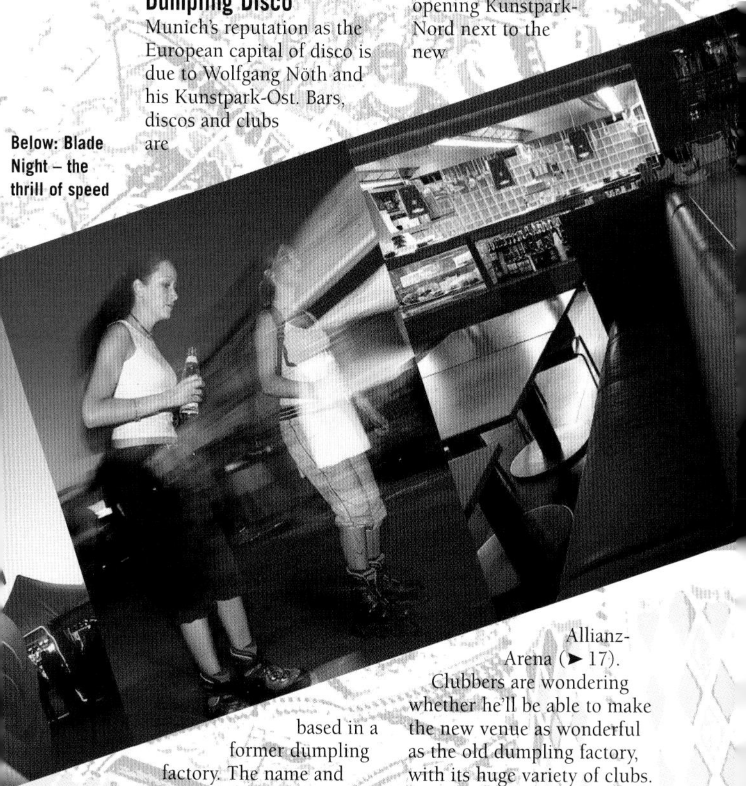

Below: Blade Night – the thrill of speed

Right: parties everywhere

Ultimate Office Party

Techno beat in the office? Cocktails on the desk? Dancing between the filing cabinets? This is yet another aspect of Munich night life. With more office space than is needed, unoccupied municipal buildings can be given over for use by the party people. New clubs spring up here and there, only to close down or move on three months later. You can find out where and when it's all happening today on www.nightlife-muenchen.de.

Blade Nights

There's trouble when the Blade Nights begin: between May and September, every Monday night, thousands of rollerblade, skateboard and inline skaters roll and race through Munich on a number of different routes. Entire roads are closed off for this event, something that necessarily sets the car drivers against the bladers. (Information on starting points and routes is available from www.muenchner-blade-night.de.)

FOOTBALL CRAZY

The football stadium regularly has to change colours in this town. When the two big Munich clubs play a home game, the Allianz-Arena is dressed either in red or in blue, depending on which club is playing inside.

Cabaret star Ottfried Fischer sums up the relationship between Munich's football fans and its two major clubs: "In Munich it doesn't matter so much which club you *do* support as which you *don't*". Some fans will boo the "Lions", Munich's blue club TSV 1860, others will shout down the reds at FC Bayern Munich. Of the two clubs, Bayern has long been the more successful. Unlike the Lions, they have not had to contend with relegation to the Second League. Yet the team boasting "18 national players from nine countries and three continents" has at times been accused of playing a soulless game, while the Lions are said to raise the fans' excitement to fever pitch. Pay a visit to the stadium to see for yourself: the atmosphere seems just as overwhelming during the Bayern games (tickets from www.fcbayern.de).

Red and Blue can rub along together

Football Legends

Franz Beckenbauer, Gerd Müller, Uli Hoeness and Sepp Maier were all part of the legendary line-up when FC Bayern won the World Cup in 1976. All four players have stayed connected with their club. Beckenbauer is now its chairman and Hoeness the manager. Maier trains the future goalkeepers, while Müller works as one of the

The best fan shops in town can be found all around the Hofbräuhaus

FC Bayern during a training session

In the background: the football stadium

No die-hard fan will miss a home game

co-trainers of the Regional League of Amateurs.

A Suitable Stadium

Both football clubs are large commercial enterprises with high-flying ambitions; Bayern is even listed on the stock-market. The new football stadium, which was built in the north of the city for the 2006 Football World Cup, is jointly financed by the council, who will own the grounds, and the clubs, who will fund the building of the stadium. The new Allianz-Arena in Fröttmanning, which will hold 66,000 spectators, is a futuristic showpiece, popularly known as the "life-belt" or the "rubber dinghy". The design, by Swiss architects' firm of Herzog/de Meuronin, features a smooth transparent shell made up of hundreds of inflatable cushions acting as a projection surface to cover the stadium in waves of colours. It's convenient for the two clubs: there is a choice of red or blue!

The Kaiser

Bayern star, national player, trainer of the national team, President of Bayern and Vice President of the German Football Association – this was a rapid rise for a boy from a simple background: Franz Beckenbauer was born in 1945 in München-Giesing; in 1964 he had his first season with FC Bayern, then the weaker of the two Munich clubs. The elegance of his game, his tactical superiority and the "football duet" he performed with forward Gerd Müller, helped to earn him the nickname "The Kaiser" (the emperor). Beckenbauer twice became world champion (in 1974 as a player and in 1990 as trainer), took part in 103 internationals between 1965 and 1977 and won numerous cups together with the Bavarians.

Biennale and SpielArt

Two of Europe's most important cultural festivals take place in Munich on alternate years. The Musik-Biennale, which premieres contemporary music, in years with an even number (www.muenchenerbiennale.de), and, in years with odd numbers SpielArt, a theatre festival featuring exciting guest performances and new international productions (www.spielart.org).

Stages past and present

With world-renowned directors, first-class music theatre and avant-garde eccentrics – Munich boasts a cultural scene that is among the best in Europe.

Ballet and drama

There is a lively theatre scene in Munich, with a large number of independent theatre companies. The two largest are the Staatsschauspiel and the Kammerspiele, with international reputations, and around which a storm of controversy recently raged. In 2001, the city council decided not to renew their contract with Dieter Dorn, prize-winning director of the Munich Kammerspiele (➤ 94), after 25 years. It was time, they felt, for a change of direction, despite the fact that he had given the theatre an exceptionally high profile, and remains a favourite with Munich theatre-goers. A compromise was eventually reached whereby Dorn was re-employed by the Bavarian provincial state government to run the Bayerisches Staatsschauspiel. His replacement at the Kammerspiele, Frank Baumbauer is committed to new and challenging experimental works, rather than classical high culture. He has had an uphill struggle to establish a new audience for the theatre. A task made harder by the fact that Dorn's original team are just across the road, on the other side of Maximilianstrasse.

Tradition and Innovation

August Everding (1928–99), another traditionalist, has left his mark on the State Opera House, the Bayerische Staatsoper (➤ 94). His love of

Colourful Character

"A bit of a character", is how people tend to refer to Alexej Sagerer. For over 30 years he and his avant-garde theatre ProT (www.prot.de) have been providing audiences with challenging experiences. For a recent production, Sagerer placed 14 actors and 7 sheep in a metal cube for 28 hours. Spectators were required to walk and dance around the cube "if you like it!"

Richard Strauss and Richard Wagner determined the programme and was :esponsible for the July Festival. However, the 1umorous, provo-:ative spirit of lirector Sir Peter onas (ex English National Opera) has ,wept through the ıallowed halls nriching the state ›pera's repertoire vith grotesque, narchic productions ›f Händel operas and nodern musicals.

atirical Cabaret

nother venue where he Old and the New lways feature is Münchner Lach- und Schiess-gesellschaft (the Munich Laughing and Shooting Society). Founded in 1956 by Dieter Hildebrandt and Sammy Drechsel, the sharp political satire of this cabaret acts sets politician's nerves jangling and has the audience in stitches. In 1972, the original cast split up, but their successors are equally talented. Dieter Hildebrandt, who has now been awarded many cultural prizes, still makes the occasional guest appear-ance (► 118).

The National-theater beckons

Dieter Hilde-brandt and his Lach- und Schieß-gesell-schaft

DRAMATIC Y

Soviet republic, Hitler putsch, seat of the National Socialists during the unsettled years of the Weimar Republic and the rise of Hitler – Munich has hosted some turbulent events, on the political left and right.

"Politicians will be replaced by Worker's Councils, factories will be nationalized" – on 7 April, 1919, Ernst Toller, Erich Mühsam and others declared the "Soviet Republic of Munich". Just under a month later, on 3 May, the volunteer corps put an end to the experiment. After three days of fighting more than 600 people had died. Many leading figures in the soviet republic were of the Jewish faith, and nationalist parties and politicians increasingly directed their propaganda against the Jews, whom they likened to "bolsheviks" and "anarchists".

The Beer Hall Putsch

Adolf Hitler, who had lived in Munich since 1912, staged his first major bid for power here in 1923. Accompanied by his SA storm troopers, and with the support of Field Marshal Erich von Ludendorff, he occupied the Bürgerbräukeller, the city's largest beer hall (➤ 130), where a political meeting was being held. He declared that both provincial and national governments had been deposed. The next morning Hitler and Ludendorff marched together with thousands of followers to the Feldherrnhalle (➤ 79). But support had ebbed away and the uprising was supressed.

The Munich Agreement

On 29 September, 1938, Great Britain, France, Italy and the German Empire, represented by Hitler, signed

Below, left to right: the National Socialist putsch, 8 and 9 November, 1923; Hitler's "proclamation" 9 November, 1923; Hitler in the Löwenbräukeller in 1941, on the anniversary of the putsch attempt

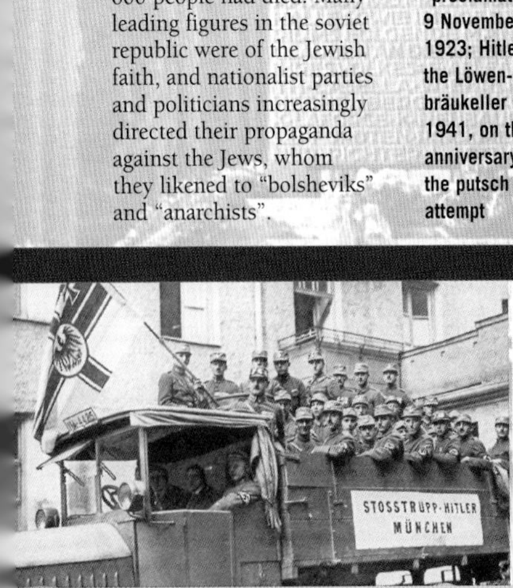

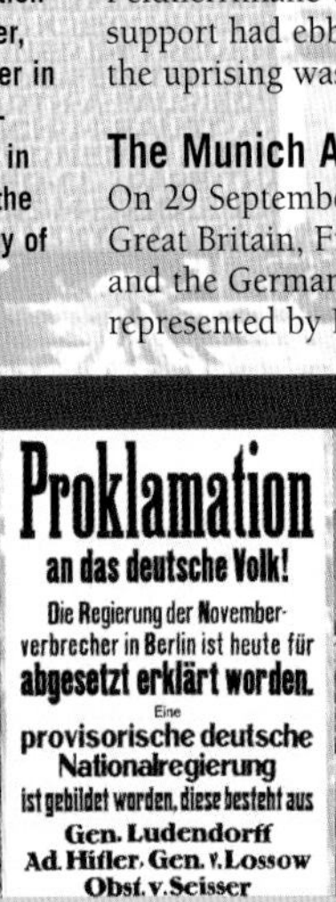

Proklamation
an das deutsche Volk!
Die Regierung der November-verbrecher in Berlin ist heute für
abgesetzt erklärt worden.
Eine
provisorische deutsche Nationalregierung
ist gebildet worden, diese besteht aus
Gen. Ludendorff
Ad. Hitler, Gen. v. Lossow
Obst. v. Seisser

Opposite, left to right: anarchist playwright Erich Mühsam; writer and activist, Ernst Toller; overthrow of the soviet republic on 1 and 2 May, 1919

Forced labour at Dachau Concentration Camp,1943

1945: Dachau Concentration Camp after the liberation

Background left: Feldherrnhalle, a memorial to those who fell in the Hitler putsch

an agreement, which forced Czechoslovakia to cede the Sudetenland to Germany. This was intended to appease Hitler and to ensure peace, but instead it gave him *carte blanche* to invade Czechoslovakia.

Dachau Memorial Site

Dachau, 17km (10½ miles) northwest of Munich, was Germany's first concentration camp, set up in 1933 by Heinrich Himmler. Political opponents of the National Socialist regime were the first to be incarcerated in this former munitions factory – mainly communists, socialists and trade unionists. After Crystal Night in 1938, 10,000 Jews from Munich and its surroundings were deported to Dachau. When war broke out in 1939 these were joined by tens of thousands of Poles, Czechs, Russians and nationals from many other countries. Of a total of 200,000 registered prisoners, only 32,000 were officially recorded as having died. Many more were killed, or died from exhaustion, medical experiments and epidemics. US troops finally liberated the remaining 67,000 prisoners on 29 April, 1945. Survivors campaigned to have a fitting memorial created for those that were lost.

Synagogue and Cultural Centre

In June 1938, Munich's main synagogue, in Herzog-Max-Strasse, was demolished. In November of the same year, during the infamous Kristallnacht (Crystal Night) the last remaining Jewish synagogue (left) was burned down. The foundation stone for a new Jewish Cultural Centre in Jakobsplatz, in front of the Stadtmuseum (➤ 60), was finally laid in 2003. The combined museum, meeting place and synagogue will be a new focus for Jewish life in Munich.

3 2 1 AND

Many a glorious moment for both German and international cinema was captured on celluloid in the Bavaria Film Studios. They were founded in 1919, in Munich's southern suburb of Geiselgasteig.

Bavaria Studios opened for business in 1919. After World War II, when their main rival, the Ufa Studios at Berlin-Babelsberg, disappeared behind the Iron Curtain, they became Germany's largest dream factory. The productions that saw the light of day here, did not originate solely from Germany, Hollywood was there too: in 1952, Elia Kazan filmed *Man on a Tightrope* with Gerd Fröbe. Ten years later, John Sturges brought James Coburn, Charles Bronson and a young Steve McQueen to Munich to film *The Great Escape*. Finally, in 1971, the Berlin of the 1920s was recreated in the Bavaria halls for *Cabaret*, directed by Bob Fosse and starring Liza Minelli and Michael York. A new era for the Studios began in the 1980s, with Wolfgang Petersen's large-scale productions. The U-boat used in the film *Das Boot* and Fuchur, the dragon from the *Neverending Story*, (1984) became attractions in their own right. "Bavaria Film Tours" began. Today a 90-minute guided tour of the Studios, with visits to well-known sets of popular TV soaps, is one of the undisputed highlights of a visit to Munich (Bavariafilmplatz 7, Geiselgasteig, tel: 089/ 64 99 23 04, daily Mar-Oct 9 am–4 pm, start of the last tour; Nov–Feb 10 am–3 pm, Tram 25

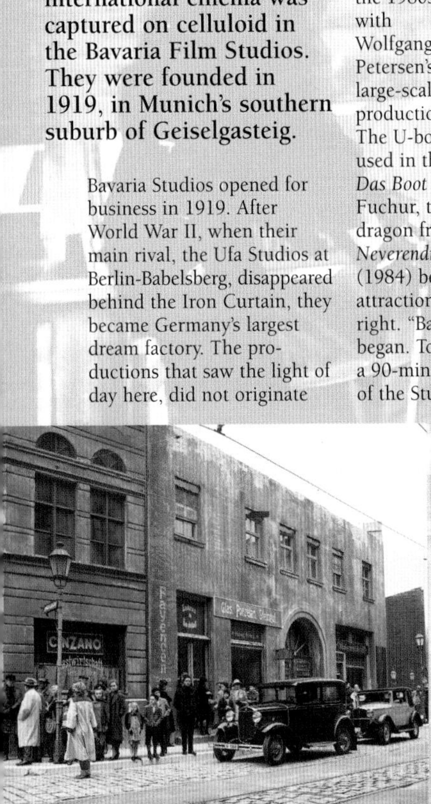

Top left: riding on Fuchur, the Dragon

Top and above: *Das Boot*

Left: reconstruction of a post-war street in Berlin

Background: stunt show

Bavariafilmplatz; admission: expensive, www.bavaria-filmtour.de).

Fassbinder and Friends

In the 1960s, pioneer of New German Cinema, Rainer Werner Fassbinder (1945–82) and a group of his friends set out to revitalize film and theatre in Germany. Together with Peer Raben and Hanna Schygulla, he founded the actors' collective "antitheater" in Munich in 1968. Their unconventional productions caused a stir. In 1969, he directed his first feature film, *Liebe ist kälter als der Tod* (*Love is Colder than Death*); a year later, he had already been awarded the Bundesfilmpreis (Federal Film Prize) for *Katzelmacher*, a film about the life of an immigrant worker. Fassbinder was a workaholic, shooting one film after another, managing theatre productions on the side and writing radio plays. For his 13-hour TV production *Berlin Alexanderplatz*, post-war Berlin was rebuilt in the Bavaria Studios. Tragically, Fassbinder died in Munich in 1982, probably from taking a mixture of sleeping pills and cocaine.

Internationally renowned director Volker Schlöndorff at work

Munich Man

Nobody personified Munich man as well as the late Walter Sedlmayr. The actor, who was tragically murdered in 1990, excelled in numerous TV and film roles, such as Fassbinder's *Fear Eats the Soul* (1974). The best-loved *derblecker* (critic of politicians), he became the face of Paulaner beer and Munich (► 12).

Scene from Fassbinder's ***Berlin Alexanderplatz***

HI-TECH

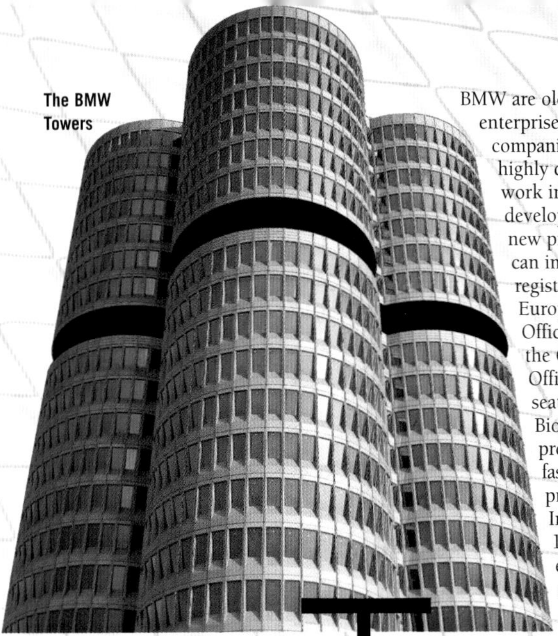

The BMW Towers

Microchips, biotechnology and fast cars – as a location for high-tech businesses, Munich ranks right at the top of the global league.

Munich has the world's fourth-largest concentration of high-tech businesses, with some 250,000 employees working for about 20,000 large and small enterprises. Microsoft and Infineon have large branches in Munich, and global players such as Siemens and BMW are old Munich-based enterprises. In these two companies alone, 16,000 highly qualified staff work in research and development, creating new products that can immediately be registered with the European Patent Office, which, like the German Patent Office, also has its seat in Munich. Biotechnology also profits from these fast-track patenting procedures.

In the late 1990s, Munich experienced a flood of new registrations of companies working in the field of biotechnology; today some 120 enterprises employ around 3,000 staff who work and research in this area, mostly in close cooperation with the Max-Planck-Institute for Biochemistry, which is based in the district of Martinsried, in the town's southwest. The EADS (European Aeronautic Defence and Space Company), the world's second-largest aviation and space travel company, is also based in Munich. And in addition, in 2003, Ottobrunn near Munich was chosen as the main site for Galileo Industries, which will build the first four satellites for the European Satellite Navigation System, which should be fully operable by 2008.

High-tech products made In Munich

Turnstile Munich

Shortly after its opening in 1992, approximately 10 million passengers passed through Munich airport. In 2003, a second terminal was opened to cope with the estimated 40 million passengers that are projected to use the airport by 2010. Munich's Franz-Josef-Strauss Airport in Erding is considered an architectural masterpiece, with Helmut Jahn one of the main contributing architects. You can go on a guided tour of the airport (Besucherpark "DimensionM" tel: 089/97 54 13 33, Apr–15 Oct, daily 9:30 am–6 pm, 16 Oct–Mar until 5 pm; admission: expensive).

A New Look

At first glance, Munich doesn't look like a hi-tech powerhouse. If the presence of high-rise buildings and daring architecture are an indication of a town's readiness to innovate, then Munich has not, until very recently, been in the running. The cityscape was dominated not by glass towers but by the onion domes of Frauenkirche. Whenever a new high-rise building is planned the planning laws continue to insist that the existing view of the Old Town must not be affected under any circumstances. The recent move towards innovation began in 2003/2004 with plans to build Helmut Jahn's "Skyline Tower" in Parkstadt Schwabing, "Münchner Tor" (Munich Gateway) with its two HighLight Munich Business Towers in Berliner Strasse and "Uptown Munich" on Georg-Brauchle-Ring near the Olympic Stadium. The Towers on the edge of the inner city are still the subject of bitter controversies. Opponents of high-rise buildings fear the "Frankfurtization" of the city; their supporters, on the other hand, want to rid the town of its provincial image.

Desirable Location

In fact, it is probably exactly this mixture of metropolitan arrogance and provincial tranquillity that makes Munich such an ideal location for many businesses. Its great recreational facilities, the

Opposite page: prototype of a BMW

View from the Patent Office

No Star for Mercedes

In 2003, Munich Council banned the new DaimlerChrysler Niederlassung building at Donnersberger Brücke from displaying the Mercedes star, its company logo, on top of its tower. In order to preserve the elegant skyline of Munich's Old Town, advertising on high-rise buildings was not permitted. However, the Bavarian provincial government quickly lifted the ban, and today the star is turning again, high above the town.

picturesque hinterland and the lovely weather make a move to Munich attractive for qualified staff, despite the often exorbitant rents. Munich, unlike any other German city, is a metropolis for single people. About half of all apartments, in Maxvorstadt nearly 70 per cent, are occupied by singles – there's no question then that the Bavarian capital's so-called "flirt factor" is exceptionally high. Even the Oktoberfest, which used to be a family event is now called "Singl'wies'n" because of the sociability of its visitors.

HITECH

The Future is Underground

For an exciting architectural experience, try a ride on some of Munich's newest underground lines. Embark on lines U2 or U8 for the futuristic station Am Hart (architects Hilmer/Sattler) and experience its blue glass mosaic walls and gleaming aluminium ceiling. Crudely rendered walls and glass add a special touch to U1 station Westfriedhof (architects Auer & Weber). And lines U2 or U7 will take you to Messestadt-West, a station with a daring lighting concept that bathes the entire station in shades of red, thus emphasizing the texture of the concrete.

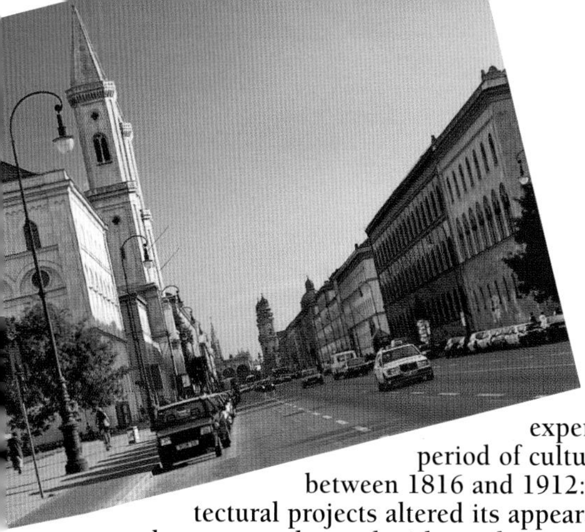

Contrary to King Ludwig's wishes, trees now grow along Ludwigstrasse

Munich experienced a period of cultural change between 1816 and 1912: new architectural projects altered its appearance; the opera houses reverberated with revolutionary sounds; and the first museum was opened. A bohemian population of painters, writers and anarchists settled in Schwabing. Life in this Bavarian town became stimulating and dynamic.

KINGS & ARTISTS

Classical arcades on Königsplatz

Respect for Antiquity

Munich's architectural transformation in the 19th century was largely due to the personality of King Ludwig I, and his love of art. An ardent admirer of the architecture of Ancient Greece and Rome, he found a fellow-enthusiast in the architect Leo von Klenze (1784–1864). In 1816, while still only Crown Prince, Ludwig commissioned the Glyptothek, as an appropriate setting for the antiquities he had collected on his travels. It became Germany's very first museum, and houses some splendid examples of sculpture and statuary.

The development of Königsplatz (➤ 102), modelled on the Forum in ancient Rome and surrounded by temples, was completed in 1862. One of these neo-classical buildings, the Propyläen, also designed by Klenze, was inspired by the

Greek vase from the collection of antiquities

Equestrian statue of Ludwig I on Odeonsplatz

Acropolis in Athens. As early as 1817, the king and the architect started a project which symbolized their artistic vision: Ludwigstrasse (► 110), a cold, severe, mile-long showpiece of a street, running from Feldherrnhalle to Siegestor. No frescoes, statues, trees or gardens were allowed to detract from the sublime architecture. Despite subsequent structural changes, it remains today a unique and majestic, but somewhat soulless, monument.

The King and the Composer

When he was only twelve years old, Ludwig II became entranced by Richard Wagner's music, and as soon as he became king in 1864, he invited the composer to Munich. Wagner knew how to use his influence on the impressionable young king, who promised him vast sums for his monumental opera productions. Architect Gottfried Semper was commissioned to design the largest festival theatre in the world, on the upper banks of the Isar River – a project that was never realized. The close working

Left: King Ludwig II, Wagner enthusiast

The King and the Dancer

Ludwig I was not only interested in antiquity, he also had an eye for beautiful women, from noble as well as less noble backgrounds. On his behest, Ludwig Stieler painted a series of portraits of attractive Munich ladies for Schloss Nymphenburg (► 149). Among them was Maria Dolores Gilbert aka the Spanish dancer Lola Montez, and the King soon succumbed to her charms. The people of Bavaria were infuriated by this scandalous liaison and, in 1848, the dancer had to flee and the King was forced to abdicate only two weeks later.

KINGS & ARTISTS

relationship between King Ludwig II and Richard Wagner lasted for a year and then, bowing to pressure from his civil servants and subjects, the King had to ask the composer to leave. In a fury, Ludwig also left town and transferred his energy to the construction of his fairytale Gothic castles, Linderhof and Neuschwanstein (➤ 164). In their interior design, the mythological world of Richard Wagner's operas lives on today.

Satirical Magazine

In 1896, publisher Albert Langen and cartoonist Theodor Heine founded the Munich magazine *Simplicissimus*, which remained Germany's leading satirical magazine until it closed in 1944. Its select circle of contributors included Ludwig Thoma, Frank Wedekind, Lovis Corinth, Rainer Maria Rilke, Olaf Gulbransson, Thomas Mann and Alfred Kubin.

Ludwig II's consolation prize – the fairytale castle of Linderhof

Bohemian Art Scene

When "mad king" Ludwig II was declared insane in 1886, his uncle, Prince Luitpold, became Bavaria's regent. During this peaceful era, which lasted until 1912, a bohemian art scene flourished in the city. In 1911, Munich-born artist Franz Marc (1880–1916) founded the artists' association Der Blaue Reiter (the Blue Rider) together with Vassily Kandinsky, a Russian immigrant who had arrived in 1896. August Macke and Paul Klee were two of its pre-eminent members. Richard Strauss (1864–1949), another famous son of Munich, composed *Salome* (1905) and *Rosenkavalier* (1911). The writer Thomas Mann (1875–1955) moved here in 1894; he later coined the phrase "Munich shone", in recognition of the city's lively art scene. This phrase is still used today. The suburb of Schwabing, incorporated into the city in 1890, was the hub of Munich's creative life. This was a cosmopolitan community of writers, poets, actors, painters and intellectuals, including exiled revolutionary Vladimir Ilyich Lenin (1870–1924) waiting to burst onto the world's political stage.

Beer and Sausages

Munich specialities are not known for being low in calories, and with such substantial delicacies on offer, local waistlines tend towards the expansive.

You'd think there could be nothing simpler than a sausage, but the Munich *weisswurst* (white sausage) illustrates just how specific the rules for both preparation and eating can be. The correct provenance is absolutely essential: according to a 2004 EU directive, if it was not made by a Munich factory, it cannot be called a "Munich white sausage". The sausage should be filled with veal – never pork –, onions and fresh parsley. Once the sausage has reached the table, the ritual continues: the skin is slit open along the length of the sausage, which is then halved so the sausage meat slips elegantly out of its skin. Now it can be enjoyed for Brotzeit, together with sweet Bavarian – never French! – mustard and fresh pretzels. By the way, white sausages should normally be served singly, not in pairs (unlike shown in the picture above), and eating them after midday is strictly taboo!

Brotzeit

An indispensable part of a Munich *brotzeit* is *leberkäse* (literally liver cheese), which has nothing to do with liver or cheese, of course. Rather, it is a shaped loaf of minced beef and pork, bacon and onions, baked in the oven until it has developed a crisp crust. A much-loved summer *brotzeit* speciality is *obatzda* consisting of ripe camembert, butter, onion, pepper, salt, caraway seeds and sweet paprika. There's also a ritual around slicing and salting of the *radi*, a large white horsradish. As soon as you know how to do it, you're ready to get married. But no *brotzeit* is complete without a brez'n – a pretzel!

Who can down the most tankards?

Roast Meat and Dumplings

Potato and bread dumplings accompany many local meat dishes, such as *schweinsbrodn* (roast pork), which to be just right has to boast a very crisp crackling. *Schlachtplatt'n* (meat platter) consists of a variety of sausages, *sauerkraut* and dumplings, of course. But it is only the genuine article if black pudding and liver sausage are included. Munich *kronfleisch* is served either as a mid-morning snack or as a main course. The fibrous cooked beef goes particularly well with freshly grated *kren* (horseradish). *Sauerbraten* (pickled beef) is a popular Sunday dish, its subtle, sour taste is best washed down with a glass of draft beer.

White sausages – a Bavarian's idea of gourmet heaven

Local Brews

Even in Munich, the breweries have noticed that people have started drinking less beer and more wine – but for the time being the city remains a paradise for beer drinkers. The classic Bavarian beer is *helles* (lager). Its fizzy equivalent brewed from wheat is *weissbier* (white beer) or *weizen* (wheat beer). There are special beers for special occasions: after Lent you'll find the strong, malty *starkbier* (strong beer) or *doppelbock* (double bock), which at 7% alcohol takes some getting used to – it's more than some customers can take. The Oktoberfest *wies'nbier* is also a strong beer, but the *mass* (tankards) are often filled so haphazardly that it would take several such one-litre glasses to topple a typical hard-drinking Wies'n guest.

Roast pork tastes best with a beer

DID YOU KNOW...

...that at the end of January every year a mountain of artificial snow is created in the Munich Olympic Stadium for the FIS Snowboarding World Cup's Big Air/Straight Jump competition? DJs make this a night to remember.

...that Munich's permanent Lord Mayor, Christian Ude (Social Democratic Party), is a talented cabaret artist, with sell-out performances? His humorous books about urban life (*Stadtradeln, Chefsache*) are bestsellers in Munich.

...that during the Oktoberfest some 6 million visitors drink 60,000 hectolitres (1.32 million gallons) of beer and eat 91 oxen, half a million roast chickens and just under 200,000 pairs of *schweinswürstl* (sausages)?

...that according to a survey the FC Bayern soccer club has 10 million fans around the world?

...that the fashionably updated folk costume is no longer in? Instead, the good old dirndl and the classic krachlederne, the lederhose of old, are what's worn today?

...that after New York, Munich is the world's second most important publishing town?

...that FC Bayern München has not always been Munich's top soccer club? While TSV 1860 von München has been playing in the National League since 1963, Bayern only managed to manoeuvre itself into the front row in 1965.

...that Munich is the only town in Germany with an untamed mountain stream? In 2001, the restoration of the Isar, which ran along in a riverbed constricted by weirs and canals, was begun. In southern Munich, the Isar has now returned to its former natural state.

Finding Your Feet

First Two Hours

Munich Airport at Erding

Munich's international airport, Franz Josef Strauss Airport, is about 30km (18.6 miles) northeast of the city. Most international lines fly to and from Terminal 1, while Terminal 2 is reserved for Lufthansa, its partners and Thomas Cook charter flights.

Airport Transfers

- A **taxi** into the city will take about 30 minutes, longer during rush hours; it costs about 50 euros.
- **Lufthansa Airport Bus** connects the airport with Hauptbahnhof (central station); there is only one stop, at U-Bahn station Nordfriedhof, where you can change for destinations in the north of the city. Tickets are available from the driver. A return ticket costs 15 euros, a single 9.50 euros. Buses depart every 20 minutes, from 5 am to 9 pm.
- **S-Bahn** line S8 also goes to Hauptbahnhof, as do the last carriages of line S1. The transfer takes about 40 minutes. At busy times, trains leave every 10 minutes (no departures from the airport 1:36 am–4:05 am and from Hauptbahnhof 0:52 am–2:35 am). The S-Bahn stations are situated underground at the airport and at Hauptbahnhof (costs ► 36).

Telephone Helplines

Flight information, tel: (089) 97 52 13 13; car park information, tel: (089) 97 56 51 10; lost property, Central Area Level 03, tel: (089) 97 52 13 70.

Railway Station

All trains to Munich Hauptbahnhof terminate there. Numerous shops and services can be found inside Hauptbahnhof. Some long-distance trains also stop at Ostbahnhof if they come from the east, and at München-Pasing if arriving from the west.

Telephone Helplines

Train information: free tel: (0800) 150 70 90, for advice tel: 118 61; lost property: main hall opposite platform 26, tel: (089) 13 08 66 64.

Car

Motorways A9 from Nuremberg, A94 from Passau, A8 from Salzburg, A95 from Garmisch and A96 from Lindau all join the **Mittlerer Ring**. Motorway A8 from Stuttgart terminates in Munich's western suburbs.

Tourist Information

- Information can be obtained in advance of your visit from **Fremdenverkehrsamt**, 80313 München; tel: (089) 233 03 00; from outside Germany tel: +49 89 233 03 00; fax +49 89 23 33 02 33, www.muenchen-tourist.de; Mon–Thu 9:30–3, Fri till 12:30 pm.
- There is a tourist information office in **Hauptbahnhof**, Bahnhofsplatz 2, Mon–Sat 9–8, Sun 10–6 (U-Bahn Hauptbahnhof), and at **Marienplatz**, Neues Rathaus, Mon–Fri 10–8, Sat till 4 pm (U-Bahn Marienplatz).
- Tourist information offices also sell several versions of the **München Welcome Card** (► 35/186).

Getting Around

Munich has an excellent network of underground/subway (U-Bahn) and local commuter (S-Bahn) railway lines, as well as numerous bus routes and the famous white-and-blue trams. Some 700km (434 miles) of cycle paths make the town a real joy for bicyclists, and if you don't feel like pushing the pedals yourself, you can always take a ride in a rickshaw (► 37).

Public Transport

- **S-Bahn lines** connect the centre with the environs; the S-Bahn runs underground on the central stretch, between Hauptbahnhof and Ostbahnhof. There are convenient crossover points between this central stretch and **U-Bahn lines** U1 to U8, which cover almost the entire town.
- Apart from U- and S-Bahn, Munich also has ten **tram routes**. They all end up at Hauptbahnhof or Karlsplatz (Stachus).
- The system is completed by a network of **bus routes**. During rush hours, congestion may lead to delays. Bus route No 53 is also known as the museum route because it passes all the most important museums.
- **Night services:** Some buses and trams run every 30 minutes throughout the night, especially at weekends. Some U-Bahn lines also continue running later at weekends.

Tickets

- U-Bahn, S-Bahn, buses and trams are part of a unified transport system, the Munich Transport and Tariff League (MVV). Many visitors find the pricing system a little complicated. The easiest option is to buy a **München Welcome Card** (► 34/186) from one of the tourist offices.
- There are **ticket machines** at every stop. Machines accept coins, bank notes and charge cards, and print out **Einzelfahrkarten** (single tickets; adults 2.10 euros, children 1 euro) and **Streifenkarten** with 10 strips (multi-trip tickets; adults 9.50 euros, children 4 euros; sufficient for five journeys within one zone). You can also buy **Tageskarten** (one-day travel cards) and **Dreitageskarten** (three-day travel cards, not to be confused with the München Welcome Card) from the machines.
- You need to stamp your ticket in one of the **validating machines** which are situated on the way to the platforms (multi-ticket cards need to be folded so the right number of strips show before validating). Validating machines for buses and trams are inside the vehicles.
- **Children** under six years travel free; from six to 14 years children pay a flat fee for the entire network (special single and multi-trip tickets); passengers under **21 years** only need to validate half the number of strips of an adult card.
- Munich has concentric **price zones,** shown on maps as a white central zone, and green, yellow and red outer zones. The **ticket price** depends on the number of zones you pass through. If you leave one zone and re-enter it later, it counts as two zones.
- For one journey within the centre (marked white on maps) you need a **Standard-Einzelfahrkarte** (standard single ticket) or **two strips** of the multi-trip ticket (changing lines is permitted, circular journeys aren't). A single ticket remains valid for three hours.
- For **journeys crossing two or more zones** you will need to validate two ticket strips per zone. Multi-zone tickets are valid for four hours. For a journey to the **airport** you need to validate eight strips.
- **Short journeys** (adults 1.10 euros or one strip of the multi-trip ticket)

are valid for a maximum of four bus or tram stops or a maximum of two U-Bahn or S-Bahn stops (it does not matter whether the bus or train actually stops at all the stations or not). These tickets are valid for a maximum of one hour.

- **Bicycles** can only be taken into U-Bahn and S-Bahn (although not during the rush hours Mon–Fri 6–9 am and 4–6 pm); you have to buy a separate ticket for the bicycle.
- The penalty for travelling without a ticket or without a validated ticket, is 40 euros.

Taxi

There are many taxi ranks throughout the city. Alternatively you can book one by phone from the central booking office (tel: 089/216 10 or Isar-Funk tel: 089/45 05 40).

Cycling

- From April to September, you can rent a bicycle from **Radius-Touristik**, in Hauptbahnhof adjacent to Platform 32 (tel: 089/55 02 93 74).
- Munich has a flexible system of bicycle rental known as **Call a bike**. You'll spot the silver-red bicycles at every major road junction. Once you have registered as a customer (online at www.bahn.de or by phone at tel: 0700/05 22 55 22), all you need to do is select a bicycle, dial the number that is displayed on it and announce your customer number. The bicycle is then automatically released, and you can return it when you are finished. Phone to report that you've returned the bicycle and where it can be found; the rental fee (approx. 15 euros a day or a per-minute fee) will simply be deducted from your credit card.

Cars

There are inexpensive park-and-ride spaces on the outskirts of the city, for example at U-Bahn stations Studentenstadt in the north (U6), Messestadt-Ost in the east (U2), Fürstenried-West in the south (U3) and at the S-Bahn stations Karlsfeld (S2) and Westkreuz in the west (S5, S6). You are strongly advised to make use of this facility as parking spaces in the centre are rare and expensive. It will cost you at least 3 euros per hour to park your car for one hour inside Altstadtring. There are car parks in the southern city, for example in Herzogspittalstrasse and at Altheimer Eck, and in the northern city in Hochbrückenstrasse.

City Tours

- **Coach sightseeing tours: PanoramaTours** (Arnulfstrasse 8, tel: 089/55 02 89 95; fax: 089/54 90 75 70) offers a variety of tours, lasting between one and five hours, depending on the theme; some include guided tours of the museums. Tours depart from 10 am to 4 pm, once every hour, in front of the Hertie department store in Bahnhofsvorplatz.
  The **Yellow Cab Stadtrundfahrten** double-decker buses also depart once an hour from 10 am to 5 pm (Sendlinger-Tor-Platz 5, tel: 089/26 02 51 83; fax: 089/26 02 51 85), in front of Elisenhof in Bahnhofsvorplatz. In summer, the upper deck is open-air.
- **Walking tours:** Every Saturday and Sunday, and between May and August also on Wednesday and Friday evenings, **Stattreisen** (Frauenlobstrasse 24, tel: 089/54 40 42 30; fax: 08954 40 42 99, www.stattreisen-muenchen.de) offer guided walking tours of various parts of town. Walks take about two hours. There are also guided tours by tram and an inline-skating tour of the Olympiapark.

Spurwechsel (Sankt-Martin-Strasse 9, tel: 089/692 46 99; fax: 089/ 69 37 00 02; www.home.t-online.de/home/spurwechsel.stadtfuehrungen) aims to reveal little-known squares and (hi)stories. On themed walks you'll find out all about, for example, bourgeois Munich, the soviet republic, the National Socialist period or the town of beers.
Weis(s)er Stadtvogel (Sankt-Anna-Strasse 6, tel: 089/29 16 97 65; fax: 089/29 16 97 65; www.weisser-stadtvogel.de) offers guided tours in several languages as well as in the Bavarian dialect (tour of the Old Town every Friday and Saturday 10:30 am and 1 pm; meeting point is Mariensäule on Marienplatz, booking not necessary).

- **Guided bicycle tours:** City Hopper (Hohenzollernstrasse 95, tel: 089/ 272 11 31; fax: 089/273 10 16) and the companies listed under "Walking tours" above help you explore the city by rented bicycle.
- **Sightseeing in a horse-drawn carriage:** The Hans Holzmann Company (Schwere-Reiter-Strasse 22, tel: mornings 089/18 06 08), Munich's last remaining carriage company, will drive you through Englischer Garten or the Old Town. You don't need to book ahead; the carriage waits at Chinesischer Turm in Englischer Garten from noon every day.
- **Sightseeing in a rickshaw:** Rikscha-Mobil, the cycle taxi (tel: 0700/80 90 10 20; fax 0700/80 90 10 10; www.rikscha-mobil.de), will bounce you across Munich's streets. The main rickshaw rank is at Marienplatz, but you can usually also find one on Odeonsplatz. You can even rent a rickshaw without driver and chauffeur your friends and family through the city yourself.
- **Private taxi tours:** Taxi-Guide-Sight-Seeing-Tours (tel: 0175/481 28 48; www.taxi-guide-muenchen.de) are conducted in several languages by drivers that have been trained by the tourist office.
- **Munich from the air:** You may be a bit far off the ground, but you certainly won't be able to complain about the views! Besides, you'll have the pleasure of flying in a venerable old Juncker JU-52, the so-called *Tante Ju* (Auntie Ju) – it makes an appalling noise but it's an adventure nevertheless. (Reservations JU-52 Booking Service, Oberdillerstrasse 29, 82065 Baierbrunn, tel: 0700/58 52 35 84 or 08157/90 02 79; fax: 08157/90 02 78).

Rafting

For a very special adventure, travel by raft down the Isar River, from Wolfratshausen up to the quay in Tierpark (from May to September): the atmosphere is merry and the surroundings damp – not only because you'll get splashed by the waters of the Isar but also because there's plenty of draft beer and brass music on board. (Information: Herr Angermaier, Kalkofenstrasse 14, 83661 Arzbach, tel: 08042/12 20; Franz and Sebastian Seltner, Heideweg 9, 82515 Wolfratshausen, tel: 08171/183 20; Josef Seltner, Lindenweg 1, 82515 Wolfratshausen, tel: 08171/785 18; www.flossfahrt.de.)

Admission Charges
The cost of admission to museums and places of interest mentioned in this guide is indicated by three price categories:
inexpensive: under 3 euros
moderate: 3–6 euros
expensive: over 6 euros

Accommodation

For its 3.5 million visitors a year, Munich has almost 40,000 beds in more than 340 hotels and guest houses in all price categories. The same number of visitors again stay with friends and acquaintances. Forty per cent of all visitors come from abroad, making Munich Germany's most-visited city. It is also by far the most expensive city to stay in, although hotel costs do not compare with prices in London, Rome or Paris, where the average price per bed is about 50 per cent higher than in Munich. Everybody is assured suitable accommodation – be it on a campsite, in a youth hostel, in a family-type middle-range hotel chain or in the most luxurious top hotel.

City Districts

There are hotels distributed throughout the entire city area. **Many hotels** are in the vicinity of the central station. If the sex shops on the south side of the station bother you, seek out a place to stay a little farther afield. Security, however, is generally not a problem. The most **luxurious hotels** are clustered around Theatinerstrasse, and this is where celebrities in politics or business, film or radio will flock. The large hotel chains have based their prestigious postmodern fortresses beyond the Old Town. To find a relatively **inexpensive hotel,** look near the station, but you should also find one elsewhere in the city.

Reservations

You can book a room at one of the tourist office's partner hotels by post, phone or email (Fremdenverkehrsamt, Sendlinger Strasse 1, 80331 München, Mon–Fri 8–7, Sat 10–6 tel: 089/23 39 65 55; fax: 089/23 33 02 33; www.muenchen-tourist.de). Alternatively, book in person, either at Bahnhofplatz 2 or at Neues Rathaus. The website also has a complete list of all Munich hotels with links to the hotels' own websites.

Private Accommodation

Bed and breakfast accommodation as well as furnished apartments, flats and houses, for shorter or longer periods, can be rented privately via Statthotel (Bavaria-Film-Platz 4, 82031 Grünwald, tel: 0180/530 55 30; fax: 0180/530 55 40; www.statthotel:de).

Youth Hostels and Guest houses

There are several youth guest houses in the **city centre**.

The YMCA near the station, CVJM-Jugendgästehaus (Landwehrstrasse 13, tel: 089/552 14 10; fax: 089/550 42 82; www.cvjm-muenchen.org) offers accommodation to boys, girls and adults (singles, doubles and triples, restaurant, closing time 0:30 am).

Youth Hotel Marienherberge (Goethestrasse 9, tel: 089/55 58 05; fax: 089/55 02 82 60; invia.muenchen.marienherberge@t-online.de), run by the Catholic Church, only admits girls and women (singles, doubles and dormitories, closing time midnight).

The ecological youth hotel 4 you münchen (Hirtenstrasse 18, tel: 089/552 16 60; fax: 089/55 21 66 66; www.the4you.de) has singles, doubles and dormitories, with ensuite or shared bathrooms; adults are also admitted (crèche service, cafeteria, no closing time).

The youth hostel in **Neuhausen** (Wendl-Dietrich-Strasse 20, tel: 089/13 11 56; fax: 089/167 87 45; www.djh.de/jugendherbergen/muenchenneuhausen) also has doubles; available to young people under

26 and families with at least one child under 18 (no closing time).
Kolpinghaus in **Neuhausen/Gern** (Hanebergstrasse 8, tel: 089/12 60 50; fax: 089/12 60 52 12) accepts everyone irrespective of age (singles, doubles and dormitories, no closing time).
The **Thalkirchen** Jugendherberge (Miesingstrasse 4, tel: 089/723 65 50; fax: 089/724 25 67; jghmuenchen@djh-bayern.de), run by the German youth hostel association, DJH, has doubles and dormitories for people under 26 years and families with at least one child under 18 and no closing time.

Camping

There are four campsites on the outskirts of town.
Thalkirchen is the closest to the centre, near Zoo U-Bahn station (Zentralländstrasse 49, tel: 089/723 17 07; fax: 089/724 31 77; 15 Mar–31 Oct).
Obermenzing (Lochhausenerstrasse 59, tel: 089/811 22 35; fax: 089/814 48 07; 15 Mar–31 Oct) is near the end of the Munich–Stuttgart motorway.
Langwieder See is 2km (1.2 miles) from the end of the Stuttgart–Munich motorway (exit Langwieder See, Eschenriederstrasse 119, tel: 089/864 15 66; fax: 089/863 23 42; 1 Apr–15 Oct).
Nord-West (Auf den Schrederwiesen 3, tel: 089/150 69 36; fax: 089/15 82 04 63; open all year) can be reached by going north on Dachauer Strasse, almost to Karlsfeld. To stay at a public campsite, young people under 18 need to be accompanied by an adult; there is no such restriction at the Kapuzinerhölzl youth camp (see below).

Youth Camp

The Kapuzinerhölzl youth camp Das Zelt (Kapuzinerhölzl, In den Kirschen 30, tel: 089/141 43 00, fax: 089/17 50 90, www.the-tent.com) can be reached by tram No 17 from Hauptbahnhof to Botanischer Garten. The camp, run by Munich Council and open from May to August (no closing time), is a global destination for young people. Young – and young-at-heart – visitors from around the world meet here in large dormitory tents for single travellers, group tents for travel groups and at the youth campsite. You can use either your own sleeping bag or borrow one of the camp's blankets and insulating mats; breakfast is served here too. A programme of sports and games, sightseeing walks plus bicycle rental, bonfires and a beer garden all contribute to an enjoyable stay.

Hotels

Accommodation Prices
Prices for a double room with ensuite WC/bath and breakfast:
€ under 75 euros
€€ 75–150 euros
€€€ 150–250 euros
€€€€ over 250 euros

Hotel prices in Munich are relatively expensive for Germany, and they rise considerably during big fairs or the Oktoberfest.

Adria Hotel €€

This small hotel is decorated to create a Mediterranean atmosphere in the centre of the city. Tasteful, contemporary furnishings make the Adria in Munich's Lehel district an elegant and tranquil base for exploring the city as well as for visits to the opera or museums or a leisurely stroll through Englischer Garten.

197 F4 Liebigstrasse 8a (089) 242 11 70; fax (089) 242 11 79 99 Lehel www.adria-muenchen.de

Advokat €€–€€€

Clear lines, bright, unfussy rooms – Munich's first boutique hotel, in the smart Gärtnerplatz district, attracts both businesspeople and holidaymakers who prefer elegance over luxury. The rooms, although small, are tastefully furnished, and in the evening you will find an apple on your pillow instead of a chocolate.

191 E1 Baaderstrasse 1 (089) 21 63 10; fax (089) 216 31 90 Isartor Bus No 52 Gärtnerplatz www.hotel-advokat.de

Anna €€€

This hotel has 56 attractive rooms, with a great flair for design evident throughout. Everything is minimalist here, with an obvious Japanese feel. Indeed, the hotel offers regular weekend specials including courses in the preparation of sushi. You can also use the facilities of the Hotel Königshof, under the same ownership, which has been awarded a Michelin star.

190 A4 Schützenstrasse 11 (089) 59 99 40; fax (089) 59 99 43 33 Karlsplatz www.annahotel:de

Bayerischer Hof €€€€

In 1840, Ludwig I asked for a comfortable place in Munich to accommodate his guests, so Reich Councillor Joseph Ritter von Maffei built Bayerischer Hof. The Austrian Empress Elisabeth "Sissi" was one of the first guests. The Volkhardt family took over the running of the hotel in 1897, and developed it into today's grand hotel over four generations. Bayerischer Hof incorporates the neighbouring Montgelas-Palais, from where the Munich soviet republic was declared in 1919. The hotel's Night Club Bar is renowned all over the city for its cocktails and lively ambience, the adjacent gallery for its exhibitions and Kleine Komödie for its entertaining comedies.

190 C4 Promenadeplatz 2–6 (089) 212 00; fax (089) 212 09 06 Marienplatz Tram No 19 Theatinerstrasse www.bayerischerhof.de

Cortiina €€€

Swamp-oak panelling, parquet floors and natural jura stone in the bathrooms – this is not a cosy, old-fashioned place but a modern boutique hotel where relaxation of body and soul have determined the choice of materials and layouts used in the dramatic design. The hotel has 33 rooms, a lounge where you can relax to the sounds of classical music, enveloped in leather armchairs around a fireplace or taking the air in a green inner courtyard. This is perfect if you want a change from both chintz and postmodernism. The bar is popular with the locals too.

191 E3 Ledererstrasse 8 (089) 242 24 90; fax (089) 242 24 91 00 Marienplatz www.cortiina.com

Cosmopolitan €€

Bright and cool is the style adopted in the 71 rooms furnished by Ligne Roset. The bedrooms have soundproof windows – an important feature as the Cosmopolitan is based right in the heart of Schwabing's pulsating nightlife, perfect for a night out. You won't find any fussy details here, only functional features, but everything is tasteful and of a high quality, all at a reasonable price.

194 C2 Hohenzollernstrasse 5 (089) 38 38 10; fax (089) 38 38 11 11 Münchner Freiheit Bus No 33 Hohenzollernstrasse www.cosmopolitan-hotel.de

Deutsche Eiche €€

This old-established hotel, in the centre of Munich, with a restaurant and its own bath-house, is situated in the middle of the gay area. Close to all the popular pubs and clubs, it attracts a largely gay and lesbian clientele. The rooms are furnished in a comfortable but functional style; there's a rustic restaurant and occasional live entertainment.

197 E3 Reichenbachstrasse 13 (089) 231 16 60; fax (089) 23 11 66 98 Marienplatz Tram Nos 17, 18 Reichenbachplatz www.deutsche-eiche.com

Econtel Hotel München €€

A modern hotel, located in the western half of Munich, in a quiet spot only two minutes walk from the S-Bahn station. Comfortable rooms are available at various prices. The hotel also boasts family-friendly "Mickey for Kids" rooms. Brightly coloured, each room offers accommodation for parents and up to two children under 12 years. Children under six years can also help themselves for free to the breakfast buffet.

192, west of the A1 Bodenseestrasse 227 (089) 87 18 90; fax (089) 87 18 94 00 Neuaubing www.econtel.de

Englischer Garten €€

Based in a converted 18th-century mill, a listed building, this oasis will make you feel as if you're staying in a country villa rather than in the heart of Schwabing. In summer breakfast is served in the garden. The family-run hotel has 12 elegantly and tastefully furnished rooms, and service is exceptionally attentive. Munich's famous Englischer Garten is not far away, and you can explore it on foot or by bicycle on loan from the hotel. Also part of the complex are a number of outbuildings, with a further 16 apartments, each equipped with its own kitchen.

195 D2 Liebergesellstrasse 8 (089) 383 94 10; fax (089) 38 39 41 33 Münchner Freiheit Bus No 44 Osterwaldstrasse www.hotelenglischergarten.de

Hauser €€

This family-run hotel, situated in the university district, is popular with younger visitors. After a day's cycling through the city, with bicycles on loan from the hotel, you can spend a relaxing evening in the solarium, sauna or steam bath. The 34 rooms have modern and functional furnishings, and the noise-proof windows ensure a good night's sleep, despite the hotel's proximity to Türkenstrasse with its many pubs.

194 B1 Schellingstrasse 11 (089) 286 67 50; fax (089) 28 66 75 99 Universität Bus No 53 Schellingstrasse www.hotel-hauser.de

Haus International €

This guest house, situated half-way between Munich's Old Town and the Olympic Stadium, was built for the 1972 Olympics. It is one of the most popular places to stay for young people (although there is no age restriction), and you are advised to reserve well in advance. The full-board option is particularly good value for money. There is a choice of singles, doubles and dormitories, with either ensuite or shared bathrooms. The furnishings are functional but comfortable. In summer, a multicultural crowd gathers in the courtyard, and the in-house disco is lively and popular all year round.

194 A2 Elisabethstrasse 87 (089) 12 00 60; fax (089) 12 00 66 30 Josephsplatz Bus No 33, Tram No 12 Barbarastrasse www.haus-international.de

H'Otello Boardinghouse €€

Apartments with cheerful modern furnishings and cooking facilities for self-catering. This boarding house in Westschwabing is popular with business travellers, and also with families and young people who appreciate the chance to heat up their own meals or to make their own breakfasts. If you prefer to have everything ready prepared for you, you will find a plentiful choice at the breakfast buffet.

194 B2 Fallmerayerstrasse 22 (089) 307 92 00; fax (089) 30 79 20 97 Hohenzollernplatz www.hotello-boardinghouse.de

Kempinski Vier Jahreszeiten €€€€

Munich's flagship hotel is placed in the city's main shopping street, close to all city-centre attractions. One story tells of a guest, Count Toerring, who rode his horse through the lobby, up the stairs and into his room. Times have changed but staff still aim to satisfy their guests' whims. An elegant ambience prevails – sip your afternoon tea in the lobby, under a glass cupola, surrounded by mahogany and brass. There are 316 rooms and suites, furnished to the standard you would expect from a four-star hotel. There are panoramic views from the roof terrace, which also has a beauty spa and swimming pool. Ask for special offers.

191 E/F3 Maximilianstrasse 17 (089) 212 50; fax (089) 21 25 20 00 Marienplatz Tram No 19 Kammerspiele www.kempinski-vierjahreszeiten.de

Lex €–€€

Not far from Königsplatz, this modern hotel with contemporary furnishings is great value in an excellent location: Lenbachhaus, Königplatz and the Pinakothek museums are all just around the corner. Special apartments are available for longer-term stays at reasonable prices; there's a kitchen, and internet and fax connections for business travellers. The Lex doesn't have a restaurant but there are many nearby.

193 F1 Briennerstrasse 48 (089) 542 72 60; fax (089) 523 24 23 Königsplatz Tram No 20 Stiglmaierplatz www.hotel-lex.de

Mandarin Oriental €€€€

Book early – the 53 rooms and 20 suites in the Mandarin Oriental (formerly Hotel Rafael) quickly get booked up thanks to its perfect location on a very quiet side street, right next to opera. Opera divas and tenors are regulars here, like everyone else appreciative of the fine furnishings. If celebrity-spotting isn't your thing, just take the lift up to the magnificent roof terrace, leap into the pool and enjoy the views over Munich's townscape towards the mountains. Free minibar.

191 E3 Neuturmstrasse 1 (089) 29 09 80; fax (089) 22 25 39 Marienplatz Tram No 19 Nationaltheater www.mandarinoriental.com

Mona Lisa €€

This small guest house has only seven rooms, but each one has been lovingly furnished to a highly personal style and in a different colour scheme (rooms are named for their colours: blackberry, blue and so forth). Service is very attentive. The family-run business is popular and often fully booked.

197 F4 Robert-Koch-Strasse 4 (089) 21 02 83 80; fax (089) 21 02 83 82 Lehel Tram No 17 Lehel www.hotelmonalisa.de

Opéra €€€

Built in 1898 by the Bavarian supplier of seafood and game to the royal court as his private residence and food store (he used the Eisbach stream under the hote to keep oysters and lobsters fresh before serving them at the royal table), the palace did not open its doors to the first hotel guest until 1976. Each room is individually furnished with antiques, much appreciated by an elegant clientele. Balmy summer evenings are best spent sipping a cocktail in the courtyard; the Gandl restaurant next door is one of Munich's best.

197 E4 Sankt-Anna-strasse 10 (089) 210 49 40; fax (089) 21 04 94 77 Lehel Tram No 17 Lehel www.hotel-opera.de

Pension Am Siegestor €

One of Munich's more basic guest houses, where the rooms are only equipped with a washbasin; showers and toilets are shared by guests on each floor. To compensate for this lack of luxury the pension charges only moderate prices and is in a hard-to-beat location: quiet, near the Siegestor, yet right in the heart of lively Schwabing.

194 C1 Akademie-strasse 5 (089) 39 95 50; fax (089) 34 30 50 Bus No 53 Universität www.siegestor.com

Pension Greiner €–€€

Based on the first floor of this town house near the university, the nine rooms are beautifully and individually furnished, with ensuite or shared bathroom. Contemporary furniture may be offset by an eye-catching rustic armoire. You can also choose to stay in the farm-house parlour. The family who run the hotel will help you get the best from your city visit.

194 C1 Ohmstrasse 12 (089) 380 18 80; fax (089) 33 92 46 Giselastrasse Bus No 54 Martiusstrasse www.pensiongreiner.de

Prinz €€–€€€

One of the main advantages of this pleasant hotel, run with great attention to detail, is its excellent position: for lots of culture, Gasteig and Deutsches Museum are just around the corner, and if you book a room at the front of the house, you'll get magnificent views over Munich (but also some noise from the streets below). The rooms are tastefully and elegantly furnished; there's a garage on the lower floor and guests are spoiled in the excellent restaurant.

197 F3 Hochstrasse 45 (089) 441 40 80; fax (089) 441 40 83 33 Rosenheimer Platz www.hotel-prinz.de

Ritzi €€

The Ritzi has 25 rooms, each one individually and unconventionally furnished. So, while close to the Maximilianeum, you can sleep in an African lodge or imagine your-self on a beach holiday on Bali. The restaurant serves light, Far-Eastern inspired food. The Ritzi is over 100 years old and has kept the authentic art deco style in its communal areas. In the lobby you can lounge on red velvet seats – originally from La Scala in Milan.

198 A4 Maria-Theresia-Strasse 2a (089) 419 50 30; fax (089) 41 95 03 50 Max-Weber-Platz Tram No 19 Max-Weber-Platz www.hotelritzi.de

Romantik Hotel Insel-Mühle €€€

Idyllically surrounded by a large, old garden, this romantic, rustic hotel, part of an estate dating back more than 400 years, is an attractive choice for all those seeking peaceful surroundings. The rooms are furnished in a comfortable Bavarian style, the restaurant serves Bavarian specialities and there's a well-stocked wine cellar. The only drawback is that it's hard to get to the city by public transport (S-Bahn to Pasing, then bus).

192, westl. A4 Von-Kahr-strasse 87 (089) 810 10; fax (089) 812 05 71 Bus No 76 Friedhof Untermenzing www.inselmuehle-muenchen.de

Food and Drink

Roast pork with crackling and dumplings, white sausages, wheat beer and *leberkäse* (see page 31) – Bavarians are justly proud of their food and drink. Bavarian dishes feature on the menus of most of the cosy and comfortable taverns, bistros and stylish restaurants. Unless, of course, you've chosen to eat at one of the many Italian, Asian or French restaurants…

Chefs from around the world have settled in Munich and opened their own restaurants here. Today there's a vast selection of international eateries, offering an alternative to Bavarian inns. But wherever you go, you'll always find a tavern with a traditional atmosphere, where some tables are reserved for regulars and where strong waitresses carry large plates with even larger portions of food to the table, accompanied by tankards of beer. For the smaller appetite, butchers' shops usually have an excellent selection of light meals, which Bavarians call *schmankerln*. Most will offer a simple hot meal at lunchtime: *leberkäse* or a *fleischpflanzerl* (a burger without bread), a hot sausage with potato salad or a slice of roast meat on a *semmel* (a bread roll).

When to Eat

Breakfast is served at many cafés until the early afternoon; you will find a wide selection of themed breakfasts, ranging from hangover or champagne to healthy. At lunchtime, the restaurants usually open their doors for food orders from noon to 3 pm, in the evening they start serving food at about 6 pm. Some serve food all day, but it is unusual for guests to arrive at a restaurant later than about 9 pm for a full evening meal – although you will always be able to get a post-theatre or opera supper.

Traditional Bavarian Restaurants

Altes Hackerhaus (➤ 66); Schuhbeck's in Südtiroler Stuben (➤ 90); Zum Franziskaner (➤ 91); Andechser am Dom (➤ 66)

The Best Cuisine

Ess Neun (➤ 66); Lux (➤ 67); Dukatz (➤ 89); Wine bar Message in a Bottle (➤ 91); Fouquets (➤ 112)

Eating Tips

- Many restaurants, especially the smarter ones, will fill up from about 7 pm, and you are advised to **book a table**.
- In the **beer gardens**, most areas are self-service: you have to queue (line) up at the counter to order your food, which tends to be typical local fare. You are, however, also allowed to bring and consume your own food. Beer is served at the table.
- It is standard practice to add a **tip** of about 5–10 per cent to the bill. If you want to express displeasure about the service or the food, don't add anything.

Prices

Prices are per person for a meal without drinks as follows:
€ under 12 euros **€€** 12–25 euros **€€€** over 25 euros

Shopping

Munich is a paradise for shopaholics. You'll find everything within the confines of the city – from the temples of high fashion, numerous department stores and designer boutiques right down to the factory outlet.

Souvenirs

Ein Herz'l fürs Herz'l ("a sweet heart for the sweetheart") is a gingerbread or chocolate heart. Unfortunately this typical Munich speciality is only available during the Oktoberfest or at the Auer Dulten, a funfair taking place three times a year (► 136). Outside these events, you'll have to contend yourself with a Münchner Kindl. This little monk, dressed in black and yellow, is one of Munich's emblems, and is available in countless guises, from doll to sticker. If you're after something a little more wacky, have a look at **servus.heimat** (► 92). Here you'll find King Ludwig and his dream castle Neuschwanstein as a snow paperweight, T-shirts with humorous or Bavarian slogans, and also beautiful coffee-table books. Fans of the two Munich soccer clubs will find accessories and paraphernalia in the fan shops around **Platzl** (► 92).

Fashion

Rudolph Moshammer stands, a little lapdog in his arms and his eyes expectantly scanning the horizon, in his shop (► 92) in Maximilianstrasse, waiting for his well-to-do clients. **Maximilianstrasse** is Munich's most expensive shopping street, boasting the most elegant shops of all top designers. Nearby **Theatinerstrasse**, with its Fünf Höfe (Five Courtyards) also targets wealthy customers. If your budget does not stretch this far, aim for the city, where you're bound to find something in one of the many international fashion chains such as Zara or H&M. If you're after an item that's a little more unusual, by lesser-known designers, try shopping in **Haidhausen** (► 136) or **Schwabing** (► 115). The streets around **Münchner Freiheit** (► 115), meanwhile, have become a shopping paradise for hip-hop fans. The best shop for classic folklore clothes is **Lodenfrey** (► 92).

Art, Design and Antiques

A large number of galleries have settled in **Maxvorstadt** and **Schwabing** (► 95). Here you may chance upon some interesting discoveries while you're ambling through the streets, or when you take a closer look at one of the courtyards. Stores selling designer furnishings and accessories are extremely popular; many are clustered around the **University** (► 115) and **Münchner Freiheit** (► 115). A highlight for everyone who enjoys browsing is **Antikpalast** (► 136), an antiques palace next to Ostbahnhof.

Junk, Crafts and Flea Markets

- **Riemer Flohmarkt**, Bavaria's largest open-air flea market, takes place every Saturday from April to October, from 9 am to 4 pm, in the grounds of the new exhibition centre in Riem (Alfons-Goppel-Strasse 3, tel: 089/ 950 39 60; www.flohmarkt-riem.de).
- Three times a year, antiques dealers and booksellers set up their stalls on Mariahilfplatz for the duration of the **Dult** (► 136). This combined junk market and funfair is popular with families, as there are many attractions for children.
- Crafts from around the world are sold by young traders during the two **Tollwood-Festivals**, in June or December respectively, (► 14) and at the **Schwabing Christmas Market** on Münchner Freiheit.

Entertainment

For a long time, Munich was considered a bit staid and unadventurous in terms of its entertainment value, but then the Kunstpark-Ost (known today as Kultfabrik) opened, and one of Munich's long-standing and hitherto sacrosanct bureaucratic institutions was at last abolished – closing time.

Today, a broad repertoire of opera, theatre and lively alternative productions are typical of the city's cultural life. Munich also has an active jazz community, which has been using the Haidhauser **Unterfahrt** (➤ 138) as its base for decades. The dance and club scene congregates in one of the converted market halls. An overview of current events is available from the free magazine, *In München*. English-language listings are in *New in the City Today* (free) and in *Munich Found* (3 euros) which also has reviews.

Theatre and Opera

Bayerische Staatsoper (➤ 94) with its top productions is regarded as one of Germany's best music theatres. **Pasinger Fabrik** (August-Exter-Strasse 1, tel: 089/829 29 00; www.pasinger-fabrik.com), meanwhile, has an alternative take on opera, enthusiastically producing one opera each year in summer. **Residenztheater** and **Kammerspiele** (➤ 94) compete with renowned stage productions of the highest calibre. A great place for children and young people to experience quality drama (in German) is the **Schauburg** (Elisabethplatz, tel: 089/23 33 71 71; www.schauburg.net).

The Music Scene

Munich's Philharmonic Orchestra performs at the **Philharmonie** in Gasteig (➤ 130). Mammoth concerts take place in Olympiahalle, and in summer also in the Olympiastadion and on Königsplatz. One of the most popular smaller music venues is **Muffathalle** (➤ 137), and many clubs, such as the **Atomic Café** (➤ 94), also have live music.

Dancing, Watching, Drinking

In summer, fans of ballroom dancing can indulge in some Latin dancing each Monday, at the open-air **Tango-Montage** on the Prater Island behind the Müller'sches Volksbad public baths (➤ 130, www.praterinsel.de). Throughout the year, salsa and fifties evenings will get you in the mood at **Max Emanuel's** (➤ 116). If dancing is not your thing, you'll find a like-minded crowd at **Kultfabrik** (➤ 137) or **Backstage** (➤ 158).

Gays and Lesbians

Munich's gay heart beats around Gärtnerplatz and in the Glockenbach district. Here you'll find numerous cafés, pubs and clubs, even patisseries and bookstores, aiming at a gay and lesbian clientele. One of the hot spots in the city centre is the popular disco **Soul City** (Maximiliansplatz 5).

Booking in Advance

You can order tickets for most events online from München Ticket (www.muenchen-ticket.de). There are several advance booking offices, for example München-Information in the town hall (➤ 55). Opera tickets can also be booked online (www.bayerische-staatsoper.de) or at the advance booking office in Maximilianshöfe (Marstallplatz 5, tel: 089/21 85 19 19, Mon–Fri 10–6, Sat until 1 pm; the box office opens one hour before the performance).

The Southern City

Getting Your Bearings

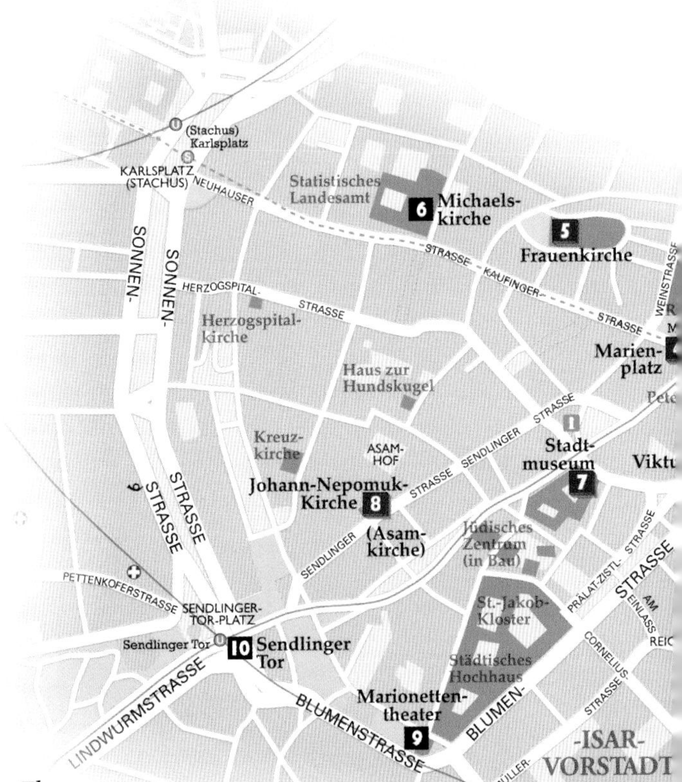

The southern half of the city, delineated by Isartor, Karlstor (Stachus) and Sendlinger Tor, has a lively, contemporary face, with many modern buildings. Its historic area is bounded by three medieval town gates. From Marienplatz you can easily explore the markets, churches and shops on foot.

The axis extending from Isartor via Viktualienmarkt and Marienplatz to Stachus (officially known as Karlsplatz) is Munich's main shopping boulevard. There's a cheery hustle and bustle at almost any time in the pedestrianized stretch around Marienplatz: performing mime artists and buskers, shopping families and hurrying business people; Peruvian flutes competing with Russian accordions and Italian violins,

★ Don't Miss

- **1 Viktualienmarkt ➤ 52**
- **4 Marienplatz ➤ 55**
- **5 Frauenkirche ➤ 58**
- **7 Stadtmuseum ➤ 60**
- **8 Asamkirche ➤ 62**

At Your Leisure

- 2 Zentrum für Aussergewöhnliche Museen ➤ 64
- 3 Isartor ➤ 64
- 6 Michaelskirche ➤ 65
- 9 Marionettentheater ➤ 65
- 10 Sendlinger Tor ➤ 65

Come right in! All the fun's in the city centre

and both locals and visitors enjoying a break while listening to their music. The Bavarian sense of humour with its appreciation of the absurd finds ample expression in the Valentin-Musäum and the nearby Zentrum für Aussergewöhnliche Museen (Centre for Unusual Museums). Fruit, vegetables and delicacies from around the world are on display at Viktualienmarkt, behind the old Peterskirche. Among the architectural highlights in this area are Altes and Neues Rathaus (Old and New Town Hall), both sited on Marienplatz, the magnificent Gothic Frauenkirche and rococo Asamkirche.

Page 47: Mariensäule, flanked by the onion domes of Frauenkirche

Munich's towers: Rathaus, Frauenkirche and Olympic Tower

Munich's city centre, around Viktualienmarkt and Marienplatz, has more to offer than historic buildings and museums. This part of town is also the liveliest and most important shopping area in the city.

The Southern City in a Day

9:00 am

How about croissants and fresh fruit juice for breakfast? Or why not sample a Bavarian white sausage breakfast? Check i out on **1 Viktualienmarkt** (left; ➤ 52). You have about an hour before the first museum opens its doors, time to listen to the sales patter of the market traders and to marvel at the tempting array of local and exotic foods on offer, while admiring Peterskirche in the background. At the **2 Zentrum für Aussergewöhnliche Museen** (➤ 64) you can find out all about the Easter bunny, the history of chamber pots, and other oddities.

11:01 am

At **3 Isartor** (➤ 64), the eastern exit from the Old Town, is the Valentin-Musäum (right), where the doors open punctually at 11:01 am. You'll see some strange objects that sprang from the boundless imagination of Karl Valentin, the Bavarian master of all things absurd. Continue up a spiral staircase to the Turmstüberl (➤ 68) inn – and use the opportunity to enjo a brief break. At noon exactly, you should b back outside on **4 Marienplatz** (➤ 55) for this is when the carillon's coopers, knight and entertainers on Neues Rathaus start their dance on the tower's façade (left). The aptly named Café Glockenspiel (right; ➤ 66), on the

fifth floor of the building opposite, provides the best views. Combine the experience with an espresso or lunch at the café, then take a few minutes to visit Altes Rathaus (Old Town Hall).

1:30 pm

Legend has it that the devil helped build 5 **Frauenkirche** (➤ 58); don't let it put you off seeing the inside of this vast and majestically beautiful church. Afterwards join the throng on Kaufingerstrasse. This pedestrianized shopping street, continuing as Neuhauser Strasse, has the highest number of shoppers per square metre (yard) in Germany. Countless shops and street musicians from around the world vie for your attention here, and it's only a short distance to Stachus, Munich's main traffic hub, where a refreshing fountain gushes in summer.

3 pm

It's time to learn a bit about Munich's history at the 7 **Stadtmuseum** (➤ 60). Afterwards, enjoy a restorative break in the Stadtcafé (➤ 67), based in the same building, a favourite hangout with Munich's students.

4:30 pm

Prepare to be overwhelmed by the sheer opulence and splendour of the late-baroque 8 **Asamkirche** (➤ 62) in Sendlinger Strasse. In the vicinity of the church, numerous shops will inspire you to stock up with original souvenirs from Munich. Your final stop for the day is the 700-year-old 10 **Sendlinger Tor** (➤ 65), one of the Old Town gates, entirely covered in ivy. Finish your tour of the southern city with a visit to the Filmmuseum (➤ 70) or with some Bavarian culinary delights at Altes Hackerhaus (➤ 66).

1 Viktualienmarkt

The best time to visit Munich's largest and oldest food market is the early morning: night owls and early risers gather at the 140 market stalls with a glass of sparkling wine, a wheat beer or a fresh fruit juice, either to help them fall asleep or to get the energy for a new day.

A name that promises gastronomic delights

In 1807, on the orders of King Maximilian I, the municipal authorities moved the grain market, known as Schrannenmarkt, from Marienplatz to its present spot, now simply called Marktplatz. The market square soon became too small to accommodate southern Germany's most important market, and more space was created by demolishing the surrounding buildings. Even the Heiliggeistspital (Hospital of the Holy Spirit), where the great plague epidemic started in 1340, was not spared. To compensate for the loss, **Heiliggeistkirche** (Church of the Holy Spirit), on the north side of the square, was given a longer nave and a neo-baroque makeover of its interior.

A Licence to Sell

The city fathers declared that Viktualienmarkt should complement the large farmers' markets in the country. Licences to sell are strictly limited: not everyone may set up stall and sell just anything. There is, in fact, a long waiting list for permits. Only reliable individuals can expect a licence, and they must sell the widest possible range of goods, for this is supposed to be a showcase of all that Munich has to offer. And although carambolas or tamarilloes don't actually thrive in Upper Bavaria, the person packing them into a bag is usually a local. The few air-freighted oysters that find their way in will always be served with an authentically Bavarian *an guad'n* (Enjoy!).

A Rare Gem of Industrial Architecture

The former grain market halls, known as **Schranne**, were built in 1851. They burned down in 1932, but the cast-iron framework was saved. The halls are now going to be rebuilt south of Viktualienmarkt, as a gourmet food centre.

Mediterranean treats

Early birds

At 5 am, the market traders start to move their *viktualien* (goods) onto the stalls of the 22,000sq m

Fasching (Carnival)

On Carnival Tuesday (Shrove Tuesday, Mardi Gras), at 11 am, the market women start their dance on Viktualienmarkt. Dressed in dirndls, lederhosen or clowns' costumes, adorned with colourful feather boas, loud make-up, red stockings and straw hats, they dance round in a circle. But beware! These ladies are no wallflowers – they take a mischievous delight in showering their male victims with suggestive remarks.

(26,312sq yards) market square. In the stalls around the beautiful maypole, fruits from every continent, herbs and mushrooms from the Bavarian forests, fresh vegetables, delicious cheeses, game, poultry, fish, meats, several hundred different types of honey and countless wines and spirits will be on display an hour later. Healthy – as well as less healthy foods – are all beautifully arranged in colourful layers and rows and columns. Now it's time for the traders to grab a fortifying *ausgezogener*, or strudel pastry, in the Schmalznudel (► 67), before the first buyers come to market, enticed by the many lovely foods on offer and happy to succumb to temptation.

The best-dressed dog in Munich?

Comic Fountains

Inspired by the streams that once crossed the market, six **fountains** have been erected, each with a bronze statue commemorating one of the city's favourite entertainers. There's tall, skinny comedian and satirist Karl Valentin (1882–1948) and his short, stocky partner Liesl Karlstadt (1892–1960); the satirical poet and singer Roider-Jackl (1906–75); Ida Schumacher, shown in her cabaret persona as Ratschkathl with bucket and brush; actor Elise Aulinger (1881–1965), a book in her hand; and barrel-shaped actor Weiss Ferdl (1883–1949). They've all done their bit for public health by making their audiences laugh. Today, the citizens of Munich still express their gratitude by leaving flowers at their feet.

Karl Valentin, comedian, satirist and writer

Peterskirche – a baroque gem

Petersbergl

On the west side of the market square is Petersbergl, with the butchers' halls (since 1881). The people who work here are affectionately known as "Petersbergl butchers", although the "Bergl", or little mountain, does not amount to much more than a hillock. On the hill stands **Peterskirche**, the city's oldest parish church also known as Alter Peter. It was built as a Gothic church in 1278–94 on earlier foundations but burned down in the 14th century. Remodelled several times since then, it was finally rebuilt to the original plans after bomb damage in World War II. The interior of the 90-m (98-foot) long buttressed basilica is dominated by rococo stucco and gold. Nikolaus Stuber created the baroque high altar (1730), which holds at its centre a wooden sculpture of St Peter by Erasmus Grasser (1492), flanked by marble columns.

Fitness training for kids

You need to be fit to tackle the 302 steps up to the viewing platform on top of 92-m (302-foot) high tower. Children will love the bird's-eye view of the Rathaus carillon and the ant-sized shoppers in the market below.

TAKING A BREAK

Stop at one of the area's **snack stalls,** and a short break easily turns into a long one. Why not try a Sauerkraut juice for a change, or a freshly squeezed carrot juice with celeriac?

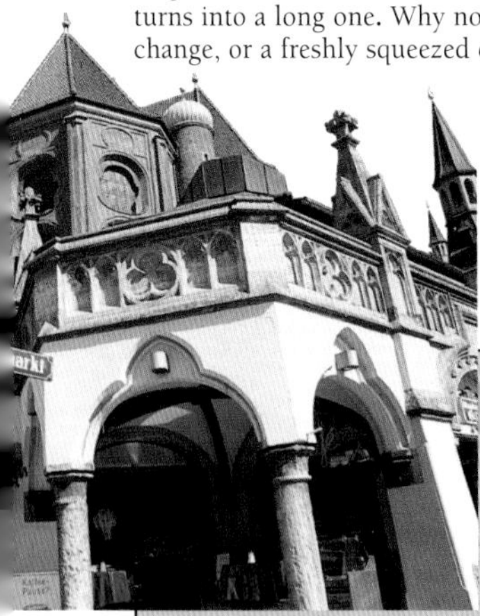

191 D2 Marienplatz
Bus No 52 Viktualienmarkt

Peterskirche
(089) 260 48 28 Thu–Tue 7:30 am–7 pm, Wed 7:30 am–noon, 5–7 pm; tower Mon–Sat 9–6, Son 10–6
Tower inexpensive

VIKTUALIENMARKT: INSIDE INFO

Top tip There are alternating **Mozart, Schubert or Haydn Masses** every Sunday at 9 am in Peterskirche, and once a month there's a Latin Choral Mass. These services are popular, so get there early to make sure you get a seat.

One to miss Don't buy any **souvenirs** here – they are less expensive elsewhere.

4 Marienplatz

Munich's central square attracts throngs of visitors from everywhere with its playful new and dignified old town halls, and a string of town houses with shops and restaurants.

There's something here for everyone, for shopaholic teenagers and camera-happy tourists, for protesting U-Bahn drivers and celebrating football fans, for noisy street musicians and well-to-do promenading ladies. Marienplatz, undeniably, is Munich's heart and its most attractive stage.

Altes Rathaus, with its splendid late-Gothic façade, stands at Marienplatz's east side. Work on the town hall was started

Turrets and eaves: the Gothic Altes Rathaus

in 1470 by cathedral architect Jörg von Halsbach, who incorporated one of the city gates. Bombing in World War II left the Rathaus entirely ruined, and reconstruction was not completed until 1972. The town hall is adorned with the bronze figure of Juliet, a gift from the town of Verona, said to bring good fortune to lovers. Munich's town insignia are displayed on the 56-m (164-foot) high town hall tower, which houses the **Spielzeugmuseum** (Toy Museum). On four floors, there are trains and planes, dolls' houses and Barbie dolls, to enthuse both younger and older visitors. The Council Chamber of Altes Rathaus is where lottery numbers were drawn in the 18th century; it is also from where, on 9 November, 1938, Hitler and Goebbels dispatched their hordes for the Night of Broken Glass, a Nazi pogrom against the Jewish community.

Neues Rathaus, with its playful neo-Gothic façade, which is almost 100-m (109-yard) long, dominates Marienplatz. Construction started in 1867, under the supervision of Austrian architect, Georg von Hauberrisser, and took over 40 years to

Münchner Kindl

A monk, known to locals as "Kindl" (little child) since the 16th century, adorns the town insignia. Trade-marked, it travels around the world on tourist brochures, enticing visitors to Munich.

complete. The asymmetric building divides into two parts – the older part on the right has a richly ornamented central gable, while the newer part on the left is crowned by the 80-m (262-foot) tower with the Münchner Kindl. The architect used rich decorative detail, continuous arcades and terraces to give the building a visual uniformity. There's a lift to the viewing platform at 60m (197 feet).

The **Glockenspiel** (carillon) plays at 11 am, noon and from March to October also at 5 pm. Here Wilhelm V and Renata von Lothringen celebrate their 1568 wedding, while on the level below the coopers dance to boost morale after the plague.

Left: Mariensäule, a popular meeting point

The Heart of Bavaria

Mariensäule is Bavaria's most central point; from here the geodesic network stretches to the farthest corners of the province. When the city was besieged by Swedes in 1632–35, Maximilian pledged to erect a monument after their withdrawal. In 1638 Hubert Gerhard's golden statue (1593) of the Virgin Mary, patron saint of Bavaria, was taken from Frauenkirche and placed on top of a Corinthian marble column. At Mary's feet, harnessed angels fight against the plague, hunger, war and heresy. The Virgin holds a sceptre and the imperial orb, symbols of the power that she has devolved to the elector.

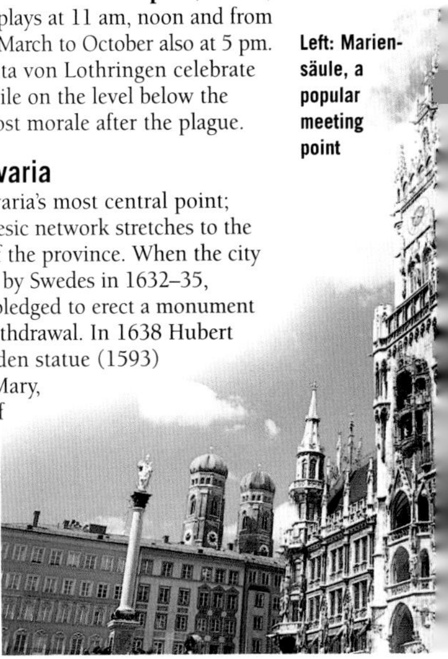

The vast Neues Rathaus

Fischbrunnen

If you're here on Ash Wednesday, make sure to wash out your purse in the Fish Fountain. This, apparently, ensures that you'll have no money worries for the rest of the year. Munich's Mayor follows the 600-year-old custom, and he did so even when the municipal coffers were not quite as empty as they are today. The fountain, cast in 1866, lost several bronze

Refreshing fountain

Debtors' notes and the plague

In March 1349, a traveller staying overnight at the hospital in Viktualienmarkt brought the Black Death to Munich but officials tortured Jewish citizens until they confessed to having poisoned the fountains. Armed with axes and spears, Munich citizens stormed the Jewish ghetto behind the town hall and killed men, women and children. They also burned their IOUs, as did the dukes who were indebted to Jewish money-lenders. The plague continued to rage until the end of the year, and the town remained paralyzed from the horrors all winter. In the spring, however, the Schäfflers (barrel-makers) tempted people back into the streets with their morale-boosting roundelay dance. Duke Ludwig, freed from his debts, decreed that in future the coopers should parade through town every seventh year during carnival. After 2005, the Schäfflers will next dance in 2012.

statues during World War II, and only few original parts could be used when it was rebuilt in 1954. The group of figures is of the "Metzgersprung" (butchers' leap), when the journeymen butchers celebrated release from their masters' contracts with a bath in the fountain. Today, people meet their friends here.

TAKING A BREAK

From Café **Glockenspiel** (► 66) you'll enjoy the best view of the dancing figures in the town hall carillon opposite.

---

191 D3 Marienplatz

Neues Rathaus
Marienplatz 8 Sitzungsdienst (089) 23 39 26 08
Sitzungsdienst (Meetings Information) Mon–Fri 9–4; tower Mon–Thu 9–4, Fri 10–1
Tower ascent inexpensive

Spielzeugmuseum in Altes Rathaus
Marienplatz 15 (089) 29 40 01 Daily 10–5:30
Inexpensive

MARIENPLATZ: INSIDE INFO

Top tip You can visit both the small and the large Council Chambers during **public meetings**; information is available from the Sitzungsdienst.

Hidden gem Are your kids bored with sightseeing? Children aged from one to five can be left to play at the **Münchner Kindl** crèche while parents continue their exploration of the city (Burgstrasse 6, tel. 089/24 23 16 00, Mon–Fri 9–6, Sat 10–4, costs about 4.50 euros/hour, www.muenchnerkindl.de).

5 Frauenkirche

Frauenkirche, the Cathedral Church of Our Dear Lady, with its towers topped with onion domes, is the city's most important landmark. The plain exterior of the brick building impresses with its sheer size. The interior is similarly vast, accommodating a congregation of some 20,000 worshippers, .

No building is allowed to dwarf the cathedral

Duke Sigmund founded the church but alas, he didn't have sufficient money to have it built. Nevertheless, the foundation stone was duly laid on 9 February, 1468. While the Duke forgot the project, and the Church contributed no more than pious words, the citizens of Munich were busy collecting money and building materials – 140 rafts carried some 2,100 tree trunks on the Isar River into town; stones for the foundations were collected from the banks of the Isar; and tiles from a demolished earlier church were reused. To save time and money, workers lived in huts on top of the scaffolding rather than climbing down and up again during every break. Even so, the money ran out. At last the Church intervened; Pope Sixtus IV granted an indulgence lasting eight days, and 250 clergymen heard confessions. This and two further indulgences absolved 124,000 people of their sins – for a fee. Each indulgence cost one week's livelihood per

Ludwig I's well-guarded tomb

Devils' footprint
At the cathedral's entrance you may spot the imprint of a foot in the floor, the "Teufelstritt", or devil's step. Jörg von Halsbach, so the legend goes, made a pact with the devil, who promised to help build the cathedral as long as it would have no windows. When the work was finished, the devil saw the light flooding the nave, and triumphantly claimed the architect's soul. But Halsbach led him to a spot near the door from where not a single window could be seen. His plans foiled, the devil stamped his foot. The Wicked One, it is said, still rages around the church today with his mighty fall winds, but he never stepped inside again.

head. After only 20 years, Munich's church was completed, although the architect, Jörg von Halsbach, died before it was finished.

Plain and Severe

The vast hall church is a typical example of *Backsteingotik*, Gothic brick architecture. Its two towers, 99- and 100-m high (325- and 328-feet), rise octagonally from the square substructure above the naves, either side of the main portal. The two characteristic onion domes don't quite seem to belong – Greek in appearance, they announce the beginning of the Renaissance. The western portal admits visitors to the majestic, almost undecorated interior, which is divided into three naves by 22 slim, octagonal columns carrying the star vaulting. Immediately to the right, in the side nave's first bay, is the resplendent tomb (1622) of Emperor Ludwig the Bavarian (his remains are in the Dukes' Crypt, underneath the choir). The reddish late-Gothic tombstone set in black marble depicts Emperor Ludwig next to Dukes Albrecht III and Ernst. The tomb is guarded by bronze statues of the Wittelsbach Duke Albrecht V in full regalia and of Wilhelm IV as Knight of the Golden Fleece, together with four standard-bearers. The stained-glass choir windows date from the 15th and 16th centuries; in a chapel in the southern side nave one, created in 1573, is an image of the Münchner Kindl. In the southern tower, 86 steps lead to a lift which takes visitors to a platform from where there are great views of the city.

The cathedral: cool and majestic

TAKING A BREAK

Richard's Backhaus (Neuhauser Strasse 2) always has a supply of fresh croissants and tasty coffee.

190 C3 Frauenplatz 1 (089) 290 08 20
Daily 7–7, Thu till 8:30 pm, Fri till 6 pm; tower ascent Apr–Oct, Mon–Sat 10–5 pm
Marienplatz Tower ascent inexpensive

FRAUENKIRCHE: INSIDE INFO

Top tip The beautiful interior of the cathedral comes into its own during **Mass:** on Saturdays at 5:30 pm, and on Sundays and holidays at 10 am, noon and 6 pm.

7 Stadtmuseum

Based in the 15th-century royal stables and armoury, the Municipal Museum presents a number of different exhibitions and collections on the town's history.

The most valuable exhibits in the museum complex, reconstructed after World War II, are the **Moriskentänzer**, or Dancing Moors, which are displayed in their own vaults on the ground floor. Of the 16 wooden figures originally commissioned by the Council for Altes Rathaus, ten are still in existence. These masterpieces of late-Gothic sculpture, carved in 1480 by Erasmus Grasser, who had been inspired by a troop of dancers from North Africa, are among the most attractive depictions of movement. The dancers, just under 50-cm (20-inches) tall, are displayed in three groups in glass cases. With cheeky expressions, they dance their exotic roundelay, their hands wrapped round their bodies in dance or suggestively stretched out, bowing to the spectator and proudly performing their art.

For children young and old

The puppet museum in the Stadtmuseum has regular alternating performances of traditional and imaginatively revisited pieces: Snow White, for example, meets up with the hunter and Dwarf No 7 at a snow-covered railway station, entirely cut off from the world around – what is going to happen next?

Left: model of Munich in the Middle Ages

The fine art of wood carving: *Moriskentänzer*

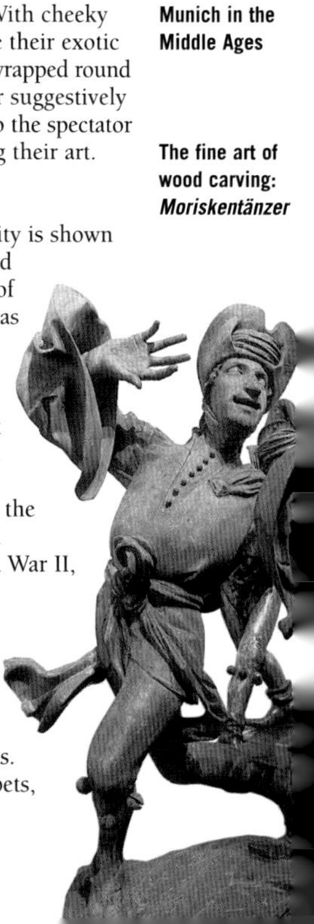

Municipal History

On the first floor, the city is shown in models, paintings and photographs. A model of 15th-century Munich has little houses huddled around the almost monstrous Frauenkirche; paintings depict the evolving townscape over the centuries; and photographs document the destruction of beautiful buildings during World War II, and their peacetime reconstruction.

Dolls Galore

On the third floor, an extensive exhibition of puppet theatres beckons. Marionettes, stick puppets,

Stadtmuseum, in the royal armoury

heads and entire stage sets track the development of the puppet theatre, which in the past was certainly not for children, unlike that at today's funfairs. The aristocracy invited puppeteers into their castles, and some became great artists. There are puppets from around the world on display, traditional and contemporary, some distorted into surreal forms. Among the more unusual displays, near the entrance, are puppets from Socialist days, including a party secretary, a collective farmer, a member of the Free German Youth, an agricultural worker, a war veteran and a demonstrator.

Further Exhibitions

On the fourth floor you'll find 1,600 musical instruments from Africa, Asia, America and Europe, including rarities such as a star orchestrion (a large mechanical harmonicon). Every Sunday at 11 am, the rooms are transformed into a museum of sound. As the former capital of German art and capital of the Nazi movement, Munich had to reappraise some aspects of its own past. This is revealed in the "National Socialism in Munich" department next door.

Idyllic: the Stadtcafé

TAKING A BREAK

Students, filmmakers and passers-by gather at **Stadtcafé** (➤ 67) for their espressos.

190 C2
St-Jakobs-Platz 1 (089) 23 32 23 70, Filmmuseum programme (089) 23 32 41 50
Tue–Sun 10–6 Sendlinger Tor
Buses Nos 52, 56 Blumenstrasse
Inexpensive (free Sun)
www.stadtmuseum-online.de, www.figurentheater-gfp.de, www.filmmuseum-muenchen.de

STADTMUSEUM: INSIDE INFO

Top tip A broad range of films, including some very unusual pieces, are shown every night at the **Filmmuseum**, which is world-renowned for its film restorations.

One to miss Don't go out of your way to visit the **Modemuseum** (Fashion Museum), unless you're a model or a tailor. The Wohnkultur (Art of Living) department is also only worth a fleeting visit.

8 Asamkirche

The official name of this magnificent baroque masterpiece of a church is Johann-Nepomuk-Kirche, but locally it is known by the names of its architects, the brothers Cosmas Damian and Egid Quirin Asam.

Skilled craftsmen – builders, sculptors, painters, stucco plasterers rolled into one– the Asam brothers created an outstanding monument in 1733–46 and donated it to the city. This splendid church was perfectly integrated into the façades of the terraced houses either side: to the left is the residential home of the Asam family, and to the right the vicarage. It wasn't easy for the Asams to build the church: the Council was not interested in private individuals founding churches, and the two famous artists only succeeded by persevering and cleverly exerting their influence.

Magnificent Exterior...

The narrow façade of the church is in the most beautiful baroque style with early rococo influences. It seems to grow out of the natural stone, decorated with small statues and floral patterns. The portal is framed by two columns, a theme that is repeated in the window above, and the top of the window ends in a curved border which recurs in the roof. The portal's ceiling depicts St Nepomuk, sanctified in 1729, as he ascends to heaven, accompanied by angels.

A voluptuous feast for the eyes

...and Festive Splendour in the Interior

Small and manageable on plan (28m by 9m/30 yards by 10 yards), the interior uses countless decorative details and optical illusions to widen the nave into a festive room of princely proportions. Feast your eyes on stucco and carving, gilding, marble sculptures and frescoes around the room. Unimpressed by finicky architects, the Asam Brothers gave their all, at a time when their artistic skills were at their peak. The high altar is divided into two levels by the wrap-around gallery, with both halves framing a halo of rays. The lower part houses St Nepomuk's glass sarcophagus. Marble columns spiral up intc

A little church for the artist-dukes

"heaven", taking the eye up to the ceiling painting, on which *trompe-l'oeil* pillars extend the room even farther upwards. Underneath the ceiling painting, the crucifix seems to be floating in space – a manifestation of the Absolute within a grotto of earthly transitoriness. The oval choir window is not original. Broken only while repairs were being made to the war-damaged church, the new window completely changed the direction of the incoming light and thus weakened the effect of the original lighting of the crucifix. To the left and right of the lower part of the altar, the two master builders are immortalized on grisaille medallions.

Putti live in the church's every nook and cranny

The Asam Family Home

Egid Quirin Asam bought the house in 1729. He remodelled it in 1733, adding rich stucco decorations to the façade. The stuccowork on the left side, which depicts the ascension of Industrious Man into a Classical Greek heaven where he is received by Apollo, is typical of Upper Bavaria. The right-hand side of the façade is adorned with allegories of sculpture, poetry, painting, architecture and music.

TAKING A BREAK

Villanis (in Asamhof, Sendlinger Str.) has been a top favourite with Munich's gays and lesbians for over 20 years; its art nouveau interior and the light snacks on offer make it an ideal place for a break.

---

190 B2 Sendlinger Strasse 62 (089) 260 91 71 Mon–Fri 7:30–6, Sat 8–7, Sun till 3 pm Sendlinger Tor

ASAMKIRCHE: INSIDE INFO

Top tip In the morning, the sun's rays entering via the large eastern window give you some idea of the **original lighting plan**. Take opera glasses along so you can better see the paintings and sculptures.

One to miss During Mass in the small church you are requested to refrain from **taking any photographs or talking**.

At Your Leisure

The Old Town's eastern gateway: Isartor

2 Zentrum für Aussergewöhnliche Museen

The Centre for Unusual Museums, ZAM, houses collections of strange and wonderful objects including so-called *bourdalous*. These intriguing objects were named after the priest Frère Bourdalou, whose sermons were so captivating that the women felt unable to leave the church before the end of Mass if they needed to relieve themselves. At first, they used sauce-boats, but soon these were replaced by purpose-made porcelain containers, the *bourdalous*. Other collections include: the Chamber Pot Museum, the Museum of Scents with countless flagons, the Sissi Museum with a collection of the Austrian empress's negligees; the Pedal Car Museum, chronicling 100 years of the pedal car; and the Easter Bunny Museum with rabbits in all shapes and sizes.

191 E2 Westenriederstrasse 41
(089) 290 41 21 Daily 10–6
Isartor Inexpensive
www.zam-museum.de

3 Isartor

The Isartor, Munich's eastern gate, on the east side of Marienplatz which used to slope down to a valley, was incorporated into the town fortifications in 1314. Remodelled in 1337 and 1499, one side features a large frieze, dating back to 1835, which faces away from the city centre. Ludwig I dedicated the gate to the memory of Ludwig IV's victory at the battle of Ampfing in 1322. The southern tower houses the **Valentin-Karlstadt-Musäum**, which, among other items, shows a "thawed snow sculpture" and a winter toothpick kept at mouth temperature by a fur.

Renaissance splendour: Michaelskirche

Karl Valentin
Munich's most famous comedian was born in 1882, in the city's Au district. First he passed his apprenticeship as a carpenter: "I learned how to plane, saw, nail. Soon I nicked a nail, nailed it into the wall, and used it to hang up for ever the entire golden craft of carpentry," he reported in his typically deadpan manner. Valentin's career as a comedian began in 1908, with his famous monologue Das Aquarium (The Aquarium). A year later he was joined by his long-term partner Liesl Karlstadt. After World War II, the Bavarians suddenly lost interest in him. He died in great poverty in 1948, from a cold.

The other exhibits are as bizarre as their creators, Karl Valentin and Liesl Karlstadt.

191 F2 · Tal 43 · (089) 290 41 21 · Fri–Tue 11:01–5:29, Sun from 10:01 · Isartor · Inexpensive · www.valentin-musaeum.de

6 Michaelskirche

In 1583, Wilhelm V (the Pious) laid the foundation stone for the Jesuit Church of St Michael, the spiritual centre of the counter-Reformation. The topping-out ceremony was three years later, but the tower collapsed in 1590, and the church, boasting the second largest barrel-vault after St Peter's in Rome, was not consecrated until 1597. The proud gabled façade, with its niches containing statues of the founder's ancestors, faces the pedestrianized zone. Between the portals, a bronze statue (1592) by Hubert Gerhard shows St Michael slaying Satan. The Dukes Crypt on the choir's west side contains the tomb of Ludwig II, Bavaria's fairy-tale king.

190 C3 · Neuhauser Strasse 52 · (089) 231 70 60 · Church Sat–Thu 9–7, Fri 11–7; Crypt Mon–Fri 9:30–4:30, Sat till 2:30 · Stachus

9 Marionettentheater

Josef Leonhard "Papa" Schmid and Count von Pocci founded the Puppet Theatre in 1858, and in 1900 it moved to the building erected by Theodor Fischer as a temple to the Muses, the world's first theatre dedicated to puppetry. The Count removed Kasperl (Punch) from market stalls and funfairs onto the stage. The repertory today includes *Däumelinchen (Thumbelina)*, *Zwerg Nase (Dwarf Nose)* and *Zauberflöte (The Magic Flute)*. Traditional performances are especially beautiful, with live music and words from behind the stage.

190 C1 · Blumenstrasse 52 · (089) 26 57 12 · Performances usually at 3 and 8 pm · Sendlinger Tor · Expensive · www.muenchner-marionettentheater.de

10 Sendlinger Tor

In 1175 Munich received its first town wall, but rapid growth meant that a new ring was needed. In around 1310 Sendlinger Tor, with its central gatetower, two hexagonal flanking towers and three passages, became the southern exit. In 1808 the gatetower was dismantled, and in 1906 the passages were linked.

190 B1 · Sendlinger Tor

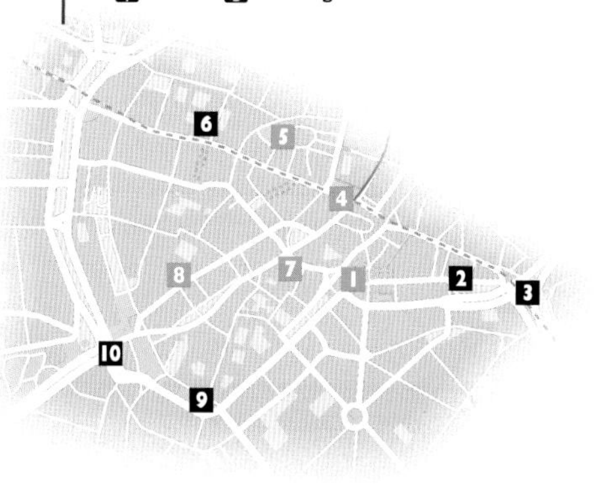

Where to... Eat and Drink?

Prices
Prices are given for one person, excluding drinks.
€ under 12 euros **€€** 12–25 euros **€€€** over 25 euros

Restaurants

Altes Hackerhaus €–€€

A typical old-style Bavarian tavern, with seating in cosy, wood-panelled alcoves or in the former coopers' vaults. Excellent, solid food – the roast pork with dumplings and cabbage salad is particularly good – or try the delicious sweet dumplings with vanilla custard. The waiting staff are always friendly and good-humoured.

190 C2 Sendlinger Strasse 14 (089) 260 50 26 Daily 9 am–midnight Sendlinger Tor

Andechser am Dom €–€€

This restaurant, right in the centre of town, is popular with locals and tourists alike. The furnishings hint at the restaurant's connections with Andechs Abbey, and the beer that is served here is Andechser Klosterbräu. The menu features Bavarian food. At lunchtime it's often hard to find a seat either inside or on the terrace. If you're not too exhausted from sightseeing, you can eat at one of the standing tables, while enjoying the view of Frauenkirche.

191 D3 Weinstrasse 7a/entrance Filserbräugasse (089) 29 84 81 Daily 10 am–1 am Marienplatz

Buxs €

The furnishings in this restaurant are plain and functional, but it's the vegetarian cuisine which is the main attraction. Guests order and collect their own meals from the counter. The choice is extremely varied, and dishes will not reappear on the menu until the month is over.

191 D2 Frauenstrasse 9 (089) 291 95 50 Mon–Fri 11 am–6:45 pm, Sat till 3 pm Isartor

Café Glockenspiel

Get the best views of the town hall carillon from here, while enjoying a Mediterranean meal or just sipping a cup of coffee. The café is busy in the daytime, when children and their parents, business people meeting colleagues, and those with plenty of time on their hands come in for coffee and cake, or just a drink. In the evening you have to order food, but by then the carillon coopers have stopped dancing anyway. At the bar people-watchers sip their cocktails.

191 D3 Marienplatz 28 (089) 26 42 56 Mon–Sat 10 am–1 am, Sun till 7 pm Marienplatz

Ess neun €€€

Staff and décor are both cool and trendy; diners are beautiful, young and well off. Design rules supreme. The cuisine is exceptionally imaginative – it features such unusual dishes as chocolate pizza with a savoury fish topping or papardelle with a white sausage poulard and lobster. Many guests are attracted by these unusual specialities, and they will happily wait in the entrance bar for a table, while enjoying an apéritif.

190 C1 Hans-Sachs-Strasse 9 (089) 23 23 09 35 Mon–Sat 7 pm–1 am Tram Nos 18, 27 Müllerstrasse

Jean de Saint Malo €€

An excellent French restaurant, specializing in fish and seafood dishes, the Jean de Saint Malo counts as a neighbourhood hangout in Glockenbachviertel,

Munich's super-trendy district. The red-checked tablecloths suit the busy, cheerful atmosphere. This popular Breton restaurant is destined for vertical take-off in Munich's gastronomic landscape. They have an excellent wine list too. Make sure you reserve a table.

190 B1 ✉ Holzstrasse 25
☎ (089) 23 00 00 77 Tue–Sun 11:30 am–2 pm, 6 pm–midnight
Tram Nos 18, 27 Müllerstrasse

Lux €€

A small, friendly bistro-type restaurant, decorated with 1990s-style stencilled flowers, serving quality French food and frequented by a lively media crowd. For his late guests, the chef serves up canapés and oysters *fines* No 2, to go with the excellent cocktails that are mixed by eye rather than using standard measurements.

191 D1 ✉ Reichenbachstrasse 37
☎ (089) 20 23 83 93 Mon–Thu 6 pm–1 am, Fri–Sat till 2 am
Fraunhoferstrasse

Weisses Brauhaus €

Brewing wheat beer used to be the privilege of princes, but in 1852 the Schneider family became the first bourgeois family to brew their own beer. Their base, then as now, is Weisses Bräuhaus and the Schneider-Weisse they brew here may well be the best white beer in the world. The kitchen produces authentic Bavarian food: *kronfleisch* (braised beef) with chives and horseradish, or knuckles of veal baked in Aventinus (a strong beer). Soured cuts of meat also feature on the traditional menu as does crème bavarois. There's a mixed crowd of guests, comprising both visitors and locals.

191 D2 ✉ Tal 7 ☎ (089) 290 13 80
Daily 7 am–3 am Marienplatz

Zum Straubinger €€

A cosy, traditional inn. Bavarian classics, from liver dumpling soup to white sausage or mushrooms in cream with dumplings, are served up by friendly locals, either indoors or in the small beer garden. Rapid service comes with a "10 or nothing" guarantee – if you have to wait for more than ten minutes to be served, you won't have to pay for your meal.

191 D2 ✉ Blumenstrasse 5
☎ (089) 232 38 30 Daily 9 am–1 am
Buses Nos 52, 56 Blumenstrasse

Cafés

Mozart

New owners have retained most of the furnishings of the popular original coffee house, and you can sit either at a wooden table or, more comfortably, in an armchair or on a sofa. The café is close to the university clinics, and so its customers are typically medical staff – doctors, students, nurses – as well as tourists who've finished their sightseeing tour of the city at Sendlinger Tor.

190 A2 ✉ Pettenkoferstrasse 2
☎ (089) 59 41 90 Sun–Thu 10 am–1 am, Fri–Sat till 3 am
Sendlinger Tor

Schmalznudel

Munich's traditional gathering point for both night owls and early risers, who seek sustenance for body and soul from the eponymous Schmalznudel (also known as Ausgezogene – a fritter), doughnuts or a steamed pastry with their coffee. Beer is not served here, but sparkling wine and champagne flow aplenty in a jolly, Bavarian atmosphere.

191 D2 ✉ Prälat-Zistl-Strasse 8
☎ (089) 26 82 37 Daily 5 am–5 pm
Bus No 52 Viktualienmarkt

Stadtcafé

The furnishings may have seen better days, but this doesn't bother the mainly younger clientele who come here for a cappuccino or an espresso and one of the delicious cakes, or the equally tasty small French-inspired pastries from the glass cabinet. There is a friendly, informal atmosphere, and it gets very busy in the evening, when the student regulars pour in. This is the place where cinema-goers seek refreshment before watching a film at the Filmmuseum, or mull over what they've seen afterwards.

190 C2 St.-Jakobs-Platz 1 (089) 26 69 49 Sun–Thu 11 am–midnight, Fri–Sat till 1 am Buses Nos 52, 56 Blumenstrasse

Turmstüberl

The café is on the top floor of one of the towers of the Isartor, in the Valentin-Musäum (➤ 64/65).
A visit is well worth it; you can see the exhibits on the way up, and from the top you get panoramic views of Munich. The furnishings are as eccentric as the managers, Petra Perle and Frau Sylvia. Well-known in Munich, Frau Petra achieved fame as an MTV presenter. Try the potato soup or pretzels, the white sausages, a white beer or a home-made cake, while listening to gramophone music.

191 F2 Tal 43 (089) 29 37 62 Fri–Tue 11:01–5:29, Sun from 10:01 am Isartor

Where to... Shop

Two entirely different shopping universes meet between Marienplatz and Glockenbach district. All around Marienplatz you'll come across department stores and fashion chains that you might see in other towns, but also fashionable boutiques. Italian shoe shops and shops with all kinds of decorative and lifestyle objects for the home dominate the scene along Sendlinger Strasse. Viktualienmarkt and the surrounding shops, selling specialities from around the world, are a paradise for food lovers and gourmets, and the stores in the elegant Glockenbachviertel around Gärtnerplatz are the most aspirational in the city, their goods changing as rapidly as the fashions.

Between Marienplatz and Stachus

The Munich fashion house **Ludwig Beck** (Marienplatz 11) has one of the best-stocked music departments on the fourth floor, specializing in classical, folk and jazz. Next to it, the Hautnah perfumery department abounds in seductive scents, pots of cream and perfume bottles. **Hieber am Dom** (Liebfrauenstrasse 1) is traditionally the best place in Munich to buy sheet music and musical instruments.

Around Viktualienmarkt

Since 1936, **Kamm Weninger** (Viktualienmarkt 2) has been the place for those in the know to find everything they need in the way of hair-care products. **Kräuterhaus Lindig** (Blumenstrasse 15) is filled with exotic aromas from the many scented and healing plants that are on sale here. A few steps along, you can buy speciality oils, vinegars, brandies and grappa at **Vom Fass** (Reichenbachstrasse 2). The name of the shop means "from the barrel", and appropriately everything is sold straight from the barrel. On Viktualienmarkt itself, **Exoten Müller** sells Vietnamese dragon fruit and Colombian guavas; **Duftschmankerl** has aromatic herbal bouquets and mobiles made from scented ingredients. There's a more pungent smell at **Rottler** which sells fresh sauerkraut, pickled cucumbers and mustard-dill pickles from the barrel as well as a vast selection of spices. Aromatic clouds also hang around **Caseus**, the top cheese seller in the market. As one might expect, **kaffee & mehr** (Viktualienmarkt 1) sells coffee. The wide-ranging selection is as unusual as the well informed service. Customers will be certain to find what they want. **Poseidon** (Westenriederstrasse 13) is the place for fish fans, who can buy fish or enjoy a quick fishy snack on the spot, standing at one of the tables. Two houses along,

Chocolate and more (Westenriederstrasse 15) tempts chocoholics with exquisite calorie-laden Lauenstein pralines and aromatic hot chocolate. They sell pretty gifts too. If you're looking for Bavarian folk art items such as beer jugs and tin tankards, look no further than **Antiquitäten Herold Neupert** (Westenriederstrasse 8). Finally, there's another aromatic shop: **Georg Huber's** (Tal 66) wood-panelled pipe and cigar shop. The excellent service makes every customer feel special.

Between Sendlinger Strasse and Gärtnerplatz

Kienmoser (Sendlinger Strasse 36) sells rope made from natural fibres, any length, ranging from 1 to 50mm in diameter, as well as nets and belts. The world's largest jeans store, stocking all brands in all sizes, is **Jeans-Kaltenbach** (Herzogspitalstrasse 4).
Optimal (Kolosseumstrasse 6), in Glockenbachviertel, deals in vinyl. There's a phenomenal selection of new and second-hand records, and it attracts a varied clientele with the eclectic range of music. **Slips** (Am Gärtnerplatz 2), one of Munich's leading fashion shops, has much more on offer than lingerie – it stocks well-known and less-well-known designer labels. Meanwhile, **Gasoline Alley** (Corneliusstrasse 5) specializes in items that will make a biker's heart beat faster: leather and shiny chrome, authentic US clothes as well as rare motorbike accessories. A couple of roads along, in the elegant Glockenbach district, **Siebter Himmel** (Hans-Sachs-Strasse 17), which means "seventh heaven", resists the trend to be cool and minimalist. It's a chaotic jumble of lots of fashionable brands, wonderfully varied and disorganized, which reminds you of shops from times past, where you could browse for hours and always come up with another new discovery.

Where to be... Entertained

Bars Serving Food

The **Buena Vista Bar** (Am Einlass 2a, tel: 089/26 02 88 11, Mon–Thu 6 pm–1 am, Sun 11 am–1 am, Fri–Sat till 3 am, food served till midnight), a Cuban bar, is run by a Portuguese owner, who regularly travels to Castro's island and stocks up with valuable paintings to hang on the bar's unplastered walls.
Attached to the bar is a small avant-garde theatre, the Team-Theater. Service before and after the shows is sometimes a little slow, but there's always a tremendous atmosphere in the crowded bar. Late at night, at the weekends, young and old dance in the corridors and between the tables to hot Latin salsa rhythms played by the resident DJ.

Morizz (Klenzestrasse 43, tel: 089/201 67 76, 7 pm–2 am), at the back of Gärtnerplatz, has become an institution in Munich's gay club scene. Guests lounge in comfort in the red leather armchairs, slurping excellent cocktails and having apparently deep conversations, while studying themselves and others in the mirrored walls.
Straight guests are also welcome, and everyone gets on famously.
The kitchen dishes up Thai food until late into the night.
Baader Café (Baaderstrasse 47, tel: 089/201 06 38, Sun–Thu 10 am–1 am, Fri–Sat till 2 am) is one of the oldest trendy pubs in the district around Gärtnerplatz, and still one of the most popular. The café never tries to follow the latest fashions; since the early 1980s it has just been the ideal place to spend the evening over a glass of beer or wine, a crunchy salad or Italian and Austrian delicacies.
People of all age groups congregate here to enjoy themselves.

The **K+K Club** (Reichenbachstrasse 22, daytime tel: 089/20 20 74 63, Sun–Thu 8 pm–2 am, Fri–Sat until 3 am) begins to fill up from about 10 pm, when the in-crowd from Glockenbach start their evening with a vodka lemon or beer, in the elegant, grey and black interior. DJ music, as well as occasional readings and exhibitions, provide a stimulating background for an audience mainly from the music and food industries.

Bars

Brown is the predominant colour at the **Lizard Lounge** (Cornelius-strasse 34, tel: 089/20 00 98 27, Mon–Sat 8 am–1 am, Sun 10 am–6 pm) – the wood, walls and cube seats are all styled in brown. The colour scheme could be depressing, but it isn't – the customers inject colour to the place as they sip their drinks – although some prefer existentialist black. Hips swing confidently to the cool DJ sounds, beer is casually drunk from the bottle, and cocktails are held by hands with fingernails adorned in all the colours of the rainbow.

Ksar Club (Müllerstrasse 30, tel: 089/26 40 38, daily 9 pm–3 am) is a permanent fixture in Munich's nightlife. The small bar gets crowded at weekends, and there's often a long line of those who either are waiting or who can't get in. Regular guests know each other, and sit chatting together, if the music isn't too loud, but newcomers are always welcome too.

Discos

Monofaktur (Sonnenstrasse 27, tel: 0162/749 59 05, Mon–Sat from 9 pm), a club styled in contemporary shades of orange, offers a different music programme every day, ranging from jazz to Sixties music to drum and bass. The average age of the customer reflects the music that is being played; the majority of the audience tend to be over 20.

Theatre

Staatstheater am Gärtnerplatz (Gärtnerplatz 3, tel: 089/21 85 19 60) was first founded in 1865 by a company of Munich citizens who wished to set up their own theatre. However, the enterprise failed and the king intervened to ensure it remained open. Since then it has been state-owned. The programme is wide-ranging, from opera and operetta to ballet evenings and jazz concerts. **Team-Theater Tankstelle** (Am Einlass 2a, tel: 089/260 43 33), based in a former petrol station, specializes in modern German and international drama, to great critical acclaim. **Theater im Fraunhofer** (Fraunhoferstrasse 9, tel: 089/26 78 50), with its programme of artistic cabaret performances, attracts a mixed crowd. The main emphasis is on critical and satirical cabaret, especially by up-and-coming artists. After performances, the long wooden tables at the *Fraunhofer* pub nearby provide the right atmosphere for a beer, a Bavarian snack and long post-cabaret discussions.

Cinemas

The **Filmtheater am Sendlinger Tor** (Sendlinger-Tor-Platz 11, tel: 089/55 46 36) shows the latest releases in a large auditorium. If you get there early, you may get one of four box seats from where you can watch the film in splendid isolation and with excellent views. The **Filmmuseum** (► 61), based in the Stadtmuseum, is world-renowned for its film restoration and conservation work. On the programme are, among others, retrospectives from the archive, classics of film-making and avant-garde films from around the world. **Werkstattkino** (Fraunhoferstrasse 9, tel: 089/260 72 50) is Munich's wackiest cinema, with a weird and wonderful mix of films – including horror B-movies – shown in an auditorium of just 60 seats.

The Northern City

Getting Your Bearings

With its stylish designer shops, smart restaurants and, at the centre, the residence of the Bavarian kings, the area around Theatinerstrasse, Residenzstrasse and Maximilianstrasse is Munich's finest district, with one great contrasting feature: the authentically Bavarian Hofbräuhaus.

The boulevards around the Residenz are so elegant they compare favourably with similar areas in the world's leading cities. There are stylish shops everywhere, especially since the chic minimalism of the Fünf Höfe (Five Courtyards) was added to the city centre, otherwise dominated by more conservative architecture. A careful balance has been observed here between the traditional and the modern. This is evident in the numerous theatres and the opera, but also in newly built structures. In fact, the historical and well established are so highly respected that *trompe-l'oeil* façades were erected in Maximilianstrasse to hide the futuristic Maximilianshöfe behind them. Outward appearance and showiness are also apparent among the theatregoing crowds in the vicinity of Theatinerstrasse, the heart of Munich's so-called *Bussi-Gesellschaft* (kissing society, the art and media scene or "luvvies").

Page 71: View down Theatinerstrasse

Bicycle stop at the Platzl

Sample both musical and culinary delights at the Opera

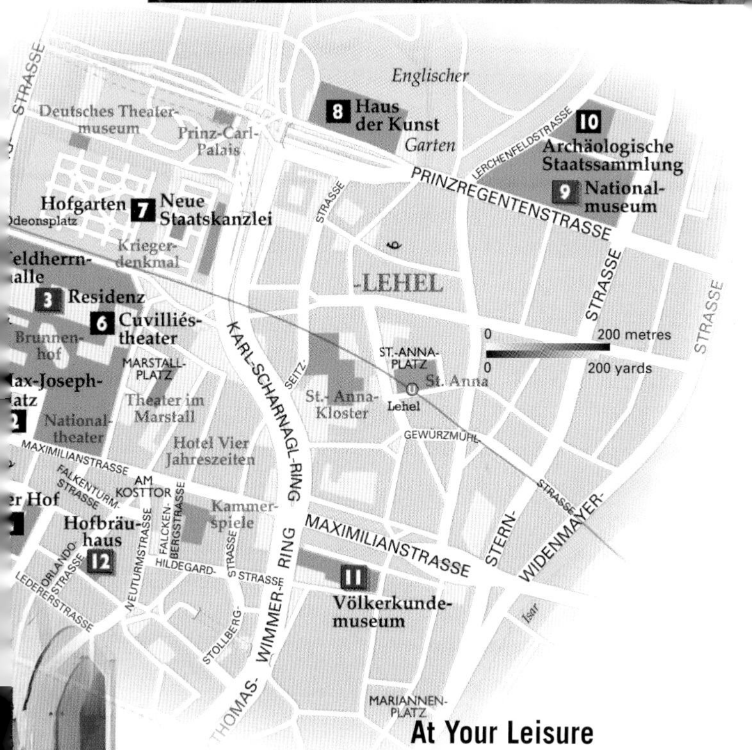

★ Don't Miss

- **3** **Residenz** ➤ 76
- **5** **Feldherrnhalle** ➤ 79
- **9** **Nationalmuseum** ➤ 80
- **11** **Völkerkunde-museum** ➤ 82
- **12** **Hofbräuhaus** ➤ 84

At Your Leisure

- **1** Alter Hof ➤ 86
- **2** Max-Joseph-Platz ➤ 86
- **4** Theatinerkirche ➤ 87
- **6** Cuvilliéstheater ➤ 87
- **7** Hofgarten and Neue Staatskanzlei ➤ 87
- **8** Haus der Kunst ➤ 88
- **10** Archäologische Staatssammlung ➤ 88

The princely buildings of the Residenz, with its splendid rooms and glorious collections, are today's highlights. And in the evening you can relax, digesting what you've seen over a glass of beer at the world-famous Hofbräuhaus.

The Northern City in a Day

9:00 am

A hint of the Middle Ages lingers in the narrow lanes and passageways around 1 **Alter Hof** (left; ➤ 86). In contrast, immediately behind it, are the modern and ultra-elegant Fünf Höfe passages (five courtyards, below; ➤ 92), where you can take a break with a latte macchiato or a lemon grass tea. In 2 **Max-Joseph-Platz** (➤ 86) you can sample the arts. Behind a neo-classical columned portico, the Bayerische Staatsoper delights with its musical repertory, while next to it, at the Residenz-theater, the best of the world of drama can be enjoyed.

10:00 am

It takes time to visit the extensive 3 **Residenz** (➤ 76) complex. Different rooms are open to the public in the morning and in the afternoon – so it's a a good idea to take some time off in the middle. After leaving the arcaded 5 **Feldherrnhalle** (➤ 79), as you walk along Ludwigstrasse, you will see on your right the sunny terraces of the Tambosi (left; ➤ 90) at Hofgarten. This is an ideal spot for your lunch break, from where you can study the Feldherrnhalle at your own leisure.

12:30 pm

Return to the Residenz where the remaining rooms are now open for visitors. Leave sufficient time for

a visit to the enchanting 6 **Cuvilliéstheater** (➤ 87). Now stroll through the geometrically laid out 7 **Hofgarten** (above; ➤ 87), continuing past **Neue Staatskanzlei** to Prinzregentenstrasse, which will take you to the Isar River, alongside Englischer Garten. You will only catch glimpses of the park from the road, however, because the view is blocked by 8 **Haus der Kunst** (➤ 88), the art museum.

3 pm

The 9 **Nationalmuseum** (right; ➤ 80) is as interesting inside as its exterior promises. The museum has splendid architectural features, and houses exhibitions of sacred art and Nativity cribs, of folk art and Gothic relief tracery. This is a great place to find out about Bavarian history.

4 pm

Continue southwards along the green banks of the Isar, and you will get to Maximilianstrasse, with its monument to Maximilian II and the 11 **Völkerkundemuseum** (Ethnography Museum ➤ 82). You have just over an hour to learn about other cultures before it closes. A stroll along Maximilianstrasse (below) will take you past the elegant designer shops of Prada, Gucci and Munich's own fashion guru, Rudolph Moshammer.

6 pm

After a hard day's exploring, you will find the reward for your efforts at the 12 **Hofbräuhaus** (➤ 84) am Platzl. Contrary to expectations, this brewery tavern is not frequented only by tourists; locals also like to pop inside to enjoy a beer or two in the pleasant beer garden.

If you're still bursting with energy after your visit to the Hofbräuhaus, try out the P1 (➤ 94) disco or take in some culture at one of the theatres (➤ 94).

3 Residenz

Left: The Madonna, guarding the Court

For 500 years, the Residenz was the seat of the Bavarian rulers. The complex, decorated in a fusion of architectural styles from Renaissance to neo-classicism, is so extensive that even its former residents – Bavarian dukes, prince-electors and kings – occasionally lost their way in the corridors between the 130 grand state rooms.

In 1385, the Wittelsbach rulers decided that their old court, called Alte Veste (➤ 86), had become too small, and so the Neuveste was erected on Max-Joseph-Platz, which is also known as Opernplatz. The structure, originally Gothic in style, was remodelled and extended in the 16th century, first by Duke Wilhelm V, then by his son Maximilian I, who turned it into a Renaissance palace. Hans Simon Reifenstuel from Gmund on Tegernsee is thought to have been the architect, while Peter de Witt, also called Candid, was responsible for much of the interior decoration. The Residenz was transformed once more under Leo von Klenze. The Renaissance portal in Residenzstrasse is crowned with a bronze sculpture of *Patrona Bavariae*, Bavaria's patroness, represented as the Holy Virgin. Yet King Ludwig I thought it not sufficiently impressive, and so he had the Königsbau (royal structure) added in 1826–35, featuring an imposing neo-classical façade and a new main portal facing Opernplatz – it is clear that the model was the Palazzo Pitti in Florence.

A sparkling gem from the Schatzkammer

In the morning...

Entering via the main Königsbau entrance in Opernplatz, will take you to the first courtyard and the ticket office. To one side is the **Schatzkammer** (Treasury), the most important collection with over 1,200 exhibits of royal and ducal insignia, sacred art and gems sparkling and glittering in the glass

Max I Joseph in front of the Residenz

cases. The treasures include the *Arnulfciborium*, a 9th-century golden altarpiece, and a small equestrian statue of St George, the horse carved from agate and chalcedony, with a ruby-decorated saddle dating from the late 1500s.

Behind the ticket office, between the Wittelsbach fountain courtyard and the kitchen, is one of the Residenz's prestige rooms, the 16th-century **Antiquarium**, where Duke Albrecht V stored his collection of antiquities. Friedrich Sustris adorned the vast barrel vault with allegories, grotesques and Bavarian town- and landscapes. Opposite the ticket office, 121 portraits of Bavarian princes and their families hang on the long corridor walls of the **Ahnengalerie** (ancestral gallery).

The **Reiche Zimmer** (Rich Rooms) on the first floor live up to their name. The apartments, originally built for Elector Max Emanuel, were remodelled by François Cuvilliés in the rococo style, on the orders of the elector's son, Karl Albrecht. Gilded carvings and stucco work compete in resplendence, but the pinnacle is the **Miniaturen-kabinett** (Cabinet of Miniatures) at the end of the suite of rooms. Restored in 2001, it displays delicate miniature paintings set into the gilded wooden panelling in the rooms.

A corridor leads to the **Päpstliche Zimmer** (Papal Rooms), the rooms of Maximilian's daughter-in-law, Electress Henriette Adelaide. Pope Pius IV stayed here in 1782. Diagonally opposite, in the **Schlachtenzimmern** (Battle Rooms), a number of paintings commemorate the Napoleonic Wars, when Bavaria

Antique sculptures and Renaissance frescoes

A chapel, part of the Reiche Zimmer

RESIDENZ: INSIDE INFO

Hidden gem One of the summer highlights is the series of **classical music or jazz concerts** in the Residenz's Brunnenhof.

fought on the side of the French emperor, profiting well from the enterprise. Your morning tour of the Residenz concludes with the anterooms to **Kurfürstenzimmer** (Prince Elector's Rooms) in Brunnenhof where valuable objects are exhibited: 19th-century French and German porcelain as well as beautiful 17th- and 18th-century East Asian pieces.

...and in the Afternoon

The **Königsbauapartments** behind the battle rooms were built by Leo von Klenze for King Ludwig I and his wife. The talented architect also designed the wall and ceiling decorations as well as the Empire-style furnishings. From here, the Golden Room takes you into the older part of the Residenz, to the **Silberkammern** (silver chambers), where 3,500 pieces of Wittelsbach table silver can be seen. The **Steinzimmertrakt**, richly decorated with stucco marble, west of Kaiserhof, leads to **Vierschimmelsaal** and **Kaisersaal**. The latter served as a festival room, its ceiling decorated with allegorical figures, a painted frieze, and tapestries by Peter Candid.

TAKING A BREAK

At **Casa del Caffè** (Residenzstrasse 2) you can enjoy an espresso that tastes authentically Italian.

Munich's most stylish concert venue: Brunnenhof

191 E4 Residenzstrasse 1 (089) 29 06 71 Fri–Wed 9–6, Thu until 8 pm, Apr–15 Oct; 10–4 rest of year Odeonsplatz Moderate www.schloesser.bayern.de

5 Feldherrnhalle

The Bavarian army's hall of fame, an open arcaded hall closely modelled on the Loggia dei Lanzi in Florence by the architect, Friedrich von Gärtner, marks the beginning of Ludwigstrasse, the prestigious boulevard leading to Siegestor.

The Feldherrnhalle, built in 1844, has three arches. The two side arches hold bronze statues by Ludwig von Schwanthaler; Count von Tilly, military commander in the Thirty Years War, stands guard on one side, while Prince Wrede, general during the Napoleonic Wars, occupies the other. In 1892, during the reign of Prince Regent Luitpold, Ferdinand von Miller's Army Monument was added.

Avoiding the issue

During the Third Reich, everyone passing the Feldherrnhalle memorial plaque, was forced to salute Hitler. Many instead made their way through Viscardigasse, which has since been known as "skivers' alley".

Dedicated to the glory of the great commanders

Putsch Attempt

It is from Feldherrnhalle that Adolf Hitler attempted – and failed – to stage a putsch on 9 November, 1923 (► 20). From 1933 to 1945, the Nazis used the "march to Feldherrnhalle" as a major propaganda event. A memorial plaque at the side of the hall, in Residenzstrasse, was guarded by SS soldiers. It was removed in 1945.

TAKING A BREAK

Café **Rottenhöfer** (Residenzstr. 26) is said to sell the best chocolates in the city.

191 D4 Odeonsplatz Odeonsplatz

FELDHERRNHALLE: INSIDE INFO

Top tip If your feet are sore, take a **bicycle rickshaw** and have yourself chauffeured through Hofgarten and into Prinzregentenstrasse.

9 Nationalmuseum

When the city of Nuremberg founded a Germanic Museum in 1852, King Maximilian II responded to the challenge by beginning the construction of a "patriotic" museum in Munich. Today the National Museum houses one of Europe's most important art and cultural history collections.

Originally the National Museum was based in the building which today is the home of the Museum für Völkerkunde (► 82), the Museum of Ethnography. The building was soon overcrowded, and the collection moved to its new premises in Prinzregentenstrasse in 1900. Gabriel von Seidl designed the museum to be in harmony with its exhibits: where Gothic items were to be shown, it was built in the Gothic style, while Romanesque and baroque exhibits are displayed in a setting appropriate for them. This makes for an eclectic exterior,

Fun for Kids

On one Sunday every month, a special programme allows children over six to listen to adventure stories, join the gang of museum explorers, try on a knight's chainmail, watch exciting plays, make puppets or stained-glass windows, and much more.

Maximilian II in front of his museum

which is as worthwhile to visit as the paintings, sacred art, crafts, armoury, weapons and farmhouse interiors on display inside.

Ivory and Other Treasures

Among the prize exhibits of sacred art are filigree ivory relief pieces such as Reider's 5th-century plaque of *Christ's Ascension* (measuring 19cm by 12cm/7½ by 4¾ inches) and *Christ's Crucifixion* from 870 (22cm by 10cm/8½ by 4 inches), as well as Gothic sculptures by Tilman Riemenschneider and others.

Costumes, furniture, valuable clocks, goblets and wall decorations give a vivid introduction to life at court during

the baroque and rococo eras. There are also superb examples of the neo-classical, historicist and art nouveau styles. Items from the world of wealthy citizens contrast with exhibits in the department of folk art on the lower floor. This is dedicated to the secular life of ordinary people, with farmhouse interiors and everyday objects.

Away in a Manger

Also on the lower floor is one of the museum's highlights: the exhibition of Christmas cribs. The 18th- and early 19th-century Alpine and Southern Italian cribs, conjure up the magic of Christmas. The cribs, collected by the distinguished Munich businessman Max Schmederer in the late 1800s, depict the angel's visit to the shepherds, the adoration of the Wise Men, the search for shelter or the flight to Egypt. They are atmospherically displayed, vividly bringing each scene to life. A particularly attractive crib shows a Neapolitan street market, several metres (yards) long, with 38-cm (15-inch) tall statues. There are butchers and bakers, market sellers and passers-by with finely woven baskets, as well as walls overgrown with vines. Such street scenes which do not show "historically accurate" Bible scenes, are typical for Neapolitan crib art before the late 1700s.

A scene from the exhibition of cribs

TAKING A BREAK

The museum's café-bistro **Marco-Aurelio** serves drinks and Italian snacks, ideal for taking a break.

197 F5 · Prinzregentenstasse 3 · (089) 211 24 01 · Tue–Sun 10–6, Thu till 8 pm · Lehel · Tram 17, Bus 53 Nationalmuseum/Haus der Kunst · Inexpensive, free on Sun · www.bayerisches-nationalmuseum.de

NATIONALMUSEUM: INSIDE INFO

Top tip There are **specially themed guided tours** of the museum every Sunday at 11 am and Thursday at 6 pm.

Hidden gem Don't miss the **wooden town models.** A particularly fine example, created in 1850–63 by Johann Baptist Seitz and his son Franz, is worked in such painstaking detail that the family nearly bankrupted themselves producing it.

11 Völkerkunde-museum

Germany's second-largest Museum of Ethnography takes visitors on a cultural journey around the world, with exhibits of Native American tepees, African masks and Asian statues.

Ritual sculptures from the heart of Africa

The Völkerkundemuseum looks slightly Moorish on the outside. This is because its playful façade was not designed for this museum but for an exhibition of Bavarian art that is now in the Nationalmuseum (► 80). The Wittelsbach rulers were very interested in ethnography and early on started collecting objects from other cultures. Princess Therese of Bavaria even went travelling herself, returning from a tour of North America in 1893 with 125 Native American artefacts. Today they form the core of the exhibition in the North America room. The museum holds a total of some 150,000 exhibits, arranged in seven permanent exhibitions themed by region (Africa, India, East Asia, North and South America, Oceania and the Islamic Orient). Exhibits are constantly rearranged and assembled to make as many pieces as possible available to the public. Special exhibitions deal with present-day issues, such as the genocide in Rwanda, nutrition around the world or the current state of Afghanistan.

Wittelsbach philanthropists

A botanical and zoological field trip took naturalists Carl Friedrich Philipp von Martius and Johann Baptist von Spix to Brazil in 1817. They returned to Munich in 1820, bringing back numerous animal and herb specimens as well as two native Brazilian children. Queen Karoline immediately took the children into her care. However, she was powerless against the ravages of the climate. The boy died in 1821, the girl one year later. Both children are buried on Munich's Südfriedhof. Their tombstone bears the inscription "Merciless is the rough winter in the north...".

Asiatic Treasures

In the Asian department on the first floor, masterpieces made from stone, bronze and wood are displayed to re-create the ambience of a Hindu or Buddhist temple, inviting meditation. The Wittelsbach East Asian Collection and Japan explorer Franz von Siebold's collection were the basis on which the museum was built, and they are still its pride and joy today. New permanent exhibitions on Oceania and the Islamic World will soon be added to the museum's programme.

Wood, Plastic and Feathers

Permanent guests in the Africa department on the second floor are two artists of the "Blaue Reiter" (Blue Rider) group, August Macke and Wassily Kandinsky. Statues and masks inspired many of their images. But there's more to see in this department than traditional sculptures; also on display are contemporary household objects that have been made into idols, as well as superb ornamental textiles. Native American songs invite the visitor to enter the North America room; apart from Princess Therese's original collection, it features the world's earliest preserved kayak, dating back to 1577. The South American Indian department has a magnificent display of textiles, some worked with feathers. A picture of everyday life in an Indian tribe can be gleaned from the exhibits of agricultural tools, cooking utensils and hunting weapons.

TAKING A BREAK

In the museum café **Bel Mondo,** light snacks such as soups, salads, pasta or cake, are available.

197 E4 · Maximilianstrasse 42 · (089) 210 13 61 00 · Tue–Sun 9:30–5:15 pm · Lehel · Tram Nos 17, 19 Maxmonument · Moderate, free on Sun (fee special exhibitions) · www.voelkerkundemuseum-muenchen.de

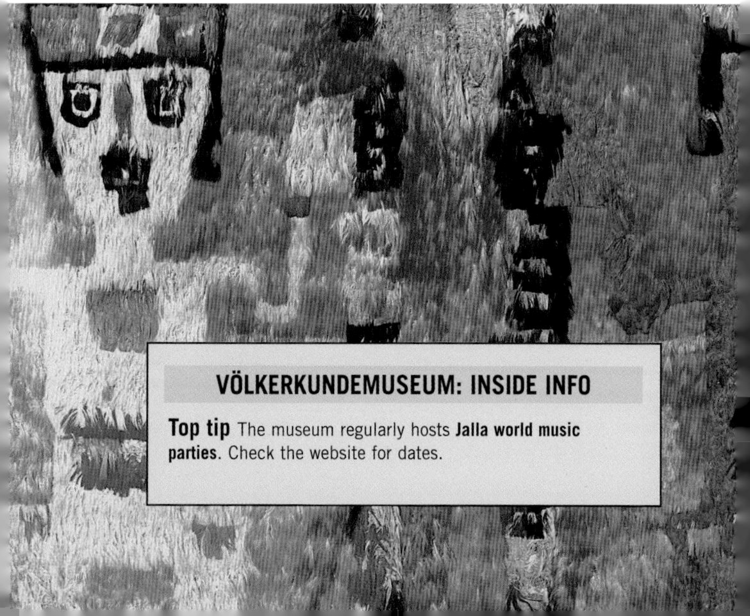

A Native American feather masterpiece

VÖLKERKUNDEMUSEUM: INSIDE INFO

Top tip The museum regularly hosts **Jalla world music parties.** Check the website for dates.

12 Hofbräuhaus

Munich families, elderly Bavarians and tourists from around the world all flock to the legendary royal brewery. The inn was even immortalized in a song and, according to one local story, the porter Alois Hingerl still has his regular table here (► 85).

In the 16th century, the aristocracy generally preferred wine to beer. But as Duke Wilhelm V found the imported wine too costly, he ordered in 1589 that in place of the Alte Veste's (today's Alter Hof, ► 86) chicken coop, a royal brewhouse should be built, to supply the royal court with beer. The brewery moved to the Platzl (Square) in 1644, from where the state continued to supply the taverns. In 1830, the brewery was granted permission to sell to the public, and this temple to beer opened its doors at the Platzl in 1896. It soon became a legend, and now some 10,000 litres (2,200 gallons) of Hofbräu beer a day flow from its barrels, while the staff break new records in the number of tankards they carry.

Always cheerful: the service at Hofbräuhaus

Sing Along

As soon as the brass band starts playing the Hofbräuhaus song everyone joins in. The song talks of the Isar and Bavaria and so on. But the famous refrain goes "oans, zwoa, gsuffa" (one, two, down the hatch), and the guests don't hesitate to follow this command.

Good cheer prevails indoors and in the garden as soon as the brass band starts up

Hofbräuhaus on the Platzl

There is a vast, rustic room, the "Schwemme", with wooden tables on the ground floor. In the evenings, the atmosphere can get so lively here that it puts up a strong competition to the Oktoberfest. Even the regulars, the old-standing Hofbräuhaus guests, may be carried along by the atmosphere and happily toast the visiting tourists. The large number of regulars at the Hofbräuhaus is evident from signs marking the tables as "Stammtisch". At these traditional tables, groups of men – and occasionally also groups of women – regularly meet once a week. Several companies have a Stammtisch reserved for their employees at one of Munich's pubs. Some regulars even have their own tankards, which can be locked away in the "tankard safe" until their next visit.

TAKING A BREAK

If you're not a beer drinker, visit the stylish **Cortiina Bar** (Ledererstrasse 8), just around the corner, open from 6 pm.

191 E3 Platzl 9
(089) 29 01 36 10
9 am–midnight Marienplatz
www.hofbraeuhaus.com

A Munich Man in Heaven

According to legend, there's a Bavarian wearing a blue cap seated in one corner of the Hofbräuhaus. That's the Angel Aloisius, the late Alois Hingerl, a Munich porter whose story was told by Ludwig Thoma. Alois, felled by a stroke, went to Heaven as the Angel Aloisius. Very unhappy, because he only had manna to nourish him, he began to rebel. And so God appointed him a messenger, whose task it was to deliver his heavenly edicts to the Bavarian government. With his very first letter in hand, Aloisius ended up at the Hofbräuhaus – and there he still sits today, while the Bavarian government is still awaiting heavenly inspiration.

HOFBRÄUHAUS: INSIDE INFO

Top tip The public rooms and the Festsaal on the **1st and 2nd floors** are more elegant than those on the ground floor.The brass band starts playing at 7 pm.

Hidden gem Even some locals don't know that the Hofbräuhaus also has an attractive, shaded **beer garden**.

One to miss Don't stay until **closing time**; much alcohol is consumed over the course of the evening and it will be taking its full effect by now.

At Your Leisure

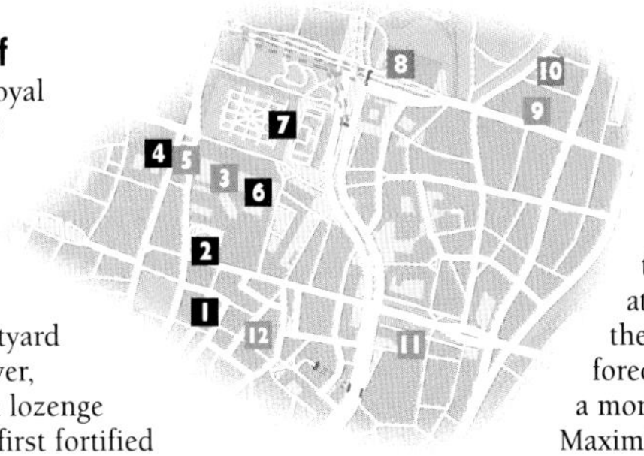

1 Alter Hof

The former royal residence has plenty of medieval trappings: a vaulted passage, a cobbled courtyard and a tall tower, adorned with lozenge shapes. This first fortified complex along the town wall was built in the late 12th century, and the German emperor, Ludwig IV the Bavarian, lived here from 1328. The court moved to the more prestigious newly built Residenz (► 76) in the late 14th century. Alter Hof can only be seen from the outside; various national and cultural institutions are based here. It is due to be converted into apartments.

191 E3 Burgstr. 8 Marienplatz

2 Max-Joseph-Platz

The square is also known as Opernplatz after the **Bayerisches Nationaltheater** (► 94), Munich's opera house, which is based here. It was founded by King Max I Joseph in 1818, but burned down only five years later. The rebuilding work by Leo von Klenze was completed in 1825. The neo-classical building has magnificent rooms including a royal spectator room. Five of Wagner's operas were financed by Ludwig II and had their premiere at the Nationaltheater. In the forecourt stands a monument to Maximilian I Joseph.

King Maximilian II commissioned Friedrich Bürklein to build a splendid boulevard flanked by townhouses, from 1852. The road extends eastwards from the Residenz to the Maximilianeum (► 131) on the opposite bank of the Isar. Today, **Maximilianstrasse** is Munich's most expensive shopping street, home to the luxury hotel Vier Jahreszeiten as well as the renowned Kammerspiele and the elegant Maximilianshöfe next to the opera.

Trompe-l'Oeil

Walking along Maximilianstrasse out of town, take a close look at the first building behind the opera house on your left. If you can't see any marked difference between this building and the ones next to it, then the architect succeeded. Until 2003 there was an ugly gap here in the line of buildings. It was to be closed by the Maximilianshöfe, erected behind a façade built according to the original plans.

***Swan Lake* performed at the Nationaltheater**

Italian baroque style: Theatinerkirche

191 E4 Odeonsplatz Tram No 19 Nationaltheater www.bayerische-staatsoper.de

4 Theatinerkirche

Theatinerkirche, the church of St Cajetan, may strike you as oddly baroque, yellow and solid in among all the Klenze-inspired neo-classical buildings around it. Electress Henriette Adelaide vowed to have the church built in 1662, and since she was originally from the House of Savoy, she introduced Italian high baroque style from her homeland to Munich. A century later, Cuvilliés added some rococo features. At the front, slender towers with baroque helmets flank the central part of the structure with its large copper dome. The interior is light and attractive with splendid stucco decorations.

191 D4 Theatinerstrasse 22 (089) 210 69 60 Church Mon–Sat 7–7, Sun 8–7; Ducal Crypt May–Oct Mon–Fri 10–1, 1:30–4:30, Sat 10–3 Odeonsplatz

6 Cuvilliéstheater

In 1751, François Cuvilliés together with the best court artisans of his day created Germany's most beautiful rococo theatre. Mozart's *Idomeneo* was premiered here in 1781. The theatre was bombed in 1944, and it took until 1958 to rebuild it according to the original plans. Only the wooden decorations of the boxes remain of the former building. Unfortunately, the theatre is now dilapidated, and there is no money to restore it.

191 E4 Residenzstrasse 1 (089) 29 06 71 Apr–15 Oct 9–6, 16 Oct–Mar 10–4, Thu till 8 pm Odeonsplatz Inexpensive www.schloesser.bayern.de, www.bayerische-staatsoper.de

7 Hofgarten and Neue Staatskanzlei

Through a small triumphal arch you pass from Odeonsplatz to Hofgarten. The garden was created in the 17th century, with geometric flowerbeds and paths leading towards the central temple of Diana. A bronze statue of *Tellus Bavarica*, "Bavarian Earth",

Glamorous boxes in the Cuvilliéstheater

Old and new: Bayerische Staatskanzlei

stands guard on top of the temple. On its eastern side the gardens are closed by the new state chancellery. The people strongly protested against the expensive government building, which encloses the army museum, built in 1907, with glass and reinforced concrete.

191 E4/5–F4 Karl-Scharnagel-Ring Odeonsplatz Bus No 53 Von-der-Tann-Strasse

8 Haus der Kunst

The entire leadership of the National Socialist party attended the opening, on 18 July, 1937, of this Nazi building designed by the architect couple Troost. Until the end of World War II, the exhibitions showed what the rulers deemed to be "German art": imposing sculptures, paintings of people with chiselled features, blond hair and blue eyes. Today, the gallery alternately shows the works of 20th-century artists and modern or avant-garde art from Germany and other countries.

191 F5 Prinzregentenstrasse 1 (089) 21 12 70 Daily 10–8 Lehel Tram No 17, Bus No 53 Nationalmuseum/Haus der Kunst Expensive www.hausderkunst.de

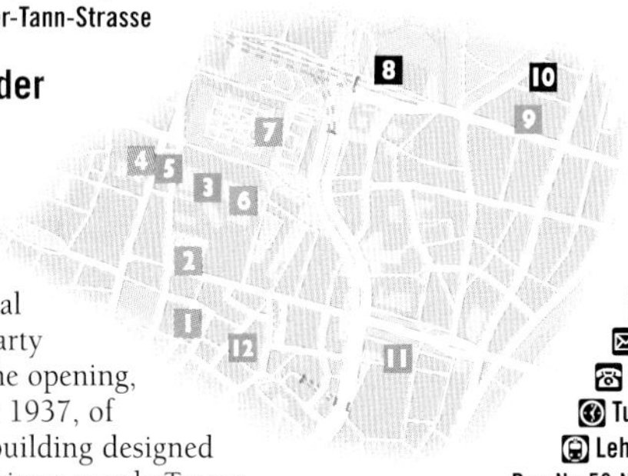

10 Archäologische Staatssammlung

The Archaeological Collection (known previously as National Collection of Prehistory) links the Early Stone Age, via Antiquity to the Middle Ages, perfectly complementing the neighbouring Nationalmuseum, which picks up the history from that time on. Burial objects provide us with an insight into the cultures of Germanic tribes, Romans and Celts; everyday objects document the life of ordinary people; and sacred art breathes life into ancient religions.

197 F5 Lerchenfeldstrasse 2 (089) 211 24 02 Tue–Sun 9–4:30 Lehel Tram No 17, Bus No 53 Nationalmuseum/Haus der Kunst Moderate www.archaeologie-bayern.de

Asterix as museum guide

The Archäologische Staatssammlung organizes children's activities: you can follow a guided tour to the Stone Age or visit the Celts with with comic book character, Asterix. Archaeological Workshop courses are for children of all ages. For details see the museum's website.

Where to... Eat and Drink

Prices
Prices are given for one person, excluding drinks.
€ under 12 euros **€€** 12–25 euros **€€€** over 25 euros

Restaurants

Austernkeller €€€
Munich's best traditional restaurant specializing in fish and seafood. The restaurant is fitted with lovely old-fashioned, chintzy furnishings, candelabra and antiques. The food is delicious; try the melt-in-the-mouth wild Irish salmon or the popular *bouillabaisse*, or splash out on caviar and oysters (the restaurant's name means oyster cellar). Service is fast and attentive, and the three-course menus are excellent value for money.

191 F3 Stollbergstrasse 11 (089) 29 87 87 Daily 5 pm–1 am Tram No 19 Kammerspiele

Dallmayr €€€
Dallmayr is one of the top suppliers of speciality foods and delicatessen items from around the world. The house restaurant offers a highly-praised imaginative menu of international dishes – game and fish feature prominently. The chef's preference is for straight, elegant dishes; he doesn't follow the latest fads. The ambience in the restaurant is quietly sophisticated; the guests tend to be from well-off circles. From the restaurant windows, diners can appreciate superb views of Marienhof and Frauenkirche.

191 D3 Dienerstrasse 14/15 (089) 213 51 00 Mon–Wed 9:30 am–7 pm, Thu–Fri till 8 pm, Sat 9–4 pm Marienplatz

Dukatz €€
Dukatz is in the House of Literature, offering readings by famous authors and new writers, while the café takes care of the literati's physical well-being. The intellectuals are joined in the bright, modern eatery by shoppers from expensive Theatinerstrasse nearby. The cuisine is fine French cooking – quiche Lorraine, *bouillabaisse*, entrecôte and delicious desserts of the highest quality. There's also an excellent selection of wines on offer. The fine porcelain is decorated with quotes by the writer Oskar Maria Graf.

191 D4 Salvatorplatz 1 (089) 291 96 00 10 am–1 am Odeonsplatz

Gandl €€–€€€
An original and tasty combination of gourmet food store and restaurant. During the day, Italian-inspired dishes are served in the shop-bistro, usually at moderate prices. In the evening the ambience is more formal, as attentive waiters serve quality French cuisine. The best time to visit Gandl, however, is in summer, when a few tables are set outdoors, on St-Anna-Platz, where you can eat in romantic surroundings, while imagining yourself in Provence.

197 F4 St-Anna-Platz 1 (089) 29 16 25 25 Mon–Sat 9 am–12:30 am Lehel

Gewürzmühle €–€€
The Spice Mill's cuisine fuses the best of European and Far Eastern cooking, using plentiful herbs and spices. As a result, delicious dishes are created, often with unusual combinations such as an unforgettable carrot and ginger soup. The guests in this popular restaurant come mainly from

the surrounding law offices and marketing companies.

197 F4 Gewürzmühlstrasse 3 (089) 21 66 81 63 Mon–Fri 11 am–3 pm, 5:30 pm–1 am Lehel

Hofer – der Stadtwirt €€

Apologies to the landlord for mentioning the building before the cuisine, but the Hofer restaurant is based in Munich's oldest building, and its Gothic vaults alone, dating back to about 1550, are worth a visit. The cuisine is traditional Bavarian (white sausages, Leberkäse and roast dumplings), with a nod to Italian influences as in the buffalo mozzarella and *vitello tonnato*. In the summer, food is served in a pleasant courtyard.

191 D3 Burgstrasse 5 (089) 24 21 04 44 Mon–Sat 10 am–1 am, Sun till 4 pm Marienplatz

Kaimug €–€€

Thai aromas waft enticingly through the elegant Fünf Höfe shopping centre, promising a fare of Far Eastern delights. Green Thai curries or tiger prawns in chilli paste are among the specialities on the menu. Guests collect their own food and drink, and seating is either at one of the crowded tables or on a bar stool along Kaimug's glass front. An insider's tip: if it's too crowded, just buy a take-away to enjoy on a bench in Marienhof, behind the town hall, or on the steps of Feldherrnhalle.

191 D4 Theatinerstrasse 15 (089) 20 60 33 25 Mon–Sat 10 am–10 pm Marienplatz

Nage und Sauge €

Popular with young people because of its moderate prices and casual atmosphere, this plainly furnished eatery (the name translates as "gnaw and suck") serves Italian-inspired food; one of the house specialities is, for example, tortellini with a spinach and gorgonzola sauce. The tiny restaurant gets extremely crowded, and as you can't book a table, make sure you get there early. At a much later hour, a trendy crowd arrives and cocktails are sipped in the cramped space, standing between tables and all the way up the stairs.

197 E4 Mariannenstrasse 2 (089) 29 88 03 5:30 pm–1 am Tram No 17 Mariannenplatz

Schuhbeck's in den Südtiroler Stuben €€€

This gourmet restaurant is owned by Alfons Schuhbeck, one of the most popular TV chefs in Germany. You can watch him prepare the food for one of his shows. The cuisine takes its inspiration from South Tyrol and Bavaria. Try, for example, *böfflamott mit gänseleber und brez'n-knöd'l* (beef, or "bœuf à la mode", stewed in red wine, with goose liver and pretzel dumplings). There is a main restaurant room, a Münchner-Kindl-Stube and a Barockstube, all boasting elegant furnishings, wooden panelling and stucco ceilings.

191 E3 Platzl 6/8 (089) 216 69 00 Mon–Sat 6 pm–1 am, Tue–Sat also noon–3 pm Marienplatz

Spatenhaus €€

On the ground floor, the rooms are panelled in wood, and guests sit either in cosy niches or at long tables where locals strike up a conversation with their neighbour. The first floor rooms are a little more formal. The cuisine is rustic Bavarian fare, with large portions served at lightning speed. The clientele is international but locals also love the Spatenhaus because it has such a friendly atmosphere.

191 D4 Residenzstrasse 12 (089) 290 70 60 9:30 am–midnight Tram No 19 Nationaltheater

Tambosi €€

A visit to this 18th-century coffee-house is a "must" on every visitor's list. The traditional interior is richly adorned with stuccowork, but it's even more popular in summer when the Hofgarten terrace is open and guests can enjoy their food with a Renaissance garden as a backdrop. The menu features good-quality

Italian snacks, such as bruschetta, crostini and pasta. At weekends you may enjoy live opera arias.

191 E5 Odeonsplatz 18 (089) 29 83 22 8 am–1 am Odeonsplatz

Weinbar Message in a Bottle €€–€€€

Excellent wines, attentive service and an outstanding cuisine are the best features of this wine bar. The meals are light and imaginatively combined, starting from an Italian base with additions from around the world, for example, sushi on a bed of prosecco mousse or monkfish with a coating of blue poppy seeds, are just two of the chef's innovative creations. The restaurant's interior is bright and friendly. Celebrities eat here, but so do those who simply appreciate a good meal.

191 F3 Maximilianstrasse 35c/ entrance via Herzog-Rudolf-Strasse (089) 24 21 77 78 Daily 6:30 pm–1:30 am, Mon–Fri also noon–3 pm Tram No 19 Kammerspiele

Zum Franziskaner €€–€€€

After refurbishment, this traditional old-Bavarian inn is now lighter and brighter without having lost any of its old-world charm. The typical Bavarian snacks, or *schmankerln*, all feature on the menu, from roast pork to *presssack* (brawn), from white sausage to *lüngerl mit knödel* (offal in a sour vinegar sauce with dumplings). Business people and tourists alike value the rapid service and the solid food.

191 D4 Perusastrasse 5, second entrance in Residenzstrasse 9 (089) 231 81 20 8 am–midnight Marienplatz

Cafés

Bar Centrale

It's crowded and smoky in this bar which has been popular for years. Young people and business people enjoy the ambience: the wooden panelling, the comfortable armchairs as well as seeing and being seen, before moving on to the clubs.

191 E3 Ledererstrasse 23 (089) 22 37 62 8 am–1 am, Sun from 10 am Marienplatz

Kreutzkamm

The "coffee *klatsch*" meets at this brightly styled coffee-house, elderly ladies who always sit in the same spot as they order a slice of Munich's best *baumkuchen* (tree cake).

191 D3 Maffeistrasse 4 (089) 29 32 77 Mon–Fri 8 am–7 pm, Sat till 6 pm, Sun noon till 6 pm (closed on Sun in summer) Tram No 19 Theatinerstrasse

Schumann's Tagesbar

Playboy and barkeeper Charles Schumann, although not originally from Munich, is well known here and beyond the city. His Daytime Bar in Fünf Höfe complex is a great place to drink a cappuccino and enjoy one of the excellent snacks as well as the pleasant atmosphere.

191 D4 Maffeistrasse 6 (089) 24 21 77 00 Mon–Fri 8 am–9 pm, Sat 9:30 am–5:30 pm Marienplatz

Where to... Shop

This part of town, apart from the immediate surroundings of Hofbräuhaus, is the smarter and therefore more expensive half of Munich's city centre. This is where international designers and famous brand names rub shoulders.

Around Hofbräuhaus

The area around Hofbräuhaus is known for its soccer club fan shops, but it has other interesting places to shop. In Ledererstrasse, for example, two unusual record shops await the visitor. **bamBam records** (Ledererstrasse 10) sells rare vinyls and CDs majoring on hip-hop, techno and rap, while **Shirokko** (Ledererstrasse 19) opposite has world music and easy listening; traditional and modern folk, salsa and highlife, jazz and merengue. There's hardly a music style that isn't represented in this old-established Munich store, and the assistants offer excellent advice. Next door you'll find a humourous Bavarian folklore store, **servus.heimat** (Ledererstrasse 17), selling cuckoo clocks and kitsch snow globes, witty T-shirts and Bavarian gingerbread hearts, King Ludwig cups and other such tongue-in-cheek items, as well as Munich travel guides. Around the corner are the typical soccer fan and souvenir shops of Orlandostrasse, and right in the middle of them is a tiny shop run by Elfriede Mertl, **Terzi Stahlwaren** (Orlandostrasse 6). It sells scissors and a vast selection of Bavarian knives, their handles fashioned from stag's antlers. Soccer fans who enjoy German football will find strips and memorabilia of clubs in the German permier league at **Fan-Shop** (Orlandostrasse 4). The two Munich clubs are represented by a dedicated shop each: Fanshop TSV 1860 München all in blue opposite and FC Bayern Shop in red next door. A rather different scene prevails at **Lebensart R. Wittgenstein** (Ledererstrasse 7). The shop window displays are designed in a minimalist style that invites the curious. In her bright Art of Living store, the owner, Frau Wittgenstein, has assembled clothing, crockery and decorative objects – everything is bright, beautiful, modern and very tasteful.

Along Maximilianstrasse

Maximilianstrasse is Munich's foremost promenading street for the well-to-do. Here, in the perfectly styled shop windows of D&G, Jill Sander or Ralph Lauren, the trends for the coming year can be gleaned today. Among all the big names, Munich's own fashion designer, **Rudolph Moshammer** (Maximilianstrasse 14), holds his own. A well known personality and eccentric, this proponent of Bavarian baroque has a predilection for oversized black wigs and an undying love for his lapdog, Daisy, whose outfits always include Moshammer-designed ties. There is another traditional Munich gem, hiding behind a tiny window display just around the corner: **Elly Seidl** (Am Kosttor 2) has specialized in chocolates since 1918. The Maximilianhöfe have a series of young and supertrendy shops: **5.senses** (Five Senses, Maximilianstrasse 11) sells unusual scents, which you would not easily find in a traditional perfumery. Exotic as well as well-loved traditional delicatessen fare is available at the famous **Dallmayr** store (Dienerstrasse 14/15) – select from salmon and oysters, coffee or white sausages, chocolates or oils, all of the highest quality.

From Maffeistrasse to Residenz

Lodenfrey (Maffeistrasse 7) started by selling traditional folk costumes but it has since become Munich's leading fashion store. The folk costume department is still one of the best in town, selling traditional lederhosen and dirndls as well as folkloric evening dress and fashionable folk costumes. Above all other shops, Munich is proud of its **Fünf Höfe**. Here fashion stores from Zara and Strenesse to Emporio Armani, the shoe paradise Camper and the Beauty Spy Wellness-Lounge can be found amidst exquisite architecture designed by such star architects as Herzog & de Meuron. But not many people know that there is also a well-stocked **supermarket** on the lower ground floor, where you can buy all those important everyday items that don't quite fit into the exclusive world above. **Bogner-Haus** (Residenzstrasse 14/15) showcases the exclusive sports fashion designs by Willy and Sônia Bogner, a label that has achieved celebrity status. The Meier family, meanwhile, have been selling shoes since 1596, and

Eduard Meier's (Residenzstrasse 22) wonderfully nostalgic, mahogany-panelled shop continues his family tradition into the 13th generation. Shoes are made to measure here, which makes them a little more expensive, but in return they will last you a lifetime. The smell of the fresh leather alone is a temptation. **Kandis** (Residenzstrasse 23) is also a Munich original; although the simple and elegant fashions with a slight African touch don't strike you as typically Bavarian. Natural materials such as linen, silk and cotton are here worked into timeless designs for women and men. Whether **Schlichting** (Weinstrasse 8) primarily addresses children or their brand-conscious mothers is not entirely certain. In any case, this is the place to go if you are looking for fabulous clothes for children, from a crochet cap to a traditional Communion dress, from babies' clothes to the hippest jeans, plus beautiful Italian shoes and great toys – naturally made from wood.

Where to be... Entertained

Bars serving food

Schumann's (Odeonsplatz 6–7, tel: 089/22 90 60, Mon–Fri 9 am–3 am, Sat–Sun 6 pm–3 am). In 2003, when barkeeper Charles Schumann let it be known that he could no longer afford the rents in Maximilianstrasse and would have to close his bar, the Munich club scene went ballistic. But the doyen of the cocktail world relented and opened this new bar in Odeonsplatz. Now all is well, and celebrities, as well as the non-famous, can continue to enjoy Schumann's charm, the tasty snacks and the excellent cocktails.

L-Opera (Maximilianstrasse 2, tel: 089/54 44 46 44, 8 am–midnight), opposite the opera house, is a truly enchanting place, particularly on balmy summer evenings, when the tables under the arcades are illuminated by torches, and customers of all age groups celebrate the night with a glass of sparkling prosecco and an Italian snack.

Blaues Haus (Hildegardstrasse 1, tel: 089/23 33 69 77, Mon–Sat 11 am–1 am) is decorated in a cool industrial style, with long wooden tables, much liked by its cultured audience and the actors from the Kammerspiele studio theatre next door. The menu is Bavarian, with the occasional culinary nod to Austria; small dishes and cakes set the scene. An excellent wine list features Italian and Austrian wines.

Roma (Maximilianstrasse 31, tel: 089/22 74 35, 8 am–3 am) is a meeting point for Munich's actors, well known or otherwise; A- and B-list celebrities congregate here as well as those who aspire to such status. The scene is absolutely typical of Munich, and as such it's well worth visiting the Roma to learn what it is all about.

Bars

The cocktails are well shaken, the audience is relaxed. The traditional American bar **Pusser's** (Falkenturmstrasse 9, tel: 089/22 05 00, Mon–Sat 5 pm–3 am, Sun 6 pm–3 am) allows you to spend a pleasant evening without unnecessary excitement.

Deep leather armchairs and a dimly-lit bar atmosphere are very conducive to trying one of the cocktails at **Tabacco** (Hartmannstrasse 8, tel: 089/22 72 16, Sun–Thu 5pm–1 am, Fri–Sat till 3 am).

Scalar Lounge (Seitzstrasse 12, tel: 089/21 57 96 36, Thu–Sat 9 pm–3 am) is decorated in a 1960s retro style. The highlight are the aquariums with colourfully shimmering fish. Munich's young and beautiful dance and drink the night away here.

The atmosphere is relaxed at **Falk's Bar** in the Bayerischer Hof hotel (Promenadeplatz 2–6, tel: 089/212 09 56, daily 11 pm–2 am), boasting rich stucco decorations and a mirror hall opened in 1839.

Discos

No matter how many new bars open in Munich, the **P1** (Prinzregentenstrasse 1, tel: 089/211 11 40, daily 9:30 pm–5 am) has ranked at the top for decades. Why? The landlord used to work at the famous Käfer delicatessen shop and the atmosphere is completely relaxed – once you've got past the bouncers.

Prinzip (Maximilianstrasse 29, tel: 0175/417 81 26, Thu–Sat from 10 pm) was supposed to be a temporary fixture, open only for a few months, but somehow it became a permanent institution. This is decidedly the best place for fans of house music.

Live music

Brit Pop used to rule at the **Atomic Café** (Neuturmstrasse 5, tel: 089/228 30 54, Tue–Sun 10 pm–3 am, Fri–Sat till 4 am), but today other styles of music are also enjoyed. The café attracts a mainly young crowd who like to listen to their kind of music. The rooms are styled in a 1960s retro look. The turntables are operated by celebrity DJs, and if a live band performs, the audience goes wild.

The **Night Club** at Bayerischer Hof hotel (Promenadeplatz 2–6, tel: 089/21 200, daily 10 pm–3 am) offers a sophisticated programme of jazz, Latin and soul for a slightly older audience; yet when a well-known band plays live, the place becomes very animated despite the elegant ambience.

Theatre

The northern half of Munich's city is theatreland. Every night, performances of the highest standard are staged, from opera to light comedy, from avant-garde theatre to classical drama. The flagship is the opera house, **Bayerisches Nationaltheater** (Max-Joseph-Platz 2), whose opera and ballet performances are usually sold out a long time in advance. Ask for tickets at the box office (Marstallplatz 5, tel: 089/21 85 19 20) or book them in advance online (www.bayerische-staatsoper.de). If you're only interested in seeing the exquisite interior and fittings, you can join a guided tour of the opera house (usually starts at 2 pm, information tel: 089/21 85 10 25, also for information about special guided tours for children). The excellent troupe at the **Residenztheater** (Max-Joseph-Platz 1) next door, under Dieter Dorn's direction, regularly get a standing ovation (tickets go on sale 14 days before each performance, the advance booking office is at Marstallplatz 5, tel: 089/21 85 19 40 or online at www.staatsschauspiel.de). The repertory features drama classics, but also younger playwrights. The ensembles at **Münchner Kammerspiele** (Falckenbergstrasse 2), at **Neues Haus** (Falckenbergstr. 1) and at **Werkraumtheater** (Hildegardstrasse 1) enthusiastically give their all in each performance. The programme at these three venues veers between the traditional and the avant-garde (tickets on sale 14 days before, from the booking office at Maximilianstrasse 28, tel: 089/23 39 66 00). Light theatre and comedy prevail at **Kleine Komödie am Max II.** (Maximilianstrasse 47, tel: 089/22 18 59) and at **Kleine Komödie im Bayerischen Hof** (Promenadeplatz 6, tel: 089/29 16 05 30, www.komoedie-muenchen.de). Well-known actors regularly draw the crowds at both theatres.

Cinema

The upholstery is a bit chintzy and worn, but the **Theatiner Filmkunst** (Theatinerstrasse 32, tel: 089/22 31 83) is one of only few remaining "traditional" picture palaces in Munich. Here you can still enjoy the cinematic treasures of times past, while seated in an authentic 1950s interior. Most films are shown in the original language with subtitles.

Maxvorstadt and Schwabing

Getting Your Bearings

Around the university, where stones were thrown during demonstrations in the 1960s, today's students live in harmony with their surroundings. Bohemian Alt-Schwabing is one of the city's trendiest shopping areas, and right next to it is Englischer Garten, Munich's green oasis, a space for sports and relaxation.

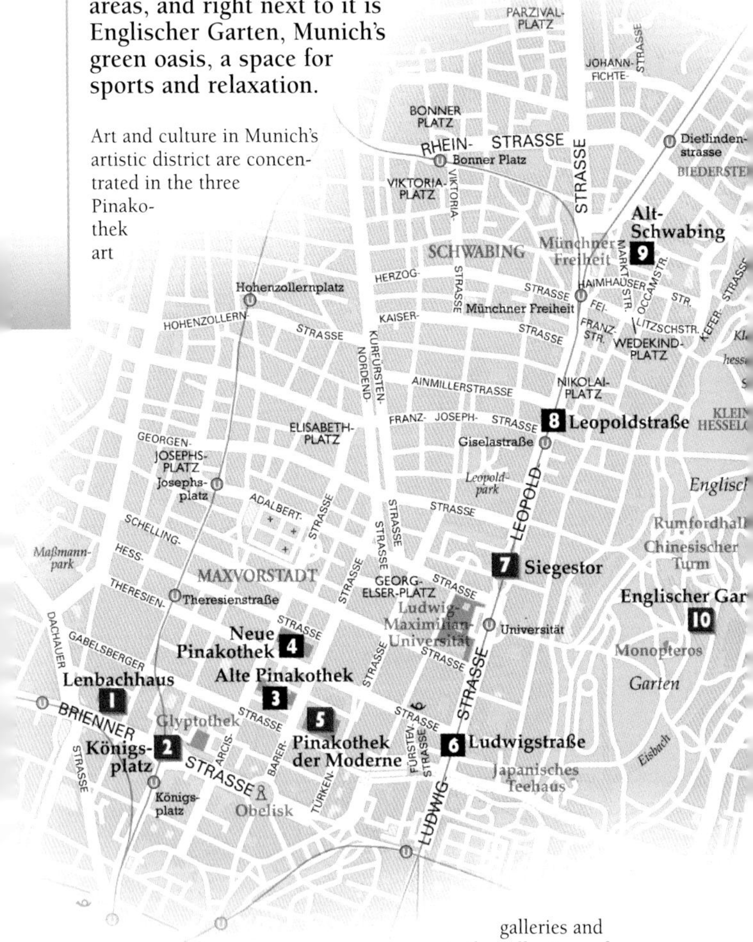

Art and culture in Munich's artistic district are concentrated in the three Pinakothek art galleries and in the collections of Expressionist works and Greek heroes. There are plenty of cafés and pubs in the student district around this enclave of the fine arts, to strike a balance between the world of art and

architecture and the colourful exuberance of real life. Leopoldstrasse, Schwabing's favourite strolling street, is the ideal place to do nothing in particular. If you sit here you will spot lots of people who are doing just that – they hang around in the street cafés, watching the world and numerous open-top cars or four-wheel drives go by, always on the look-out for an interesting person who may be hiding behind expensive sunglasses. There is certainly a tendency to display in this part of Munich, a phenomenon sometimes referred to as "Leopoldstrasse style". Alt-Schwabing, all around Münchner Freiheit, is the classic night-life district. Here you will find the most biting cabarets, the craziest pubs and the trendiest shops, especially for hip hop fans.

Girls and bikes: Schwabing in the late 1960s

Page 95: At the foot of the Monopteros temple in Englischer Garten

Soaking up the sun in Schellingstrasse

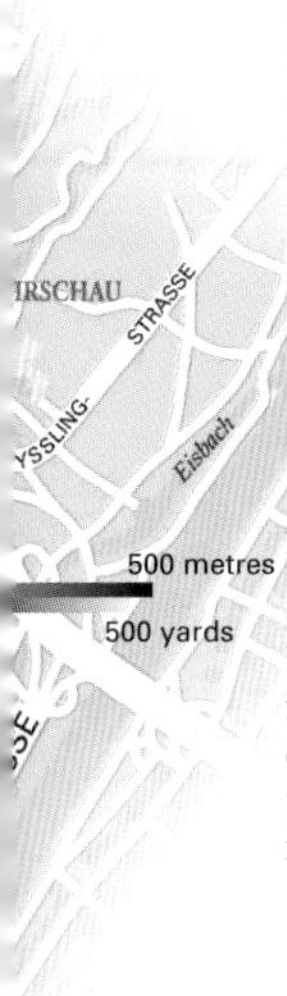

★ Don't Miss

At Your Leisure

Start the day with culture and finish in a beer garden – a perfect schedule for a visit to Munich. In between, stroll through the lively student district of Schwabing and relax in Englischer Garten.

Maxvorstadt and Schwabing in a Day

9:00 am

You start your exploration of Munich's art scene with a visit to "Der Blaue Reiter", in the elegant 1 **Lenbachhaus** (right; ➤ 100). Now return to antiquity on 2 **Königsplatz** (➤ 102), designed by Leo von Klenze. Here, Glyptothek, Staatliche Antikensammlungen (National Collections of Antiquity) and the Museum der Abgüsse Klassischer Bildwerke (Museum of Plaster Casts of Classical Sculptures) will take you back to Greek and Roman times.

12:30 pm

A short walk takes you to the much-celebrated Vietnamese restaurant Cyclo (➤ 112), where you could pause for lunch. After refreshments you can choose between visiting the Old Masters at 3 **Alte Pinakothek** or studying their younger colleagues from the 19th century at 4 **Neue Pinakothek** (below; ➤ 110). Alternatively, forget about both and rest your feet before you continue with your tour of modern art.

2:30 pm

5 **Pinakothek der Moderne** (➤ 104) is a brand-new museum, created as a holistic ensemble, combining the art, design and architecture exhibits shown inside and the building itself.

4:00 pm

6 **Ludwigstrasse** (➤ 110), between Feldherrnhalle (➤ 79) and 7 **Siegestor** (➤ 106), pays homage to the Renaissance – the street is entirely built on neo-classical lines, with light stonework. Behind the façades, students cram at the University's institutes and the National Library's reading room. Stop for a quick espresso at the Café an der Uni (above; ➤ 114) to prepare you for the rest of the day. Leave the Maxvorstadt district behind. Stroll north along the Schwabing end of 8 **Leopoldstrasse** (➤ 111), where the street cafés are always packed, even when it's cold, and the fashion shops (right) always busy. Just beyond Münchner Freiheit, are the lively streets of 9 **Alt-Schwabing** (➤ 111), with its pubs and original and amusing shops.

5:30 pm

Make your way to 10 **Englischer Garten** (left; ➤ 107) and take a break at the Seehaus (➤ 113), the Lake House on Kleinhesseloher See. As you stroll through the park, stop at Japanisches Teehaus (Japanese Tea-House) and Monopteros, a round, open-sided temple folly. All paths converge on Chinesischer Turm. This is also an excellent place for refreshments – under chestnut trees, surrounded by a mixed crowd of students, the elderly and families.

8:00 pm

If your German is good enough, try some political cabaret. The famous Lach- und Schiessgesellschaft (➤ 118) spares no one with its satirical comment. Or how about a spot of people-watching at the Reitschule (right; ➤ 116), one of Munich's favourite meeting points for singles.

1 Lenbachhaus

The Lenbachhaus City Gallery holds, among other works of art, the most outstanding pieces by the artists' group "Der Blaue Reiter" (The Blue Rider), including Germany's largest collection of paintings by Wassily Kandinsky. The building itself, designed by Munich's 'painter prince' Franz von Lenbach, is a delightful Italianate villa.

STÄDT. GALERIE
IM LENBACHHAUS
1887-91 Erbaut von Gabriel v. Seidl
1927-29 Erweitert von Hans Grässel
1969-72 von Heinrich Volbehr
und Rudolf Thönessen

Left: Historic plaque

Franz von Lenbach (1836–1904) made his name in the late 19th century by painting celebrities of the day. He had been to Rome several times and at the height of his success, he wanted to have his own Italian palazzo in Munich. Gabriel von Seidl, the architect, built the Florentine High Renaissance-style villa in 1887–91. The garden, too, is splendidly Italian, with formal, clipped hedges, splashing fountains and marble benches to invite the weary. The prestigious palace has seen many a glittering artists' celebration and has welcomed numerous famous visitors. Reich Chancellor Bismarck liked it so much that it was here that he staged his public appearances. A contemporary work of art has adorned the façade since 1994: Maurizio Nannucci's neon phrase, "You Can Imagine The Opposite".

Der Blaue Reiter

During the reign of the Prince Regent 1886–1912, Munich was a lively cultural hothouse for the arts (➤ 27). In 1909, Munich artists founded the "Neue Künstlervereinigung", an association of Munich artists who organized art exhibitions. Two years later they rejected a Kandinsky painting, *Komposition V*, and so he and several other artists resigned. Together with Franz Marc, Gabriele Münter, Alexej

Fountain in the Lenbachhaus Italian garden

An idyllic corner with a touch of Italy

Jawlensky, August Macke and Paul Klee, Kandinsky founded the "Blauer Reiter" group, to show and promote their own work. In the Schwabing workshops and Gabriele Münter's workshop at Murnau, many of the masterpieces of Expressionism were created, including Franz Marc's *Der Tiger* (1912), Alexej Jawlensky's *Reife* (1912) and Kandinsky's *Impression III (Konzert)* (1911).

Stuccowork and carvings galore

From Murnau to Munich

It was the generosity of two women that finally brought together Der Blaue Reiter and the painter prince. Twenty years after Lenbach's death, his widow decided to sell the villa and some of his works to the city of Munich, thus laying the foundation for the City Art Gallery in 1924. Meanwhile, the artist Gabriele Münter, Kandinsky's partner of many years, celebrated her 80th birthday in 1957 in Murnau, by giving rather than receiving a unique present: she donated her collection of her friends' works to the city. This generous gift transformed the City Gallery in Lenbachhaus into a museum of great significance and world renown. Apart from the works of Der Blaue Reiter and the special collection of Kandinsky's work, the Lenbachhaus also exhibits paintings by 18th- and 19th-century Munich artists, Jugendstil (art nouveau) works and contemporary art.

TAKING A BREAK

The **Museumscafé** in Lenbachhaus is cool in design terms, but you'll find that it serves an excellent hot espresso (Tue–Sun 10–6).

196 C5 · Luisenstrasse 33 · (089) 23 33 20 00
Tue–Sun 10–6 · Königsplatz · Expensive
www.lenbachhaus.de

LENBACHHAUS: INSIDE INFO

Top tip Contemporary works of art are shown in the newly-refurbished Lenbachhaus annex, the **Kunstbau**, above U-Bahn station Königsplatz.

One to miss Franz von Lenbach's **reception rooms** do little more than show his preference for an over-ornate style.

2 Königsplatz

Together, King Ludwig I's love of antiquity and Leo von Klenze's architectural genius created this unique square, an ancient forum in the heart of Munich. It is surrounded by several important buildings – the Propyläen, Glyptothek and Antikensammlungen. In summer, the square is transformed into Munich's most attractive outdoor concert hall.

From the past, the shadow of National Socialism still haunts Königsplatz. Hitler requisitioned the square as a setting for his rallies and parades, and had it paved over. The appearance of the square underwent further lasting changes: two memorial temples (destroyed in 1945) were erected for those who had died during the Hitler putsch and on the eastern side, at the Arcisstrasse/Meiserstrasse corner, a party administration building was added. In 1988, finally, the paving was ripped up and the square re-grassed.

National Socialists parade on Königsplatz, on 9 November, 1940

Visiting the Faun

The **Glyptothek** was built as an Ionic temple by Leo von Klenze in 1816–30, to house Ludwig I's famous collection of antiquities which now forms the core of the exhibition. Today the museum, restored after World War II, shows sculptures and temple reliefs, arranged in a pleasingly moody display. The *Barberinische Faun* (220 BC) stretches lasciviously, classically proportioned *Apoll von Tenea* (560 BC) looks cool and immovable, and the images of famous personalities such as the marble bust of *Emperor Augustus* (30 BC) are shown in lively and accurate detail.

Beauty contest for marble heroes

Behind a Roman Portico

Georg Friedrich Ziebland built the Roman temple opposite the Glyptothek in 1838–48. This is the home of the **Staatliche Antikensammlungen** (State Collections of Antiquities), where small sculptures and jewellery are shown, ranging

A marble Athena adorns the Glyptothek's pediment

Plaster Casts

At the Museum of Plaster Copies, over 1,700 plaster casts of Greek and Roman statues, including the ***Discus Thrower*** (5th century BC) and the ***Laocoon Group*** (50 AD), bear witness to the skills of the sculptors in antiquity. (Meiserstrasse 10, tel: 089/ 28 92 76 90, Mon–Fri 10–5. Admission: moderate, www.abgussmuseum.de)

from archaic bull sculptures from the Cyclades (3rd century BC) and Mycenaean (14th century BC) containers to a 6th-century BC Dionysos bowl. Here too, Ludwig's own collection forms the core of the museum; his Greek vases were world-famous even in his own day. The love-smitten king gave two of them to his mistress, Lola Montez (► 28), who promptly sold them on. In 1905, it became clear that both vases were fakes.

TAKING A BREAK

There's probably no better place to give your aching feet a rest than the **Café in der Glyptothek**, surrounded by perfectly formed Hellenic marble beauties.

197 D5 Königsplatz

Glyptothek
Königsplatz 3 (089) 28 61 00 Tue–Sun 10–5, Thu till 8 pm Moderate www.glyptothek.de

Staatliche Antikensammlungen
Königsplatz 1 (089) 59 83 59 Tue–Sun 10–5, Wed till 8 Moderate www.antikensammlungen.de

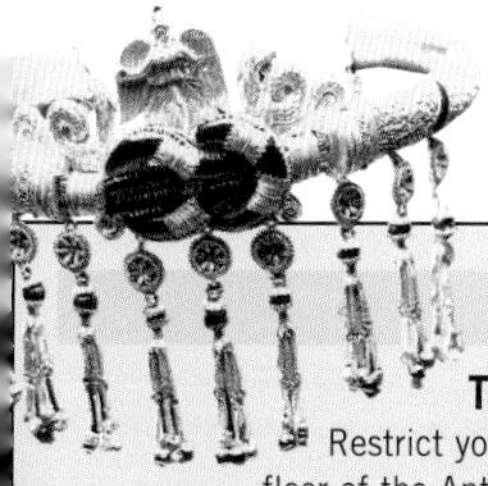

KÖNIGSPLATZ: INSIDE INFO

Top tip Don't try to see the entire collection. Restrict yourself instead to **essential pieces**. On the lower floor of the Antikensammlungen, for example, you should not miss the *Goldkranz aus Armento* (Armento Golden Wreath, 370 BC) or the *Grosses Diadem aus Pantikapaion* (Large Pantikapaion Diadem, 300 BC).

5 Pinakothek der Moderne

It was hard work to get the Museum of Contemporary Art built – the state had run out of money and private sponsors had to help – but today Munich is the proud owner of the largest museum structure in Europe, boasting extraordinary architecture and several collections of world renown.

It took 12 years before the provincial government's decision to build a third Pinakothek museum finally came to fruition in 2002. The rectangular structure, with its tall glass façades around a central rotunda, was designed by Munich architect Stephan Braunfels. The high-ceilinged rooms are flooded with light, making a wonderful setting for the collections on show. The exterior design of the Pinakothek, however, is still controversial today. The architect insisted that nothing must distract from the purist look, but many visitors don't like its plainness.

The Modern Art Collection

On the first and second floors of the Modern Art Collection, paintings, sculptures and new media are exhibited. Here you will find major Surrealist and Expressionist works, including several paintings by Max Beckmann, impressive in their intensity. René Magritte and Salvador Dalí, as well as Pablo Picasso, are represented by large numbers of their works. Major artists of the second half of the 20th century exhibited here are Joseph Beuys, Andy Warhol and Georg Baselitz. The new media section features Bruce Naumann's video installations.

Light and shade in the central rotunda

Art and architecture in a symbiotic relationship

Design

A curved staircase leads from the central rotunda down into the design section of the museum. Here the displays will take you on a colourful and exciting journey through the story of design, starting with Rudolf Thonet's work at the middle of the 19th century, continuing with revolutionary designs by the German Bauhaus and right up to Pop Art. The famous 1955 Citroën DS 19 is exhibited in this department as are Thonet's classic chairs. International contemporary jewellery is on display in the "Danner-Rotunda".

Let's go visit Pablo Picasso

Every Friday from 2:45 to 4:15 pm the Pinakothek offers special guided tours for children. "Circle, Dot, Line", for example, tracks motifs, "Click" visits the Photography Museum and other tours pay a visit to one of the great artists.

Architecture

The Pinakothek der Moderne is also the home of Germany's largest architectural collection. Drawings and models explore the development and the history of architecture, from the neo-classical structures of Leo von Klenze and Friedrich Gärtner via the great Swiss-French architect Le Corbusier to the work of German architect Otto Steidle, who died in 2004.

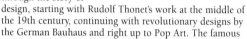

Joseph Beuys' vision of *The end of the 20th century*

TAKING A BREAK

The **Timballo** (Gabelsbergerstrasse 9), opposite the Pinakothek der Moderne, serves delicious panini and light Bavarian and Italian lunches at moderate prices.

197 D5 Barer Strasse 40 (089) 23 80 53 60 Tue–Sun 10–5, Thu–Fri until 8 Tram No 27 Pinakotheken Expensive www.pinakothek-der-moderne.de

PINAKOTHEK DER MODERNE: INSIDE INFO

Top tip The Pinakothek has a programme of regular **concerts** and **film shows**; details are on the gallery's website.

One to miss At **Pinakothekencafé 48/8**, you'll shiver, surrounded by grey concrete and artificial trees, while watching bored visitors sip their Prosecco.

7 Siegestor

The triumphal arch originally dedicated to "the glory of the Bavarian Army" marks the northern end of Ludwigstrasse. At one time, the plains started immediately beyond the gate, today it is the start of the lively Schwabing district.

Even when he was still Crown Prince, Ludwig I envisaged an arch at this spot, but it was not finished until 1849, after his abdication. Leo von Klenze planned the arch, but eventually the king commissioned Friedrich von Gärtner who proposed to build a copy of Rome's Constantine Arch. Like its Roman model, the arch is flanked by Corinthian columns. Its tall central arch, flanked by two smaller side arches, welcomes with majestic grandeur all travellers arriving in Munich from the north.

Munich's triumphal arch

Facing Out

The chariot with the figure of Bavaria was added to the Siegestor as a crowning finish in 1852. It faces town outwards, towards the two towers of the "Münchner Tor" (➤ 25/174), the gateway dominating the skyline in Schwabing. Today, the Siegestor is seen as a reminder of the cruelty of war rather than a triumphal arch. A new inscription by the writer and historian Wilhelm Hausenstein put this into words: "Dedicated to victory, destroyed by war, urging peace".

TAKING A BREAK

In summer, **CADU** (Café an der Uni, ➤ 114) sets up tables and chairs outdoors in its romantic courtyard.

194 C1 Ludwigstrasse Universität

SIEGESTOR: INSIDE INFO

Top tip If you plan to visit the Siegestor, **avoid the weekend**, when the area is transformed into a second-hand car lot, and rattling engines and slamming car doors tend to spoil the enjoyment of the arch's architecture.

10 Englischer Garten

Set up towards the end of the 18th century and handed over to the public in 1808, the English Garden was Europe's first "people's park". If you take a stroll through the park at the weekend, you'll see how appropriate the term "popular" really is. Old and young, families and couples, dog owners and cyclists, students and horse-riders, rollerbladers and elderly Bavarians, elegant ladies and punks – they all love this green oasis in the middle of Munich.

The park was founded in 1789 on the initiative of the British physicist Sir Benjamin Thompson (1753–1814), better known in Munich as Count of Rumford. He persuaded Elector Karl Theodor to put the royal hunting grounds north of the Residenz to good use by setting up an army garden here, and Friedrich Ludwig von Sckell (1750–1823), the top landscape designer of the day, created the English Garden. The park, stretching along the Isar River, between Haus der Kunst (► 88) and Oberföhringer Stauwehr

Rickshaw stop at Chinesischer Turm

Idyllic garden in the heart of the city

(a weir, ➤ 177), measures about 5km (3.5 miles) long and around 1km (0.6 mile) wide. The southern third, between Haus der Kunst and Kleinhesseloher See, is the liveliest part.

Boats and Swans

Three islands sit in the middle of **Kleinhesseloher See**, a romantic artificial lake. Swans and ducks watch the locals as they boat around the lake in summer or skate over the frozen waters in winter. By the lake stands a monument to the father of the garden, Sckell, although it is a bit austere – a column, decorated with pine cones (it was created in 1824, after a design by von Klenze). Next to it are the beer gardens of the elegant Seehaus (➤ 113) restaurant; it is always packed as soon as the first rays of sunshine can be felt.

All Paths Lead to the Chinese Tower

Walk around the lake, continuing southwards along the western path, past **Rumfordhaus**, once planned as the officers' casino but today Munich's most scenically located kindergarten. Cross over the little duck stream, on a small bridge under chestnut and beech trees, and you will get to the part of Englischer Garten that has become infamous well beyond the city limits, for its naturists. Since 1982, sunbathers have officially been permitted to shed their clothes in the area near **Schwabinger Bach**. Many did so before, including staid businessmen and women, and the police had a hard time trying to issue fines to all the naturists. Eventually the authorities gave in

Refreshments at Hirschau or Aumeister

North of Kleinhesseloher See, a footbridge takes you across a loop in the Isar into the northern half of Englischer Garten. You can still come across deer or foxes here! The Hirschau (literally "stag meadow", ➤ 114) however, does not serve game but beer, Bavarian dishes and jazz music. Continue along the Isar or along one of the many branching paths, and you'll get to one of Munich's most popular cafés, the Aumeister, at the northern end of the park (➤ 177).

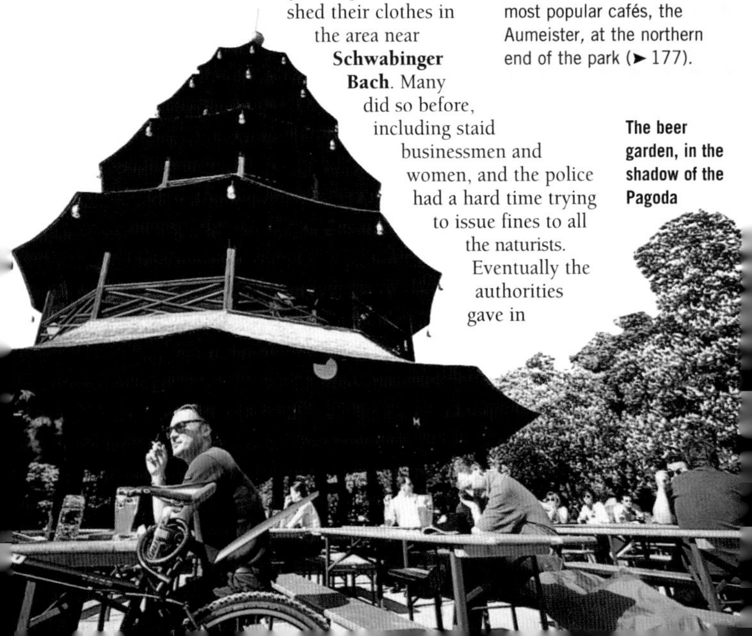

The beer garden, in the shadow of the Pagoda

A pleasant break at Kleinhesseloher See

to popular demand and made naturism legal. Now that it is no longer forbidden, however, it has become less of a challenge and its popularity has waned.

At its southern end the park is Japanese. The **Teehaus**, surrounded by a lake, was built in 1972 on the occasion of the Munich Olympic Games. During summer weekends, guests are invited to participate in a Japanese tea ceremony. If a visit to Berlin does not feature on your itinerary, you can find a fragment of the **Berlin Wall** a few steps from here, at the end of Königinstrasse. It was erected as a poignant reminder of the division of Germany until 1989. Returning north you will pass **Monopteros**, a small round Ionic temple built on a hill by von Klenze in 1836. Young people congregate here to listen to their music and enjoy the marvellous panoramic views towards Theatinerkirche and Frauenkirche. **Chinesischer Turm**, erected in the park as early as 1790 as a wooden pagoda, is also the emblem for the park's most popular beer garden, especially with young people and students (► 114). Balmy summer nights, spent here under the chestnut trees, seem to go on forever.

Merry-go-round
The antique merry-go-round next to Chinesischer Turm is fun for young and old; the children enjoy going around on it, while their parents delight in this Jugendstil treasure with its beautifully restored little horses.

TAKING A BREAK

Relax on the water: take a **boat trip** on Kleinhesseloher See,

194 C1–195 D1/2–F5
Universität, Giselastrasse, Münchner Freiheit

ENGLISCHER GARTEN: INSIDE INFO

Top tip From 1 April to 31 October, on every second and fourth weekend in the month, you can take part in a **Japanese tea ceremony** at the Teehaus (Sat, Sun 3, 4, 5, Sun also 2 pm; admission: moderate).

Hidden gem Don't worry if your legs ache. You'll usually find a **carriage** at Chinesischer Turm that will take you through the park back to your hotel.

At Your Leisure

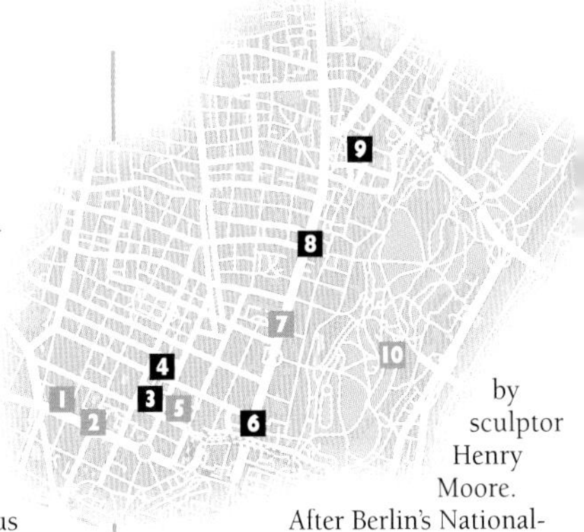

3 Alte Pinakothek

Alte Pinakothek holds one of Germany's most important collections of Old Masters. The long building is also worth seeing. It was purpose-built as a museum in 1826–1936, in the style of the Florentine Renaissance, designed by von Klenze to include features such as the optimum fall of light. The Wittelsbach dynasty had a passion for collecting and assembled many world-famous masterpieces, including Albrecht Dürer's *Four Apostles*, Albrecht Altdorfer's *The Battle of Alexander* and Raphael's *Tempi Madonna*. Among the highlights are the rooms with 17th-century Flemish paintings, including the *Medici Cycle* by Peter Paul Rubens.

197 D5 · Barer Strasse 27, entrance Theresienstrasse · (089) 23 80 52 16 · Wed–Sun 10–5, Tue till 6 pm · Königsplatz · Tram No 27 Pinakotheken, Bus No 53 Schellingstrasse · Moderate · www.alte-pinakothek.de

4 Neue Pinakothek

In front of Neue Pinakothek, visitors are greeted by the *Reclining Woman* by sculptor Henry Moore.

After Berlin's Nationalgalerie, the Pinakothek's collection of 19th-century paintings and sculptures is the second most important in Germany. Founded by Ludwig I in 1853, the gallery was destroyed in World War II and rebuilt with a monumental sandstone façade and high fanlights by Alexander von Branca. It opened to the public in 1981. It is the Pinakothek's mission to showcase the break with convention that resulted in the individualization of art in the 19th century, that permitted the development of artists such as Francisco Goya, William Turner, Edouard Manet and Paul Cézanne. The German Romanticists are also well represented.

197 D5 · Barer Strasse 29, entrance Theresienstrasse · (089) 23 80 51 95 · Thu–Mon 10–5, Wed till 8 pm · Königsplatz · Tram No 27 Pinakotheken, Bus No 53 Schellingstrasse · Moderate · www.neue-pinakothek.de

6 Ludwigstrasse

Ludwig I's prestige boulevard, which runs from Feldherrnhalle (► 79) to Siegestor (► 106), does not conform to its architect's expectations. Leo von Klenze wanted no greenery and few but large windows. The street

Enjoying the Old Masters

Not an alien, but Schwabing's *Walking Man*

was to be a straight neo-classical line, with the Siegestor as vanishing point, but those who owned or rented the palaces rebelled and demanded changes. Ludwigstrasse's success was ensured by the university's elegant round tower and the clean line of the national library, created by Friedrich von Gärtner, while the students made certain that the stonework did not make the street appear too solemn.

197 E4–5
Odeonsplatz

Out and about in Leopoldstrasse

8 Leopoldstrasse

Ludwigstrasse's continuation to the north couldn't be more of a contrast. A broad poplar-lined avenue, with buildings in a wide variety of different architectural styles, its pavement littered with street cafés, Leopoldstrasse is an animated, living street. Students and traders sell second-hand books in front of the university's refectory building. A little farther north, students stroll past the window displays of the fashion boutiques. Suddenly, you'll come across the 17-m (56-foot) high sculpture *Walking Man* by American artist Jonathan Borofsky outside the offices of the Munich Re. It sums up this Schwabing boulevard where the motto is "stroll and be seen".

194 C1–5 Giselastrasse

9 Alt-Schwabing

From Münchner Freiheit square you get into the heart of Old Schwabing, the area around Feilitzschstrasse, Occamstrasse, Haimhauser Strasse and Wedekindplatz. Schwabing, it is said, is a state of mind. There are no sights as such to visit, just a special atmosphere to soak up: it has a suburban neighbourhood feel, with lots of young people, countless pubs, cinemas, cafés and discos. One of the focal points is the Münchner Freiheit Café, which serves giant ice creams in its large Capuccino gardens. You can occasionally spot a Schwabing celebrity ordering a coffee here.

194 C2–3 Münchner Freiheit

The White Rose

Hans and Sophie Scholl, initially enthusiastic members of Hitler youth groups, became critical of the Nazi regime. In 1942, together with friends, they founded the "White Rose" at Munich University. Arrested while leafleting on 18 February, 1943, they were executed four days later.

Where to... Eat and Drink

Prices
Prices given are for one person, excluding drinks.
€ under 12 euros **€€** 12–25 euros **€€€** over 25 euros

Restaurants

Alter Simpl €
This restaurant is an institution in Maxvorstadt, especially popular with young people and students. The menu features typical German food such as beefburgers and potato salad or goulash and dumplings, all at moderate prices. A lunchtime meal here will fill you up without breaking the bank.

194 B1 Türkenstrasse 57 (089) 260 50 26 Sun–Thu 11 am–3 am, Fri–Sat till 4 am Universität

Atzinger €
Students love this corner pub, one of Munich's least-expensive eateries. But Atzinger is much more than that, a simply great place to meet friends between lectures or after a seminar, somewhere to have a heated political debate or to argue about other things of greater and lesser importance. And a tasty Wiener schnitzel, curry sausage or kebab will sustain your energies while you put the world to rights.

194 B1 Schellingstrasse 9 (089) 28 28 80 Daily 10 am–3 am Universität

Cyclo €€
Nearly everything is perfect at this excellent Vietnamese restaurant – the furnishings, the floral displays, the beautifully presented dishes and the discreet yet attentive service. And the food is wonderful. Try the deliciously spicy beef salad with crispy vegetable bouquet or chicken soup with ginger, for example. It's all available to take away too.

194 B1 Theresienstrasse 70 (089) 28 80 83 90 Mon–Fri noon–3 pm, 6 pm–1 am, Sat–Sun 6 pm–1 am Universität

Deeba €€
One thing is certain: you'd better book a table at Deeba, because it is always busy. The main reason for the restaurant's popularity is the deliciously spiced, freshly prepared Pakistani food, but the staff too are one of the attractions – passionate about their food, they dispense advice and jokes, they improvise and they're always quick and in a good mood. Try lemony chicken with a sweet and sour sauce, or lamb casserole, served with a bowl of fragrant saffron basmati rice.

194 B1 Barerstrasse 42 (089) 28 34 07 Sun–Fri 11:30 am–3 pm, 6 pm–midnight, Sat 6 pm–midnight Universität

Fouquets €€
You won't find a seat at this tiny Creole-themed restaurant if you haven't reserved one in advance. The service is charming; Afro-Caribbean music is played in the background and, cocktail in hand, guests wait curiously to find out what culinary delights the young owners have thought up this time. There's only ever a choice of three dishes (meat, fish, vegetarian), but all are imaginatively combined with fruits, vegetables and sauces.
If a snack is all you're after, just order the shrimp soup or a selection of small dishes.

194 B1 Nordendstrasse 12 (089) 27 39 97 16 Mon–Sat 6 pm–1 am Josephsplatz

H2O €€
Schwabing boasts a beerhouse (➤ 118) and a place specializing in mineral waters, H2O. On the ground floor, trendy guests lounge on cream-coloured stools while sipping one of over 50 types of mineral water. The cuisine on the first floor is German-style Japanese but you can also order simpler dishes such as turkey kebab.

194 C2 ✉ Herzogstrasse 2 ☎ (089) 38 88 71 72 Sun–Thu 8 am–1 am, Fri–Sat till 3 am Münchner Freiheit

Kaisergarten €–€€
A rustic Bavarian restaurant, on the pretty Kaiserstrasse, with an attractive and intimate beer garden which is open in summer. The cuisine is typical Bavarian and Austrian fare – such as *sauerbraten* (soured beef), *fleischpflanzerl* (meat rissoles) or *tafelspitz* (fillet of beef). Many dishes have a modern twist, making them much lighter. Guests are a mixed crowd from all walks of life.

194 C2 ✉ Kaiserstrasse 34 ☎ (089) 34 02 02 03 Daily 9 am–1 am Münchner Freiheit

Last Supper €€
This is Munich's top restaurant for heavy metal fans and punks. It's styled like a skiing hut, and food is served below images of the Virgin Mary. The waiters – all are tattooed – serve beautifully prepared meat and pasta dishes. Last Supper only offers set menus, but you can always swap between the menus if one contains a dish you don't like. The cooking is great, but the general atmosphere and the music, which gets louder as the evening wears on, may not be to everyone's taste.

194 B1 ✉ Kurfürstenstrasse 9 ☎ (089) 28 80 88 09 Daily 5 pm–1 am Odeonsplatz

Osterwaldgarten €–€€
A small, idyllic tavern, situated in Alt-Schwabing, featuring a pretty beer garden and excellent Bavarian cooking. When the weather is not so good, you can enjoy one of the favourites – *leberkäse* (meatloaf), roast pork, goulash with pretzel dumplings or *wurstsalat* (sausage salad) – in the cosy bar. At the weekends, when many bicyclists stop here, an outdoor seat may be hard to find.

195 D2 ✉ Keferstrasse 12 ☎ (089) 38 40 50 40 Daily 10 am–1 am Münchner Freiheit

Rolandseck €–€€
This is one of very few places in Schwabing where you wouldn't go to see and be seen: the outdoor tables – and your own privacy – are protected from the glances of those outside by the dense hedge surrounding the garden. The cuisine of this rustic restaurant is no-nonsense, no-fuss Bavarian food. If you love good, honest food and you're fond of large portions, this is the right place for you.

194 C3 ✉ Viktoriastrasse 23 ☎ (089) 308 37 17 Daily 10 am–1 am Bonner Platz

Seehaus €€–€€€
Beautifully situated right next to Kleinhesseloher See, this Bavarian restaurant has an elegant atmosphere and offers first-class cooking. Among the specialities are fillet of pike-perch and *tafelspitz* (fillet of beef). The Seehaus has a pleasant terrace, and there's a beer garden next door which serves slightly more down-to-earth and less expensive food.

195 D2 ✉ Kleinhesselohe 3 ☎ (089) 381 61 30 Daily 10 am–midnight Münchner Freiheit

Tantris €€€
The Michelin-starred Tantris, with its Buddhist-inspired mission to give pleasure, has been Munich's top gourmet restaurant for many years. The menu features lobster and truffles, but quality does not come cheap – an evening meal is around 130 euros per person. The interior is vintage 1970s.

194 C3 ✉ Johann-Fichte-Strasse 7 ☎ (089) 361 95 90 Tue–Sat noon–3 pm, 6:30–1 am Dietlindenstrasse

Wirtshaus Zur Brez'n €€
Originally a traditional Bavarian tavern which has been embellished with a lot of knick-nacks to become a trendy, in-crowd pub. Even so, this is one of the most popular restaurants in the street, and the chef dishes up memorable snacks such as *knöd'lgröstel* (roast bread and potato dumplings) or *tafelspitz-brühe* (fillet of beef broth).

194 C2 Leopoldstrasse 72
(089) 39 00 92 Daily 9 am–3 am
Münchner Freiheit

Beer gardens

Chinesischer Turm €
Munich's most colourful beer garden, around its wooden pagoda, has 7,000 seats where people of all nationalities and all age groups congregate to relax and have fun together. It comprises various "Brotzeitstandln" (snack bars) where you can buy food, and the beers on sale are Löwenbräu lager and Franziskaner wheat beer. Children spend their own or their parents' money on the art nouveau merry-go-round next door.

195 D1 Englischer Garten 3
(089) 383 87 30 10 am–11 pm
Universität

Hirschau €–€€
A nice, not-too-large beer garden, with 1,700 seats, in the quieter part of Englischer Garten north of the Isar ring. *Wies'nhendl* (roast chicken) and *steckerlfisch* (spicy grilled fish) are top favourites here, washed down with a Spaten beer. A jazz band provides the live musical entertainment. For children, there's an adventure playground right next to the beer garden.

195 E2 Gysslingstrasse 15
(089) 322 10 80 11 am–midnight
Münchner Freiheit

Cafés

Altschwabing
There's still a nostalgic air floating about this lovely old coffee-house, even though it has been brought up to date. Today, muffins and doughnuts are served, and *amacchiato*, but the Jugendstil (art nouveau) interior makes up for the intrusions of the present day.

194 B1 Schellingstrasse 56
(089) 273 10 22 9 am–1 am
Universität

CADU/Café an der Uni
Situated opposite the university's main building, in a quiet inner courtyard, this pleasant café is a top favourite with students. As well as coffee and cake, you can also order some inexpensive snacks here, such as baked potatoes.

194 C1 Ludwigstrasse 24
(089) 28 98 66 00 Mon–Fri 8 am–1 am, Sat–Sun 9 am–1 am
Universität

Münchner Freiheit
Delicious tarts and ice creams! This Münchner Freiheit café, with its five tiny floors, is well loved by local people from the Schwabing district – and by everyone with a sweet tooth. Older customers tend to prefer the upper floors, while a young crowd gathers in the downstairs part of the café, the Forum at the U-Bahn exit.

194 C2 Münchner Freiheit 20
(089) 383 90 80 Daily 6:30 am–10 pm Münchner Freiheit

Puck
If you ever seriously oversleep and find it's 5 pm before you've had your breakfast, Café Puck has the solution to your problem. Here you can order coffee, eggs, muesli and toast up to 6 pm, which probably appeals to some students. Even if you don't feel like eating breakfast, this is an excellent place to mull over the paper or to meet friends in the evening, the dark wood panelling making a pleasant change from the ubiquitous modern chrome and glass interiors.

194 B1 Türkenstrasse 33
(089) 280 22 80
Daily 9 am–1 am Universität

Where to... Shop

Everything in Maxvorstadt and Schwabing revolves around fashion, with the shops pandering to a young student clientele as well as stylish customers from Schwabing, while the stores around Münchner Freiheit are targeting the hip hop scene. Few shops open before 10 am.

Around the University

A Munich institution, **Därr Travelshop** (Theresienstrasse 66) caters for all your travel and trekking needs, selling both clothing and equipment. If you have not been bitten by the travel bug and aren't into fashion either, just pay a visit to **Projekt.3** (Türkenstrasse 71) – provided your wallet is well filled. Here you'll encounter an elegant simplicity, with designerware by D&G and Cinque among others. The selection is equally classy at **Carta Pura** (Schellingstrasse 71), except that everything here revolves around paper. You can buy individual sheets and also larger quantities. At **Galeria Tiffany** (Türkenstrasse 96), the shop windows are resplendent with coloured glass. If you're not interested in buying a lamp, take a closer look at the fabulous jewellery. And if you do decide on a lamp, and you now need an extra case to safely pack it in, go to **Crumpler** (Adalbertstrasse 19), which has the greatest selection of travel bags and rucksacks.

Around Münchner Freiheit

Start your shopping day with a photo session – **The Fake** (Marktstrasse 10) will turn the palest wallflower into a diva and the cheekiest child into a little angel. Sessions have to be booked in advance. Trendy clothes and house, techno or trance music are available on two entire floors at **Neutronic** (Feilitzschstrasse 15). Just around the corner, at **Delirium** (Occamstrasse 17), is where real and would-be DJs find the drum 'n' bass or breakbeat CDs they've been looking for. If you're after the proper outfit as well as the music, try **Flip** (Feilitzschstrasse 7). You'll have to leave everything you bought so far at the entrance, that's the rule. Once inside, you'll find the latest, coolest designer gear and fabulous accessories. You won't find any big labels, instead the shop sells a wacky selection of unusual gear. **Mighty Weeny** (Siegesstrasse 23) is a treasure trove for hip hop fans, (in)famous for its graffiti spray cans as well as its truly amazing selection of streetwear and sneakers. A very different world awaits you at **Kunst&Spiel** (Leopoldstrasse 48), where toys, games and creative knick-knacks delight the followers of Rudolf Steiner's anthroposophic philosophy – as well as most other playful customers.

Around Hohenzollernstrasse

Everything at the **Africa House** (Hohenzollernstrasse 50) revolves around that continent – you'll find attractive jewellery and African fabrics in the colourful patterns of various tribes. If you prefer Indian clothes, which are so fashionable in Munich, you will find a good selection at **Irina Scarpe & Vestiti** (Ainmillerstrasse 2). Alternatively, the trendiest European and US labels are available at **Off & Co** (Belgradstrasse 5) on Kurfürstenplatz, where Miu Miu, Prada and D&G adorn shop windows and shelves. Two doors farther along is the shoe paradise **Schuh-Junkies**. Lacquered tins from Thailand, postcards from around the world and, best of all, superb writing and wrapping paper are for sale at the small shop, **PS: Papier** (Kaiserstrasse 46). **Luis Trenker** (Hohenzollernstrasse 62), named after a popular South Tyrolean mountaineer, actor and writer, sells collections of original folk costumes and fashion modelled on clothes worn in Luis Trenker's romantic mountain films. Artists and DIY enthusiasts will find every possible shade of paint colour as well as great utensils, and excellent advice at **Farben Hackl** (Hohenzollernstrasse 39). **Strumpftante** (Hohenzollernstrasse 45), with its vast selection of classic and unusual silk stockings, socks and leggings, has become a Schwabing institution. The **Kinderzimmer** (Kurfürstenstrasse 55) is a shop to visit on your own, for as soon as children enter into this magic realm, selling the most wonderful toys in the world, it will be easy to get your purse out but hard to get your children to leave! And should you want to buy fresh fruit or vegetables in Schwabing, why not take a stroll to the nearby **Elisabethmarkt** (Elisabethplatz), smaller but equally well stocked and just as appetizing as its larger cousin in the city centre, the Viktualienmarkt (➤ 52).

Where to be... Entertained

Bars serving food

Brasserie Tresznjewski (Theresienstrasse 72, tel: 089/28 23 49, Mon–Thu 8 am–3 am, Fri–Sat till 4 am) is a pleasant and on the whole not too pretentious place where you can while away the evening with a good glass of beer, a crispy salad, a pasta dish or more innovative snacks. The interior and the furnishings are cosy and comfortable.

At the fashionable and popular **Café Reitschule** (Königinstrasse 34, tel: 089/388 87 60, daily 9 am–1 am) you can sit on the terrace and watch horse-riders at the riding school or enjoy the views of Englischer Garten. Most customers, however, come for a club sandwich or one of the tasty Asian and Italian snacks, and their favourite activity is people- rather than horse-watching.

The **Garibaldi-Bar** (Schellingstrasse 60, tel: 089/28 67 36 70, daily 10 am–11 pm), in the university district, offers an insight into the Italian art of enjoying food and drink – the menu lists espresso, panini, delicious antipasti and very good wines from the bar's shop.

Lardy (Leopoldstrasse 49, tel: 089/34 49 49, 5 pm–3 am) is a trendy Mexican bar offering "tapas & soul". It's the ideal place to admire one of the many celebrities who come to visit this lively establishment.

Things are more traditional at **Max Emanuel** (Adalbertstrasse 33, tel: 089/271 40 38, 10 am–1 am). There's a popular, secluded beer garden serving good Bavarian food; and every Wednesday and Friday Munich's Latin music lovers dance salsa in one of the side rooms, accompanied by hot rhythms played by Chuck Hermann, the best salsa DJ. On Sundays, the salsa bar transforms itself into a 1950s club, complete with swinging ponytails and petticoats. This is a good place to make friends – if you're willing to put in that extra bit of effort on the dance floor.

News Café (Leopoldstrasse 74, tel: 089/38 38 06 00, Sun–Wed 8 am–2 am, Thu–Sat till 3 am) is a typical Leopoldstrasse bar, where customers go to be seen, to watch others and to pick up a date. The American-inspired menu features pasta and bagels.

Nippler (Kurfürstenstrasse 31, tel: 089/27 37 30 30, Mon–Sat 6 pm–3 am), a bar with a slightly unusual name, is well known for its delicious snacks, its excellent cocktails and for its particularly cool clientele.

The trendy crowd from Leopoldstrasse goes to the **Roxy** (Leopoldstrasse 438, tel: 089/34 92 92, daily 10 am–3 am) to prepare for their night out. This is what you need to do: get a seat on the terrace, order a giant ice cream and look at least as cool as everyone else.

Near the university, **Schall und Rauch** (Schellingstrasse 22, tel: 089/28 80 95 77, 10 am–1 am) is the place to meet old friends or to make new ones.

Billiard fans in Maxvorstadt have only one thing on their minds: let's go to the **Schellingsalon** (Schellingstrasse 54, tel: 089/272 07 88, Thu–Mon 6:30 am–1 am). This ancient bar with its similarly ancient games tables has been linked with several (in)famous names: supposedly this was Hitler's local; and after the War, Bavaria's most famous politician, the young Franz Josef Strauss, was sent to the saloon bar to buy beer. But don't let this hold you back – there's a wild Bavarian atmosphere here, and you're guaranteed to enjoy yourself. Plus, of course, you'll love it if you like playing billiards.

Considered to be Schwabing's oldest inn, **Schwabinger 7** (Feilitzschstrasse 7, tel: 089/33 24 27, daily 11 am–1 am) is something of an institution. The bar didn't age that well – some of the guests seem to have sat here, bent over their glass of beer, for decades. It has also been said that a blast of fresh air might be beneficial. However, no stroll through Schwabing would be complete without at least a fleeting visit to the "7"!

Students from the nearby technical university are the regulars at the **Steinheil** (Steinheilstrasse 16, tel: 089/52 74 88, 10 am–1 am), with the giant portions served for moderate prices being one of the main reasons. At night, the bar is always crammed so full it's hard to breathe but the atmopshere is great.

If a balmy summer night beckons but you don't fancy spending it at a beer garden, why not make for the terrace at **Tijuana** (Leopoldstrasse 13, tel: 089/550 88 00, 5 pm–1 am, weekends till 3 am)? Here you can enjoy tacos and happy-hour cocktails while eyeing up everyone else. It's a popular place for stylish girls and smart guys to impress each other.

Volksgarten (Briennerstrasse 83, tel: 089/57 87 78 59, daily 10 am–1 am), like so many other Munich restaurants, has an attractive garden; this one is situated in the courtyard of the Volkstheater. Families and theatregoers congregate here over a relaxed glass of wine, good antipasti or a piece of apfelstrudel.

Vorstadt Café (Türkenstrasse 83, tel: 089/272 06 99, Mon–Wed, Sun 9 am–1 am, Thu–Sat till 2 am) is always crowded. Young and old come to this café for a delicious breakfast, a snack at lunchtime or just to chill out with a glass of red wine and a frittata.

Zest (Adalbertstrasse 23, tel: 089/280 06 66, daily 5 pm–1 am), a popular bar in the university district, has dark walls, a long bar counter and a small restaurant area. The ambience is pleasantly subdued. The dishes of the day are Italian-inspired meals and salads.

Bars and discos

Pomp (Georgenstrasse 50, tel: 089/27 11 88, daily 9 am–3 am), a baroque bar with red walls, is very small indeed but still worth a visit. The Pomp barkeeper mixes some fabulous cocktails and the DJs play first-rate music.

Rock-loving couples favour the **Ace in the Hole** (Adalbertstrasse 82), where they lounge on tiger-pattern settees, while drinking their beers from the bottle.

Titanic City (Nordendstrasse 64, tel: 089/271 72 19, Wed–Thu 10 pm–3 am, Fri–Sat till 4 am, Sun 6 pm–3 am) is a very average and normal basement disco, rather than one of the more trendy clubs. The guests here are equally unobtrusive and the atmosphere is great.

Try also the following bars on the western limits of Maxvorstadt: **Tiefenrausch** (Schellingstrasse 91, tel: 089/27 27 20 10, Wed–Sun from 8 pm) with its deep-sea setting of blue walls, aquariums, portholes and sounds to chill out to.

At **Eat the Rich** (Hessstrasse 90, tel: 089/18 59 82, Mon–Sat 7 pm–3 am) however, it's always loud and noisy, which may have something to do with the huge cocktails that are served here.

Local celebs look cool at **Pathos Transport Theater** (Dachauer Strasse 110d, Wed from 8pm, Fri from 10 pm) while listening to drum 'n' bass sounds.

Cocktail fans are well served at **Vanilla Lounge** (Leopoldstrasse 65, tel: 089/38 66 68 36, daily 7 am–3 am) as well as at **Cocktailhouse** (Feilitzschstrasse 25, tel: 39 80 19, Sun–Thu 7 pm–1 am, Fri–Sat till 3 am), where excellent drinks can be enjoyed in a pleasant atmosphere with DJ music background sounds, or on the terrace in summer.

The **Haus der 111 Biere** (Franzstrasse 8, tel: 089/33 12 48, Sun–Wed from 6 pm, Thu–Sat from 8 pm) is an absolute must for beer drinkers. Some guests are thought to have drunk their way through all of the 111 Bavarian and international beers on offer at this bar.

The **Skyline** (Leopoldstrasse 82, tel: 089/33 31 31, weekdays till 4 am, weekends till 5 am) is Schwabing's best known disco, popular with young people and visitors. On the turntable are salsa, merengue and blackbeat.

A young indie crowd feels at home at **Prager Frühling** (Ainmillerstrasse 1, Tue–Wed from 9 pm, Thu–Sat from 10 pm), to the sounds of Brit pop, while Wednesdays are reserved for jazz fans.

Best known as **Nitro** (Leopoldstrasse 194, tel: 089/36 10 62 30, Thu 6 pm–2 am, Fri–Sat 10 pm–4 am), this club changes its name often. Although the furnishings are a slightly shabby 1980s style, the club is a very popular venue, especially for its after-work party on Thursdays from 6 pm.

Theatre

The **Lach- und Schiessgesellschaft** (corner Haimhauserstrasse and Ursulastrasse, tel: 39 19 97, www.lachundschiessgesellschaft.de), famous well beyond the Munich city limits, is a political cabaret with frequently changing programme and guest productions. Well-known comedians and cabaret artists like Willy Michl and Michael Mittermeier appear around the corner at the **Lustspielhaus** (Occamstrasse 8, tel: 089/34 49 74), or at **Bel Etage** (inside the Drugstore, Feilitzschstrasse 12, tel: 089/33 90 13) where you can see the best drag artists.

The **Schauburg** (Franz-Joseph-strasse 47, tel: 089/23 33 71 71), meanwhile, presents sophisticated drama for children and young adults.

Jörg Maurer's Unterton (Kurfürstenstrasse 8, tel: 089/33 39 33) is a theatre pub with an excellent, extremely entertaining cabaret programme. The **Heppel & Ettlich** (Kaiserstrasse 67, tel: 089/34 93 59), an actor's pub, also has theatre and cabaret performances.

The **Münchner Volkstheater** (Briennerstrasse 50, tel: 089/52 35 50) is nothing at all to do with Bavarian folklore, unless of course this can be represented in a tongue-in-cheek sort of way, updated for modern tastes, as in their very successful piece *Geierwally*.

Contemporary writers and modern classics dominate the programme at **Theater 44** (Hohenzollernstrasse 20, tel: 089/322 87 48). This small theatre likes to bring actors and audience close to each other; it is also the place where theatre luminaries such as Margarethe von Trotta and Otto Sander first trod the boards.

Cinema

Many of Schwabing's student cinemas have closed down or been modernized. However, the **Arri** (Türkenstrasse 91, tel: 089/38 89 96 64), furnished with wonderfully comfortable upholstered seats, and with lots of leg room, has resisted the trend towards multiplexes with its sophisticated programme.

Every Sunday morning, children's films are shown at the theatre pub **Heppel & Ettlich** (see Theatre).

The Right Bank

Getting Your Bearings

Munich's Haidhausen, Bogenhausen and Au districts were once so remote from the city that they could only be reached via a single bridge across the Isar River, the Ludwigsbrücke, next to Deutsches Museum. Today Haidhausen, with its many bars, has become a centre for clubbers, while Bogenhausen is one of Munich's most affluent districts.

Once Haidhausen was set to become a "second Schwabing" but fortunately that never quite happened. Nevertheless, the area has come a long way from the original workers' district, where clay was collected to burn roof tiles. In the 1970s, the district emerged as the favourite hunting ground for a young, alternative clubbing scene and it has remained so ever since. The cost of living has, of course, risen in line with this transformation. Haidhausen was declared a development area in 1976, and a building boom was unleashed which sent the rents spiralling sky-high.

Page 119: Friedensengel

Haidhausen thus came closer to its northerly neighbour, Bogenhausen, where the original neo-classical and Jugendstil façades have been restored to their former beauty. Affluent urban residents reside in loft apartments or in the fine villas

The Auer Dult fun fair is open three times a year

of Mauerkircherstrasse. Meanwhile, the Au district – the former flood plains of the Isar – is much more down to earth, having preserved its former working-class nature.

★ Don't Miss

1 **Deutsches Museum** ➤ 124
6 **Villa Stuck** ➤ 128

At Your Leisure

2 Müller'sches Volksbad ➤ 130
3 Gasteig ➤ 130
4 Maximilianeum ➤ 131
5 Friedensengel ➤ 131
7 Prinzregententheater ➤ 131
8 Bogenhausener Friedhof ➤ 132
9 Haidhausen ➤ 132

A journey through the history of science and technology, a stroll along the banks of the Isar, with views across the city, the elegant Jugendstil mansions in Bogenhausen and the multicultural Haidhausen scene – your day on the Isar's right bank offers a great variety of attractions.

The Right Bank in a Day

9:00 am

Start the day with a visit to the world's largest and most important museum of technology. Time literally flies at the 1 **Deutsches Museum** (➤ 124), where real aeroplanes and chemical experiments, giant model railways and musical instruments, star canopies and flying machines are exhibited in entertaining displays that will take you on an enjoyable journey of discovery through nature and technology.

Noon

Before strolling along the banks of the Isar, pause to admire the beautifully restored Jugendstil baths, 2 **Müller'sches Volksbad** (above; ➤ 130). Take a break for a snack or a coffee at the L-Bistro (➤ 136). While in session, you can watch and listen to Bavarian parliamentarians debate issues of the day at the 4 **Maximilianeum** (➤ 131). At the next Isar bridge, you can enjoy the view from the 5 **Friedensengel** (➤ 131) down Prinzregentenstrasse and across the Lehel district.

1:00 pm

The 6 **Villa Stuck** (➤ 128) is a delightful example of Munich Jugendstil design, with interesting exterior and interior features. Changing exhibitions take place in some rooms. The attractive 7 **Prinz-regententheater** (right; ➤ 131) is also in the vicinity. Stroll through the elegant streets of old Bogenhausen to 8 **Bogenhausener Friedhof** (Cemetery, ➤ 132), the last resting place for many Munich celebrities. To rest your feet take the tram to Max-Weber-Platz.

3:00 pm

Bavarian specialities and beer will restore you to full strength at the traditional inn, Unionsbräu (➤ 134). On Sundays white sausages are served here, although according to tradition these should always be consumed before the clocks ring high noon!

4:00 pm

Now immerse yourself in lively 9 **Haidhausen** (➤ 132). Walking along Kirchenstrasse, past the Haidhausen-Museum and towards the Alte Haidhauser Kirche, you will pass the Wasserwerk club and bar, once the home of the famous Blauer Engel strip club which was open until the 1990s. This is also where you'll find the Herbergenviertel with its quaint houses. Haidhausen's many small shops, artists' workshops and fashionable boutiques are great for shopping or just browsing. This is also a good time to decide where you'd like to eat tonight – there are plenty of restaurants in the district to choose from. Eat something nourishing – you may have a long night ahead!

9:00 pm

Gradually the first stirrings of life can be detected at the Kultfabrik, in the grounds of the former Optimol factory, on the other side of Ostbahnhof (below; ➤ 137). This is the current Munich nightlife scene. There's something here for everyone – enjoy yourself.

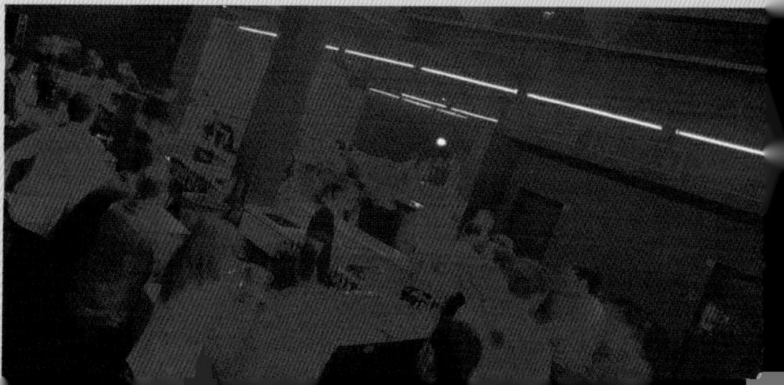

1 Deutsches Museum

The German Museum, with an exhibition area measuring 47,000sq m (over 11 acres), is one of the leading museums of its kind in the world. Opened more than 100 years ago, it shows the wonders of the development of technology, the natural sciences and research to some 1.2 million visitors a year.

A dream in green: locomotives at Deutsches Museum

Right from the start, Oskar von Miller, the museum's founding father, was committed to interactivity even though the concept hadn't even been invented then. His revolutionary idea – a museum of technology that is fun and where everything could be touched – was meant to further education, understanding and curiosity. He sought to achieve his aims through demonstrations, dioramas, the visitors' own exploration and a wide diversity of exhibits. He also set up a library and an archive to allow visitors to immerse themselves more deeply in the subject. The museum was opened at its present location on the Isar island on von Miller's 70th birthday, in 1925. The newly created Bayerischer Rundfunk radio station used the celebrations to introduce an amazing innovation: the first live radio transmission. The 65-m (213-foot) high museum tower, which housed a pendulum that illustrated the earth's revolutions, was seen by von Miller as an emblem of Munich. Its viewing platform affords excellent views across the entire city and the Isar flood plains, right up to the Alps.

It is the museum's mission, still observed by the curators today, always to be up to date with technology. And so, in 1931, visitors were able to watch the first-ever television transmission at the museum. During World War II, some 80 per cent of the building and 20 per cent of the exhibits

The solar energy department

were destroyed or damaged. After 1945, following general trends in the sciences, the museum shifted its emphasis to the natural sciences, and from the 1990s, a new spirit of integration and cooperation with the fine arts has prevailed here.

Live Technology at the Push of a Button

Von Miller's original concept still marks the exhibits today and the ethos is "Please do touch". At the push of a button, miniature waves demonstrate how sands shift in the tides, lightning flashes discharge during the demonstrations in the high-voltage display and a giant model railway proves that trains can run on time. A huge monster of a computer sends stars and planets across the projected miniature sky in the planetarium; dirty miners push heavy coal wagons in a mine; and perfect scale models illustrate the development of road and bridge engineering. There is a ship's deck for you to promenade on, complete with deckchairs, the sound of screeching seagulls and views of the German North Sea island of Heligoland; slide shows allow visitors to participate in the Wright brothers' first attempts and successes with flying; and the *Theodor Heuss* sea rescue cruiser lies outside the museum, in the dry dock. And you can also take a look at the cockpit of a fighter jet. The museum also has some special-interest departments, dealing with subjects such as glass technology, toolmaking and printing techniques.

How to Keep up With Progress

The museum is keeping up to date with modern trends by critically engaging with those branches of science that seem to have a promising future, for example pharmacy and medical technology. The department

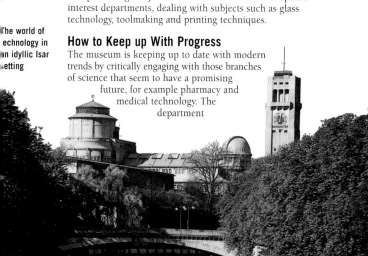

The world of technology in an idyllic Isar setting

For Kids

All children are fascinated by the mine. Young kids are enthusiastic about the model railway, while older children enjoy the technology exhibits. But the high point for all younger visitors is the children's world with its various attractions ranging from computers to water games. The planetarium also has regular performances, for example the story of "Robber Hotzenplotz" read in the dark (in German), part of the Technology Forum programme.

of gene technology was opened in 2002, an obvious consequence of current developments in research. An exhibit in this department allows visitors to go for a walk inside a cell. Other attractions include a copy of the Altamira caves in Spain, complete with prehistoric drawings, the story of musical instruments from the aeolian harp to the zither, a model of the "Spacelab" space station at its original size – the sheer diversity of the exhibits is impressive!
It's hardly surprising then that the museum's concept has been much copied elsewhere. However, the ongoing programme of adding to the exhibits has made it necessary to move some off-site. Thus, the **Flugwerft Schleissheim** (Flight Wharf, ➤ 170) has specialized in the history of aviation since 1992, while the **Verkehrszentrum** (Transport Centre, ➤ 155), which deals with all aspects of mobility, was opened in 2003 in the historic halls of Schwanthaler Höhe.

Please do touch!

The Technology Forum

The **Forum der Technik,** in the museum complex's congress building, has one IMAX cinema and two ordinary cinemas which present science content in an easy-to-understand, entertaining fashion. A screen area measuring 352sq m (3,789sq feet) plus an impressive sound system take viewers into an underwater world, lead them up to the summit of Mount Everest or show them the city of New York in amazing 3-D format. The **Planetarium** invites visitors to go on a journey through the universe. Laser-light shows attract music fans into the cupola where the top favourites for many years have been the musical and visual tributes to rock legends such as Genesis, Queen and Pink Floyd.

The colossal projector in the planetarium

TAKING A BREAK

You won't go hungry in this museum – there's a **Käfer** restaurant, a snack bar and an internet café on the 3rd floor. Perhaps the best fun is the **old railway buffet wagon** in front of the windmill outside, where you can buy snacks in summer. When the museum is closed, the **Aficionado** (daily 10 am–1 am) in the Congress Building sells snacks, salads, meat dishes and cakes. For an inexpensive alternative just bring your own sandwiches to eat on the banks of the Isar.

197 E3 Museumsinsel 1
(089) 217 91 Daily 9–5
Isartor Tram No 18 Deutsches Museum
Expensive
www.deutsches-museum.de

DEUTSCHES MUSEUM: INSIDE INFO

Top tips The movements of the futuristic box in the courtyard in front of the main entrance may remind you of a rodeo ride. But in fact this is the **Airjet Simulator** miniature cinema, where short films such as *Ice Channel* or *Children on the Big Dipper* are being shown; the sensation of moving makes the experience much more thrilling!

- Every day at 11 am and at 2 and 4 pm, museum staff set off a violent thunderstorm in the **high-voltage display on the ground floor**, where a volunteer survives being hit by lightning, protected inside the metal-lined sphere of the Faraday cage!

6 Villa Stuck

At the turn of the 19th and 20th centuries, Franz von Stuck played an important role in Munich's cultural life, which is why he has become known as the "painter prince" – and his villa was built in an appropriately princely style.

An elegant mixture of neo-classical elements and playful Jugendstil design dominates in Franz von Stuck's (1863–1928) former residence and artistic workshop. In the façade of the main building, references to antiquity immediately become apparent. The villa, with a clearly structured exterior of rectangular fields and two corner projections, is crowned by copies of four famous antique statues. Inside too, there are many mock-antique features.

A princely lifestyle for an ingenious artist

Funishings designed by von Stuck, neo-classical shapes, mosaics, paintings, carpets and accessories in the scrolled look of the day – the building was conceived as a synthesis of the arts right from the start. Since it looks like a museum, the building was always set to become an exhibition space. And, despite various obstacles, this finally happened in 1992.

Among the works of art displayed in the historic rooms, von Stuck's first success as a painter, *Der Wächter des Paradieses* (The Guard of Paradise) is remarkable. As is the painting *Die Sünde* (Sin), dating from 1893, because its erotic content caused great controversy. From the gilt-framed picture, a woman's pale

Stuck's artistic homage to his daughter

body leaps out, partially clad in dark drapery. Anna Maria Brandmaier, the mother of von Stuck's daughter Mary, was said to have been the model. Even at the time gossip and rumours were rife in polite society, and as a consequence von Stuck created numerous further versions of the "indecent" painting. The mural in the salon is equally impressive: its colours, stylistic elements and, not least of all, the figures it depicts are reminiscent of the decorations in Roman villas uncovered in Pompeii.

The eastern wing, which once functioned as von Stuck's atelier, has a decorative Jugendstil façade. Today its modern exhibition rooms show special exhibitions of Jugendstil and art nouveau style in all their manifestations around the world. Here you can find out more about the early 20th-century context of the artistic work of von Stuck and his contemporaries, with an emphasis on historical aspects and on the interaction between all the branches of fine and applied arts in the 20th century.

TAKING A BREAK

The best place to have a rest is a few paces along, at the Prinzregententheater, where, in a wing, the attractive, opulent café-restaurant **Prinzipal** (Prinzregentenplatz 12) invites you to take refreshments surrounded by walls painted with theatre scenes, or on the terrace in front of the theatre.

---

198 B4 Prinzregentenstasse. 60 (089) 455 55 10 Wed–Sun 11–6 Max-Weber-Platz, Prinzregentenplatz Tram No 18 Friedensengel Moderate www.villastuck.de

VILLA STUCK: INSIDE INFO

Top tip Take a look at the **ceiling in Franz von Stuck's "salon".** Here, the painter immortalized the constellation of the stars which could be seen in the night sky at the time when his daughter Mary was conceived.

At Your Leisure

2 Müller'sches Volksbad

This pool is regarded as one of the most beautiful art nouveau baths in the world, a veritable temple to bathing. Built in 1879–1901 by the engineer Karl Müller, the People's

Bathing fun as in the Jugendstil era

Baths were intended "mainly for people without means". Oriental and ancient Roman bathing traditions are reflected here, artfully decorated in the style of the time with stucco work, gold reliefs, decorative bannisters and scrolls. To get a view of the stunning interior, you need to go for a swim, but you will also have at your disposal Turkish baths, steam baths, Finnish sauna, solaria, massages and the last remaining tub and shower baths in Munich, for an all-round feel-good experience.

197 F3 ✉ Rosenheimer Strasse 1 ☎ (01801) 79 62 23 ⏲ Tue–Sun 7:30 am –11 pm, Mon till 5 pm 🚋 Tram No 18 Deutsches Museum 💶 Moderate

3 Gasteig

This Cultural Centre, opened 1975, is the home of the Munich Philharmonic Orchestra, the Richard Strauss Conservatory and the City Library, among others. Its architecture is controversial, likened to a cultural prison by some, while others praise the strict lines and multifaceted room layouts. A wide range of 1,700 different events is held here every year, including concerts with top musicians by the Philharmonic Orchestra as well as readings in the Carl-Orff-Saal. At the spring bookfair in March and at the Munich Book Show in November and December, Munich-based publishing houses present their catalogues. One of the liveliest Gasteig events, however, is the annual film festival at the end of June, where a vast screen is used for open-air film screenings.

197 F3 ✉ Rosenheimer Strasse 5 ☎ (089) 48 09 80 🚇 Rosenheimer Platz 🚋 Tram No 18 Am Gasteig ? www.gasteig.de, www.muenchnerphilharmoniker.de

Hitler Assassination Attempt

A plaque, set into the ground behind the oversized, water-spouting trumpet on the Kulturzentrum's southeastern side, reminds us of **Georg Elser** who tried to kill Adolf Hitler on 8 November, 1939. He planted a bomb in the Bürgerbräukeller, which once stood here. It killed 7 and injured 60 people, but Hitler was unharmed.

Munich's temple of culture

Maximilianeum, with antique statues

4 Maximilianeum

Maximilian II had this large building erected on the hills above the Isar, as a national monument to promote the people's patriotic spirit and their devotion to the monarchy. The majestic symmetrical structure, built in the neo-classical style with open-sided arcades forms the visual endpoint of exclusive Maximilianstrasse (➤ 86). Since 1949, the Maximilianeum has been the seat of the Bavarian parliament. While the House sits, visitors are permitted to observe parliamentary proceedings on the production of a passport. One of the wings is reserved for those who have gained a scholarship to the Maximilianeum – after passing an entry exam, Bavarian graduates with the best results are given the opportunity to study here with free board and lodging.

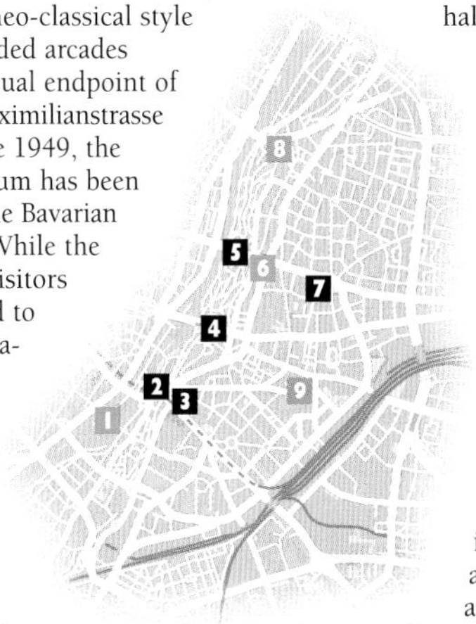

197 F4 Max-Planck-Strasse 1
(089) 41 26 27 05
Max-Weber-Platz Tram No 19 Maximilaneum Free
www.bayern.landtag.de

5 Friedensengel

Nike, the goddess of victory, was the model for the golden Angel of Peace which has stood here, high above the Isar since 1899, as a reminder of the 1871 Peace Treaty of Versailles, after victory over the French. On New Year's Eve, Munich citizens congregate under the angel's golden wings to watch the fireworks. Originally, Richard Wagner's Munich opera house, commissioned by Ludwig II, was to be built on this site. Gottfried Semper worked on the plans, but when the population opposed it, Wagner fled Munich and went to Bayreuth.

197 F4 Prinzregentenstrasse
Bus No 53 Friedensengel

7 Prinzregententheater

The idea of building a festival hall specifically for staging Wagner operas was taken up again by Ernst von Possart, less than 40 years after Gottfried Semper's work. And so the Prinzregententheater was built in 1900–01. In 1964, the theatre was declared unsafe. After extensive repairs it eventually reopened in 1996, with a Wagner opera. The programme today includes concerts, opera and readings; the theatre auditorium is renowned for its excellent acoustics.

198 B4 Prinzregentenplatz 12
(089) 21 85 28 99
Prinzregentenplatz
www.prinzregententheater.de

Viewing terrace at the foot of the Friedensengel

8 Bogenhausener Friedhof

This lovely cemetery in the elegant district of Bogenhausen is the last resting place for many Munich celebrities who wanted to be buried next to the Bogenhausener Kirche. Here, under a red star, lies the actress

Village church in elegant Bogenhausen

Liesl Karlstadt (➤ 64); a plain tombstone marks the grave of the film director Rainer Werner Fassbinder (➤ 23); and in the shade of ivy-clad trees, adorned with attractive crosses, are the last resting places of the writer Erich Kästner, of the actor Walter Sedlmayr (➤ 23), of Father Alfred Delp who was executed by the Nazis and of the German-French writer Annette Kolb. Also worth a visit is the small village church of St George, a magnificent rococo building where the great artists of the day, such as Johann Baptist Straub and Ignaz Günter, are immortalized.

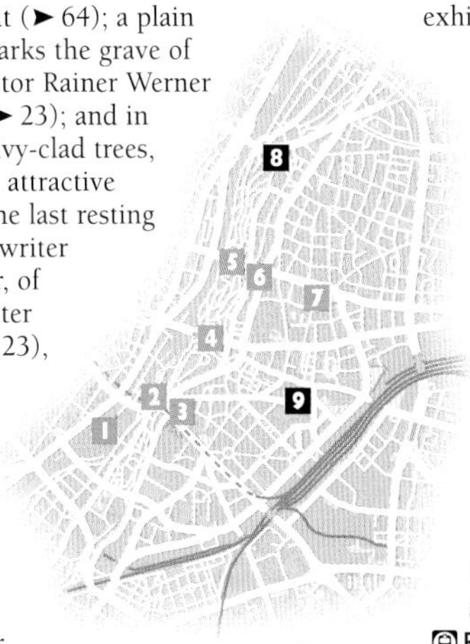

198 B5 ✉ Bogenhausener Kirchplatz 1 Daily until dusk
Tram No 18 Sternwartstrasse

9 Haidhausen

Shopping and entertainment – this neatly sums up Haidhausen today. The district has attracted a multicultural population who moved here when the rents were still affordable. You can still see glimpses of what Haidhausen was like in the 18th and 19th centuries – several small historic houses have been preserved, especially in Herbergenviertel. Here, the **Kriechbaumhof** (Preysingstrasse 71) and the Herbergenmuseum, based in the **Üblackerhäusl** (Preysingstrasse 58, tel: 089/ 480 76 79, Wed–Thur 5–7 pm, Fri, Sun 10 am–noon) bear witness to the terribly overcrowded and often very unhygenic conditions in which the workers had to live at the time. In addition, the **Haidhausen Museum** (Kirchenstrasse 24, Tel. 089/448 52 92, Mon–Wed 4–6 pm, Sun 2–6 pm), with its programme of changing exhibitions, sheds light on the cultural and social history of the district. **Alte Haidhauser Kirche** (Old Haidhausen Church, Kirchenstrasse) was once the focal point of the village, and this village atmosphere still lingers at **Wiener Platz**, with its market stalls quaintly grouped around the village maypole.

198 A/B 3–4
✉ between Rosenheimer Strasse, Orleansstrasse and Einsteinstrasse
Rosenheimer Platz, Max-Weber-Platz
Tram No 18 Am Gasteig

A bar in the Kultfabrik

Where to...
Eat and Drink

Prices
Prices are given for one person, excluding drinks.
€ under 12 euros **€€** 12–25 euros **€€€** over 25 euros

Restaurants

Augustiner Haidhausen €
Every district – even Haidhausen – needs a popular tavern such as the Augustiner. Here you sit at long, dark tables, chat and eat traditional Bavarian or contemporary Mexican or international food. Breakfast is served until 4 pm, to cater for late risers. As the evening wears on, the lights dim, the music gets louder and the atmosphere smokier.
In summer, guests sit at tables outside the restaurant where they can watch passers-by, while sipping their beers. Credit cards are not accepted here.

198 B3 Wörthstrasse 34
(089) 480 25 94
10 am–midnight Ostbahnhof

Bogenhausener Hof €€€
This exceptionally smart restaurant, with an elegance appropriate for the Bogenhausen district, is based in a listed building. The cooking is traditional Bavarian with a modern twist, accompanied by fine wines. It's hardly surprising that the restaurant attracts celebrities. There is an idyllic summer garden with a large chestnut tree, and little evidence remains to show that a lively dog market was based on this spot up to the 1950s.

198 B5 Ismaninger Strasse 85
(089) 98 55 86
Mon–Sat noon–2:30, 6–11:30 pm
Tram No 18 Sternwartstrasse

La Bretagne €€–€€€
Fish and seafood dishes are the speciality of this excellent small French restaurant. The extensive menu features unusual delicacies such as whole poached yellow gurnard. The interior is bright and modern, with light wood and cream-coloured walls. Service is friendly and helpful, and the French ambience makes you feel pleasantly relaxed. If you can't get a table, try the competition next door – Le Bousquérey has a similar menu, and the atmosphere and prices are about the same.

198 A3 Rablstrasse 37
(089) 48 72 20 Mon–Sat 6 pm–1 am Rosenheimer Platz

Dreigroschenkeller €–€€
The menu at this basement restaurant, underneath the Deutsches Museum cinema, features unusual set menus such as a "Henkersmahlzeit" (the Last Supper). Each room in the brick-vaulted building has differently themed furnishings. This "cultural dive for food, celebration and imagination" also offers an artistic programme: Mondays to Thursdays at 10 pm, drama students perform street ballads by Bertolt Brecht.

197 F3 Lilienstrasse 2
(089) 489 02 90 Sun–Thu 5 pm–1 am, Fri–Sat till 3 am
Tram No 18 Deutsches Museum

Juleps €€
American food with a Tex-Mex influence is served at this rustic restaurant, accompanied by subtle candlelight and gently revolving fans. Steaks, a variety of burger combinations or the delicious fajitas are worth trying – not a great choice for vegetarians! Finish your

evening with one of the excellent international cocktails – the restaurant bar is widely regarded as a classic by the mixed clientele.

198 B3 Breisacher Strasse 18
(089) 448 00 44
Daily 5 pm–1 am
Ostbahnhof

Käfer Schenke €€€

The kitchen philosophy in this stylish restaurant is "those who like to eat, smile a lot". And there truly is a lot to smile about in these small, private rooms. For special occasions book a table in the Porzellankabinett (Porcelain Cabinet). The cuisine is Mediterranean – the famous Käfer duck is the signature dish. Meat is cooked as a joint and carved at the table. Everything is of the highest quality; the restaurant has a great reputation to live up to and so only top quality will do.

198 B4 Prinzregentenplatz 73
(089) 416 82 47
Mon–Sat noon–1 am
Prinzregentenplatz

Lisboa Bar €€

The oldest Portuguese restaurant in Munich, the Lisboa, is a combined café, bar and restaurant. Choose one of the typical fish dishes, for example *bacalhau assado ou cozido*. Occasionally the Lisboa has live music, at times the melancholy sounds of *fado*, at other times rousing Brazilian rhythms, a great musical accompaniment for their cocktails. At the weekend, the bar often gets very crowded. The Lisboa also offers a parking service – a great help because Haidhausen is notoriously short of parking spaces.

198 B3 Breisacher Strasse 22
(089) 448 22 74
Daily 6 pm–1 am Ostbahnhof

No Mi Ya €–€€

This restaurant successfully unites Japan and Bavaria, offering sushi as well as wheat beer. Although No Mi Ya means "drinking establishment", make sure you sample the food – sashimi for example, or sushi in the smaller sushi bar. Everything is good value, the atmosphere in the small dining room is relaxed, and if you sit at an outdoor table you can watch the clubbers file past.

198 A3 Wörthstrasse 7
(089) 448 40 95
Mon–Sat 11 am–midnight
Tram No 19 Wörthstrasse

Ritzi €€–€€€

The young jet-set crowd of Bogenhausen, actors, business people and leading politicians from the nearby Landtag all congregate here; but don't let this put you off – ordinary people also like the Ritzi. The ambience is elegant and sophisticated, with a touch of art deco. Excellent food is served all day – you have the choice of breakfast, light lunchtime snacks or more extensive business lunches, afternoon coffees and cakes, or excellent evening meals inspired by Eurasian cuisine. Make sure you reserve a table if you go for Sunday brunch, served from 10:30 am. And after the meal, you could take a relaxing walk along the banks of the Isar, which flows right outside.

198 A4 Maria-Theresia-Strasse 2a (089) 470 10 10
Daily 6:30 pm–1 am
Max-Weber-Platz

Rue des Halles €€€

Bernard Le Port serves exquisite French meals at this well established restaurant. The interior is furnished in pleasantly plain Parisian style, reminiscent of a Montmartre bistro. The black-and-white photographs of the French capital work particularly well in the bright room. Menus are not cheap, but they feature so many interesting dishes that you can't confine yourself to just one course. Go on, spoil yourself!

198 A3 Steinstrasse 18
(089) 48 56 75
Daily 6:30 pm–1 am
Tram No 18 Wiener Platz

Unionsbräu Haidhausen €€

You'll find the best atmosphere in the brewery cellar. Here everyone

sits at long tables underneath the brewers' utensils with the brewing vats in view, while drinking the naturally cloudy beer. The ground-floor bar exudes Bavarian style.
In the summer you can enjoy the Bavarian snacks in the garden.
From Thursdays to Saturdays, dixie, swing and blues whip up the mood.
On Sundays, there's the traditional white sausage breakfast – and there can't be many places that still offer a sausage for just 50 cents!

198 B4 ✉ Einsteinstrasse 42 ☎ (089) 47 76 77 ⌚ Brewery Cellar Mon–Sat 4 pm–1 am, Sun 10 am–4 pm, restaurant Mon–Sat 11 am–11:30 pm, Sun until 4 pm Max-Weber-Platz

Zum Kloster €

The wall coverings may not be very up to date, but this fact may well explain the charm of this hostelry.
The friendly inn is well established, popular with Haidhausen locals and guaranteed to be free from poseurs.
In summer you can sit outside, in a traffic-calmed street, while enjoying one of the simple meals or an afternoon coffee and one of the delicious cakes from the cabinet.

198 B3 ✉ Preysingstrasse 77 ☎ (089) 447 05 64 ⌚ Mon–Sat 11 am–midnight Tram No 19 Wörthstrasse

Beer gardens

Hofbräukeller €€

In winter you'll drink your beer under the beamed ceiling of the extensive vaulted rooms, but in summer the beer garden is more inviting, where a mixed bunch shares wooden benches under the chestnut trees. Of course it quickly gets crowded. Go into the basement if you want to have a good laugh: the Valentin-Karlstadt-Theater puts on old and new pieces dedicated to a sense of the absurd.

198 A4 ✉ Innere Wiener Strasse 19 ☎ (089) 459 92 50 ⌚ Daily 9 am–midnight Tram No 18 Wiener Platz

Paulaner am Nockherberg €€

This bar is one of Munich's main beer haunts. It becomes even more popular during the "strong beer week" preceding Lent, when you'll spot as many "genuine" Bavarians in folk costume here as at the Oktoberfest. The malty Salvator beer is such a draw that the landlord even charges admission to the beer garden and the festival rooms, restored after a fire. The strong beer is accompanied by folk music and substantial food – which is served in the shade of the chestnut trees in the beer garden throughout the year.

197 F3 ✉ Hochstrasse77 ☎ (089) 459 91 30 ⌚ Daily Bar 10 am–11 pm, Beer Garden noon–11 pm Tram No 27 Ostfriedhof ? www.nockherberg.com

Cafés

Cafiko

Resisting the trend towards cool neon interiors, this café has cosy bistro tables and pictures on the walls. Guests of all ages enjoy light snacks or a coffee.

198 B3 ✉ Breisacher Strasse 8 ☎ (0173) 368 33 95 ⌚ Mon–Fri 8 am–10 pm, Sat 9 am–10 pm, Sun until 8 pm Ostbahnhof

Johannis-Café

Don't be put off by the orange floral wallpaper at the entrance nor by the conventional interior. This is where insiders meet to chill out and enjoy a Bavarian supper before bed. A surprisingly mixed clientele.

198 A4 ✉ Johannisplatz 15 ☎ (089) 480 12 40 ⌚ Daily from 11 am Tram No 18 Wiener Platz

Kilombo

This old Haidhausen café is an in-crowd favourite. Depending on the mood of the day, world music or techno are the musical background for simple, solid food.

197 F2 ✉ Senftlstrasse 9 ☎ (089) 48 52 98 ⌚ Daily 6 pm–1 am Tram No 25 Regerplatz

L-Bistro

Seating at this café is either under the glass-roofed columned hall of Müller'sches Volksbad or in the garden at the baths' decorative entrance. If you don't fancy a swim, the café offers you the chance to enjoy at least some of the Jugendstil (art nouveau) interior over a snack.

198 A3 Rosenheimer Strasse 1
(089) 48 22 22
Daily 10 am–1 am
Tram No 18 Deutsches Museum

Wiener Platz

Large-scale murals, mirrors and many cool customers mark this trendy café. Hiding behind their reflective mirror shades, they eye up other customers and watch the action outside the café as the trams rattle past. A favourite place for breakfasts, but it's equally worth recommending for evening meals.

198 A4 Innere Wiener Strasse 48 (089) 448 94 94
Daily 8 am–1 am
Tram No 18 Wiener Platz

Where to... Shop

Jewellery workshops and antique shops, book stores and boutiques, delicatessens and paper shops, art galleries and countless hairdressers – the districts on the Isar's right bank, and especially Haidhausen, offer a great and varied mixture of the extravagant, the traditional, the creative and the alternative.

Markets

The largest open-air market is the traditional **Auer Dult** which takes place three times a year – the May Dult (until May 1), the Jakobi Dult (from July 25) and the Autumn Dult (from 3rd Sunday in October). For a week at a time, the stalls are filled with an air of nostalgia. But don't be under any illusions – you will hardly find any great antiques bargains on the large square at the foot of the Auer Kirche on Mariahilfplatz! You'll have a better chance of striking it lucky at the **Antikpalast** (Friedenstrasse10) in the grounds of the Optimol factory. You could well find some beautiful pieces in this, Germany's largest art and antiques centre. The stalls at the **Markt am Wiener Platz** cater to your refreshment needs, keeping even gourmets happy. In the pre-Christmas period, the **Haidhauser Christkindlmarkt** (Weissenburger Platz) offers a quiet alternative to the bustle of the large Christmas market on Marienplatz.

Haidhausen

Attention all those with a sweet tooth: the **Confiserie Miksch** (Belfortstrasse2) is a hidden gem – the traditional confiserie has been making pralines, delicacies with ginger and specialities from Silesia since 1870, and has even supplied the royal court in Bavaria. Small things to eat, decorate or use are on sale at **Le Bazar de Cuisine** (Balanstrasse 8) – beautiful objects for the kitchen, from state-of-the-art design to nostalgia! If you enjoy browsing through old vinyl records and CDs, immerse yourself into the large selection on sale at the **M2** (Rosenheimer Strasse 77). Fashion-conscious mothers and daughters will find cool and trendy items from the leading labels at **Venus** (Wörthstrasse 1), and a few houses along, the shoes to go with it. Attractive clothes for children – new or secondhand – are sold by **Rapunzel** (Preysingstrasse 67), a shop that labels itself as the "freaked-out children's shop". Original jewellery – bracelets, rings, earrings, necklaces, broches – are waiting to be discovered at **Ventil** (Steinstrasse 17). "Living Flowers" can be bought at **Blumen, die leben** (Max-Weber-Platz 9), a beautifully decorated florists that continuously reinvents itself. Even a daisy becomes a queen of flowers here. Hundreds of different types of implements for cutting, including scissors for left-handed people, are available at **Messer & Scheren** (Rosenheimer Strasse 42). The **Münchner Blech** (Gebsattelstrasse 11) resounds from every corner, because customers are usually invited to try out the brass and woodwind instruments at this unusual shop before they make a decision. Trying out is also permitted to customers at **Liquid** (Pariser Strasse 36). However, you are advised not to overdo the sampling because the selection of excellent wines and strong spirits quickly goes to your head!

Bogenhausen

Feinkost Käfer (Prinzregentenstrasse 73) is *the* address for fine foods in Munich, selling a great – and at times unique – selection of choice foods, which look extremely appetizing and appeal to every food lover who sees them.

Where to be... Entertained

Fun Areas, Discos, Music

Nonstop fun throughout the night: the undisputed centre of Munich's nightlife can be found a little way beyond Ostbahnhof, in the former factory halls. The vast **Kultfabrik** (Grafinger Strasse 6, tel: 089/49 00 90 70, www.kultfabrik.de, opening times and admission to individual clubs vary) alone, boasting 25 separate clubs, can lay claim to the title of "Europe's longest partying mile". Then there are a further nine clubs plus additional restaurants in the grounds of the **Optimolwerke** (Friedenstrasse 10, tel: 089/450 69 20, www.optimolwerke.de, varying opening times and admission for all clubs) – you can't get bored here. You have a choice of the Ü-30-Party or hardcore heavy & nu metal at the *Club Black Raven*, of lounging on the settees at *Salon Erna* or braving the rocky thundery sounds at *Titty Twister*, of enjoying the perfect bodies of good-looking boys and girls at the *NY Tabledance* or the live performances and show acts at *Rafael*, of indulging in an après-ski ambience at the *Sound-Hütt'n* or listening to techno at the *Schall* Club – your greatest problem will be making a choice. To help you decide, check out the websites of the two "Fun Areas" or one of the two magazines, *Kultfabrik – Das Magazin* or *go Nightlife*. Alternatively, just drift around, the night is long. There are up to 30,000 visitors every weekend, and they'll have to go somewhere.

If you cannot decide which of the clubs to visit, just carry on down the road to the disco **Pacha** (Rosenheimer Strasse 145 H, tel: 0162/413 62 28, www.pacha-muenchen.de, Tue from 6 pm, Wed from 8 pm, Thu–Sat from 10 pm). Tuesday nights are reserved for Business Clubbing, Wednesdays are for a 1980s revival and on Thursdays to Saturdays the music is soul, funk and rhythm 'n' blues.

At the dance café **Maratonga** (Innere Wiener Strasse, tel: 089/48 84 25), those who stayed young at heart hit the dance floor in a relaxed atmosphere, from 1 pm to 1 am!

Where once the Auer Mühlbach turned the mighty turbines of the first steam heating power station (1894), today modern music in all its manifestations is being played at the **Muffathalle** (Zellstrasse 4, tel: 089/45 87 50 10, www.muffathalle.de). The former turbine halls with their excellent acoustics offer a stage for the stars of world music. In the beer garden, under the heritage-protected chimney, light Mediterranean meals, organic meat and fish dishes and vegetarian meals are served. The café attached to the halls is open for live performances, which means almost every day.

Munich salsa fans perform their

complicated twists and turns in front of an admiring audience at the **Palacio 2** (Friedenstrasse 10, tel: 089/14 33 56 11, Fri–Sat from 9 pm). To ensure that beginners too can enjoy the mambo, rumba and merengue rhythms, there are free 45-minute dance lessons from 9 pm every night.

Unterfahrt (Einsteinstrasse 42, tel: 089/448 27 94, Sun–Thu 7:30 pm–1 am, Fri–Sat until 3 am, www.unterfahrt.de), meanwhile, flies the flag of jazz in Munich, otherwise lacking in good jazz venues. The former beer cellars offer a varied and attractive international repertoire on stage, and the club also has a gallery.

Pubs, Bars, Clubs

The traditional Kneipe (pub) is disappearing. All bars serve at least bar snacks – most are called "café bar restaurant". **Molly Malone's** (Kellerstrasse 21, tel: 089/688 75 10, Mon–Fri 5 pm–1 am, Sat–Sun noon–1 am) is the glorious exception. The Irish community meets here to share a Guinness, Kilkenny or Irish whiskey, and for the *craic*.

Although the abbreviation **Uwe** (Metzstrasse 7, tel: 089/48 95 26 53, Mon–Fri 5 pm–1 am, Sat–Sun 3 pm –1 am) stands for "Unter-Wasser-Erlebnis" (underwater experience), this pub restaurant explicitly invites both divers and non-divers. The decor is sub-marine, with a large shark suspended above the bar.

The interior is also unusual at **Maria Pasagne** (Steinstrasse 42, tel: 089/48 61 67, daily 7 pm–1 am), crammed with African knick-knacks. To be admitted, ring the bell.

One of the top trendy venues at the moment is the underworld of the **Nektar** (Stubenvollstrasse 1, tel: 089/45 91 13 11, daily from 7 pm), where you can loll about on a white lawn in the *Salle Blanche,* while enjoying one of the excellent menus, or dance to video clips and club sounds at the *Cabinet Plasma* – one of the coolest clubs in Munich for the young and beautiful, with plenty of loose change.

Fat water pipes snake around the ceiling, an old meter decorates the wall, but otherwise the interior at the **Wasserwerk** (Wolfgangstrasse 19, tel: 089/48 90 00 20, daily 6 pm–1 am) is cool and elegant; guests love the beautifully mixed drinks.

Theatre

Cabaret performances and concerts, mainly from Bavaria yet still easily understood by German speakers, feature at the **Drehleier** (Rosenheimerstrasse 123, tel: 089/48 27 42, www.theater-drehleier.de), and the attached tavern *Szenerie* is also used for performances.

Cinema

Quality films from Hollywood and unusual shorts are shown at the repertory cinema at **Museums-Lichtspielen** (Lilienstrasse 2, tel: 089/48 24 03), mostly in their original version; many children's films are also screened in the small and cosy cinema rooms.

The **Rio** (Rosenheimer Strasse 46, tel: 089/48 69 79) has a similar programme, although at this cinema a dubbed version of the films is usually screened.

Sport and Games

Even if you're not into climbing, you can go and watch others. For the climbing installation at the **Heavens Gate** in the Kultfabrik (Grafingerstrasse 6, tel: 089/40 90 88 03, www.kletternmachtspass.de, daily 10 am–11 pm) equipment can be rented, and then used on the rocks outside or on the vertical climbing wall in the former silo plant. Children especially love to have a go. The Kultfabrik also has **Kulti-Kids**, a hall measuring 800sq m (8,611sq feet) where kids can enjoy sports, dance or try their hands at arts, literature and crafts.

West Munich

Getting Your Bearings

The elegant districts of Nymphenburg and Neuhausen in west Munich are framed by the green spaces of Olympiapark, Nymphenburg Schlosspark and Botanischer Garten. Thanks to their excellent sports, leisure and cultural facilities and attractive turn-of-the-19th-century houses and fine restaurants, these are the residential areas of choice for the well-heeled. Schwanthaler Höh', a traditional workers' district stands in vivid contrast.

Every day, hundreds of sports enthusiast and walkers flock to the green hills and silver rooftops of the sports stadiums in the Olympic park. Bourgeois Neuhausen is home to an eye-catching monument of contemporary church architecture – the modern Herz-Jesu-Kirche – while the Nymphenburg chateau and park, home of the Wittelsbach dynasty, hark back to the days when the people were devoted to their royal rulers. The residential areas of Nymphenburg and Neuhausen are becoming increasingly sought-after, despite the fact that they are expensive. Munich's citizens also flock here for their cultural edification. Whereas the West End promises a lively multicultural scene, dominated by noisy stand-up bars and ethnic restaurants, the courtyards resounding with the folk music of the Balkan countries. There is no chance of boredom here, and things get even more lively when the Oktoberfest starts up on the meadows of Theresienwiese (➤ 13).

★ Don't Miss

- **1 Olympiapark** ➤ 144
- **4 Herz-Jesu-Kirche** ➤ 147
- **5 Schloss Nymphenburg and Neuer Botanischer Garten** ➤ 149

At Your Leisure

- 2 Olympisches Dorf ➤ 153
- 3 Ost-West-Friedenskirche ➤ 153
- 6 Kindermuseum ➤ 154
- 7 Alter Botanischer Garten ➤ 154
- 8 Zirkus Krone ➤ 154
- 9 Bavaria ➤ 155
- 10 Deutsches Museum Verkehrszentrum ➤ 155

Page 139: Schloss Nymphenburg

Background: Olympiapark

You'll need to be fit for today's programme: Olympiapark, a detour to the Herz-Jesu-Kirche, Schloss Nymphenburg and the Botanischer Garten. Luckily there are plenty of places where you can rest your legs and take refreshments.

West Munich in a Day

9:00 am

For a first impression, 1 **Olympiapark** (➤ 144) is best seen from above. If the weather is fine, climb to the top of the Olympic Tower (left). The platform affords great views across the Bavarian metropolis. You can also see today's route from here. Beware of the foehn winds: it might look as if you'd be able to walk right up to Zugspitze but, however close the Alps may look, they are actually some 100km (62 miles) away!

10:00 am

Explore the Olympic grounds with a leisurely ride on the tourist train. It will take you underneath the tented roof, past the sports stadiums and around the Olympic lake, giving you an easy overview of the entire area. You can join the soccer tour of the Olympic Stadium at 11 am.
And if you are not a soccer fan, just stroll through the 2 **Olympisches Dorf** (left; ➤ 153), past the colourfully painted student bungalows.

Noon

Leave the area south of the Olympic Stadium, following the canal that will take you past the Olympic Cycling Stadium and directly to Schloss Nymphenburg. Turn into the quiet Taxisstrasse. You'll come across the attractive Taxisgarten (➤ 157) at an opportune moment as the busy morning programme is now completed. Take a break and refresh yourself with a Bavarian *brotzeit*.

1:30 pm

After your meal, continue through the sedate residential streets of Neuhausen to the 4 **Herz-Jesu-Kirche** (➤ 147). This glass cube, boasting the largest church doors in the world, is a place for contemplation and an encounter with modern architecture. Continue northwards to the Hubertusbrunnen, at the beginning of Auffahrtsallee. In the distance you can already glimpse the highlight of today's tour: 5 **Schloss Nymphenburg** (above; ➤ 149). In the splendid building you will see myriad mirrors, paintings and tapestries, as well as King Ludwig I's birthplace. After your visit to the chateau, stroll through Nymphenburg Park to admire the smaller chateaux, or visit the Bäuml porcelain collection. Whatever you do, end your visit at the Schlosscafé im Palmenhaus (left). Over a cup of coffee and a slice of cake you can muse on the paintings in King Ludwig I's gallery of the beauties of his day (➤ 150).

4:30 pm

More reasons for wide-eyed amazement: the magnificent floral displays at the 5 **Neuer Botanischer Garten** (➤ 151), accessible from Nymphenburg Park, beyond Magdalenenklause.

6:00 pm

Now hop on a tram and go towards the centre of Munich, to Romanplatz. Nearby is Hirschgarten beer garden (➤ 157), where you can recover from the day's demands over a glass of Augustiner and a radish with pretzels, while watching the red deer in the game enclosure.

1 Olympiapark

The Olympic park has a varied past. In turns the area was a parade ground, a Zeppelin landing strip, a rubble heap and finally, in 1972, the scene of the 20th summer Olympic Games. The stadium with its unusual tent-like roof structure stills attracts visitors today, for both sports and cultural events.

The Olympiapark is one of Munich's largest inner-city leisure areas. Its Olympic stadium serves as a venue for sports contests and as a giant stage for pop concerts. In the Olympic hall, sports competititons, large concerts, fairs and exhibitions

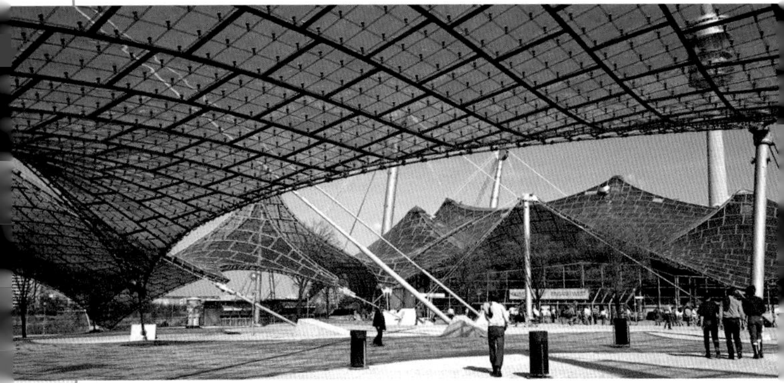

The tented roof, an architectural stroke of genius

are staged. Munich's ice-hockey team, EHC München, chases the puck across the ice on the Olympic ice rink. In winter, the Olympic mountain attracts skiers and snowboarders – professionals in the World Cup contests and amateurs for the après-ski at the original skiing hut.

In-line skaters whizz around the Olympic lake, joggers pant up the hill, children toboggan or fly their kites, and the Olympic swimming pool is today a popular public pool. During the Theatron-Musiksommer, hot new bands and international groups perform live on the stage at the lake, and rock stars, cabaret artists and the alternative arts scene meet up at the Sommer-Tollwood (➤ 14), on the other side of Olympiaberg.

The View from the Top

Towering over the entire area is the nearly 290-m (950-feet) tall **Olympiaturm** (Olympic Tower). The viewing platform, at a height of 190m (623 feet), affords truly spectacular views, especially when the foehn wind seems to bring the mountains of the Alps deceptively close to the Munich city limits. Similar panoramic views from only 52 m (170 feet) high can be

The opening ceremony of the 1972 Olympic Games

appreciated from the **Olympiaberg** (Olympic mountain); among the locals it's still known as rubble tip, because the rubble of the bombed-out city lies hidden there. The architectural element that unites the different areas of the Olympic grounds is the **Zeltdach** (tented roof), designed by the architectural company of Behnisch & Partner. Its shape reflects the topography of the area, adapting to the surrounding countryside with elegance. The structure, consisting of steel and acrylic, spans a total of 75,000sq m (18½ acres) and 58 masts, up to 81m (266 feet) high, hold up the giant roof.

During the 1972 Olympic Games, some 80,000 enthusiastic spectators watched the athletics events in the **Olympiastadion** (Olympic Stadium), which later also served as a soccer pitch. But, in 2003 the managers of Munich's two soccer clubs (► 16) decided that the stadium no longer lived up to the demands of world-class soccer today. And so, from 2006, the top clubs will compete in the Allianz-Arena in München-Fröttmaning.

Olympic match-making: hostess Sylvia (centre) became Queen of Sweden

The Twentieth Olympic Games

The Munich Olympic Games, which took place from 26 August to 11 September, 1972, were known as the "cheerful games" – at least until September 5, when Palestinian terrorists occupied the Israeli athletes' quarters. After the murder of two athletes and unsuccessful negotiations, the remaining athletes were seized as hostages and taken to the military airport of Fürstenfeldbruck, where an attempt to free them ended in a bloodbath. The Olympics continued. According to Jewish custom, visitors place stones at the monument in front of Connollystrasse No 31, commemorating the events. The highlights of the sporting events are immortalized in the winners' plaques on Coubertinplatz, where you'll find the names of Mark Spitz, Heide Rosendahl and Olga Korbut.

North of Mittlerer Ring are the headquarters of the car manufacturer BMW, the world's largest "four-cylinder structure". The "bowl" will house the **BMW Museum**. During renovations, some of the exhibits can be seen until 2007 in a temporary light-metal hall near the Olympic Tower.

Windowless BMW Museum

TAKING A BREAK

The Olympic Tower's **Drehrestaurant** (Revolving Restaurant) serves light bistro-style meals at lunchtime, which can be enjoyed together with the best views of the city and surroundings.

For Kids

If you fancy rowing across the Olympic lake, you can rent a boat near the Olympic Tower. And there's lots of fun during the summer festival in August...on countless types of vehicle!

193 E/F 3–4 (089) 30 67 24 14; Olympic Tower (089) 30 67 27 50; Olympic Stadium (089) 30 67 27 07 Olympic Tower 9–midnight; Olympic Stadium 9–6 Olympiazentrum Olympic Tower and Olympic Stadium inexpensive
www.olympiapark.de

BMW Museum
(089) 30 67 24 10–10 Inexpensive
www.bmwmobiletradition.de

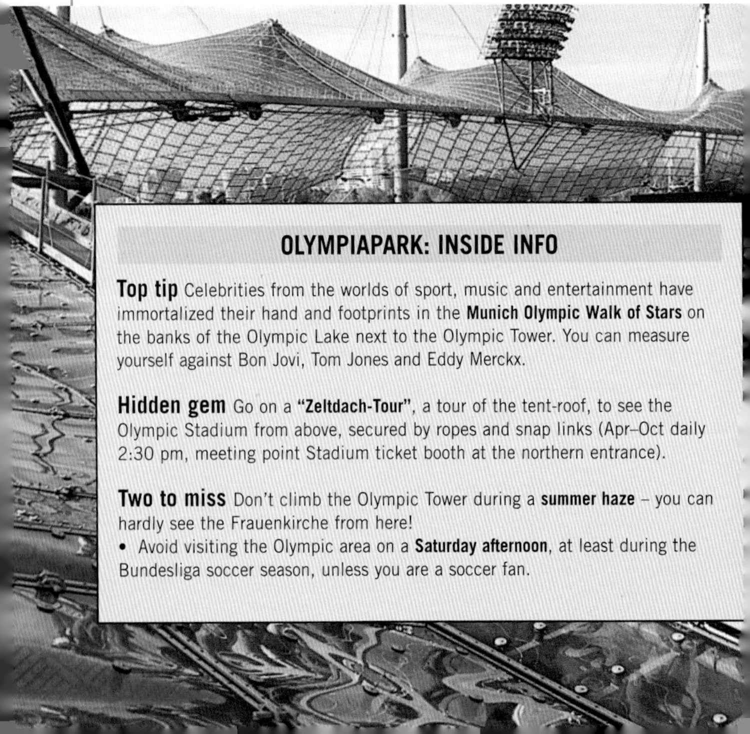

OLYMPIAPARK: INSIDE INFO

Top tip Celebrities from the worlds of sport, music and entertainment have immortalized their hand and footprints in the **Munich Olympic Walk of Stars** on the banks of the Olympic Lake next to the Olympic Tower. You can measure yourself against Bon Jovi, Tom Jones and Eddy Merckx.

Hidden gem Go on a **"Zeltdach-Tour"**, a tour of the tent-roof, to see the Olympic Stadium from above, secured by ropes and snap links (Apr–Oct daily 2:30 pm, meeting point Stadium ticket booth at the northern entrance).

Two to miss Don't climb the Olympic Tower during a **summer haze** – you can hardly see the Frauenkirche from here!
- Avoid visiting the Olympic area on a **Saturday afternoon**, at least during the Bundesliga soccer season, unless you are a soccer fan.

4 Herz-Jesu-Kirche

The world's largest church doors, glass portals spanning the entire front of the church, open in clement weather. Modern architecture in Munich has enjoyed an upturn which has now also reached church architecture: the Herz-Jesu-Kirche in Neuhausen sets new standards of design.

When a fire completely destroyed the old Herz-Jesu-Kirche in Lachnerstrasse in 1994, it was seen as an opportunity to build a new church. The congregation requested a modern structure that was to be unusual, pioneering and open. The church hall, it said on the invitation to tender, was to be conceptual, exuding "clarity, calm and a sense of security. Special attention should be given to the action of light which should enhance the church hall's solemnity and emphasize the altar as its focal point". The contract to build the church was awarded to the architectural company of Allmann/Sattler/Wappner.

The new church, dedicated in 2000, comprises – to simplify somewhat – two cubes that are set one inside the other. The walls of the inner cube are formed by slatted maple panels, and the outer glass cladding of the hall seems to have been pushed over the top of the inner sanctum. Slats and glass allowed the architects to skilfully direct the incoming light.

The play of light in the church

The Passion of Christ

Between the two cubes runs a covered walkway at high level, with modern stations of the cross. Note the crucifix in the entrance area – one of only a few objects to survive the fire of 1994. The Passion of Christ is depicted in a series of iconographical images on the 14-m (46-feet) high portal wings. Specifically for these doors, the English glass artist Alexander Beleschenko created an alphabet with each letter formed by a configuration of nails. He then encoded the passage in the Gospel of St John where Jesus is wounded in his side by a lance – a secret code, that cannot be deciphered! Inside the church, the *Fünf Wunden* (Five Wounds), five small windows

Reflected blue for the glory of God

set in the floor, symbolize the wounds of Jesus, continuing the theme of the suffering of Christ. The central focal point and the climax of the church's conceptional theme of the Passion of Christ is the crucifix curtain beind the altar. Woven in metal, using a variety of weaving techniques and varying degrees of density in its dual structure, a cross clearly emerges against the background of the curtain – an effect that is further intensified by artificial light in the evening. Thus, the crucifix curtain, just like the semi-transparent portals of small blue glass plates, takes up the leitmotif of the entire structure: to represent Christ's suffering through its use of light.

Apart from the architectural and conceptional themes realized in the church, its acoustics are also unique and quite remarkable. It is known among Munich's hobby choirs that even tiny, weak and fragile voices will not sound better anywhere else.

TAKING A BREAK

At **Romans** (Romanstr. 1), close to the Herz-Jesu-Kirche, you can enjoy fine Italian food with an elegant, modern touch. Stop for a portion of pasta or a fragrant risotto – then continue on your way, full of new vim and vigour.

---

192 C2 Lachnerstrasse 8 (089) 54 54 08 80 Daily 8–8
Rotkreuzplatz www.herzjesu-muenchen.de

HERZ-JESU-KIRCHE: INSIDE INFO

Hidden gem Listen – meditate – be amazed! Every Sunday at 7:30 pm (apart from August and September) the church offers **a special hour with music and spiritual readings**. If the weather permits, the large church portals are opened for the occasion. Afterwards you are invited to drink a glass of wine in the vicarage courtyard.

5 Schloss Nymphenburg and Neuer Botanischer Garten

When the summer was too hot for the Prince Electors, or if they were just exhausted from ruling, they fled to their summer residence. Not far from Munich, Schloss Nymphenburg exudes its southern charm right in front of the city gates.

Small gifts keep a friendship alive. And so, on the occasion of the birth of his son Maximilian Emanuel in 1663, the Prince Elector Ferdinand Maria – a generous man – gave the "Schwaige Kemnath" to his consort, Henriette Adelaide. This inn, together with its woods, fields and meadows, formed the starting point for Schloss Nymphenburg. During the following centuries, Europe's elite architects designed the palace complex. The Italian architects Agostino Barelli, Enrico Zuccalli and Antonio Viscardi contributed their expertise. Then, during the reigns of Maximilan II Emanuel (until 1726), Karl Albrecht (until 1745) and Maximilian III Joseph (until 1777), the Munich master builders Joseph Effner, François Cuvilliés the Elder and finally Johann Baptist Zimmermann advanced the construction. And so, slowly, an extensive, symmetrical palace complex in baroque and rococo style emerged, which was to remain the Wittelsbach dynasty's summer residence until the end of the monarchy, in 1918.

Rococo-style splendour and sumptuousness dominate the **interior**. Stucco, frescoes, gold, tapestries and paintings are everywhere. The most

The superb ceiling of the Audienzzimmer

impressive room is the central Steinerner Saal (Stone Room, the great hall). Here, Johann Baptist Zimmermann's giant ceiling fresco depicts Apollo in his sun chariot and a host of Olympian gods and nymphs – an allusion to "Nymphenburg"– paying their devotions to Flora, the goddess of nature.

Amalienburg, a Rococo gem

Royal Park Promenade

In 1715, Dominique Girard, the garden architect, was appointed to create the **Schlosspark** (Palace Park). People began to rebel against the aristocracy in the late 1700s, and Prince Elector Karl Theodor handed over the baroque park to them in 1792. To keep up to date with fashion, Ludwig von Sckell began to transform the park into an English landscape garden in 1804.

In the early 18th century, several smaller palaces were commissioned as outbuildings for the palace, to be used for special celebrations, for ceremonial purposes or simply as a refuge. They were seemingly "scattered" throughout the Schlosspark. The **garden palaces** Amalienburg, Badenburg (with its "indoor pool") and the Pagodenburg, styled as a Far Eastern building, are miniature expressions of splendour. The Hunting Lodge in particular, built by von Cuvilliés for Electress Amalie in 1734–39, is a true marvel of rococo elegance and lightness. In contrast, the Magdalenenklause, a romantic folly of a ruin, represents a withdrawal from the world.

Lola Montez and the other Models

In Ludwig I's Gallery of Beauties the viewer comes face to face with 35 pure and chaste ladies, appearing almost a little too naive. The court painter Joseph Stieler began painting attractive women from all social strata in 1823. It is hard to decide who is the most beautiful of them all – the shoemaker's daughter, Helene Sedlmayer, or Lady Jane Ellenborough, her gaze directed towards heaven, or Anna Hillmayr, her eyes lowered and hidden behind a book of prayers? Or, finally, is the prettiest, with her puffed sleeves and high-neck lace collar, Maria Dolores Elisa Gilbert, better known as Lola Montez (➤ 28)?

Coquetry in porcelain: Bustelli figures

Coaches and China

Mobility was important to the Prince Electors even then. However, most of the splendid coaches exhibited in the **Marstallmuseum** in the palace's southern wing, did not travel far. Reserved mainly for ceremonial purposes, all coaches and sleighs were crafted to the highest quality. The most impressive coach is the Krönungskarosse (Coronation Coach), which bumped over the cobbled streets of Frankfurt in 1742, when Karl Albrecht was crowned Kaiser Karl VII.

More delicate handiwork can be seen in the **Porzellansammlung Bäuml** (Porcelain Collection). Incredible skill and artistic flair were employed in creating the most delicate pieces, from 1747 until the 1930s Jugendstil (art nouveau). Artists such as Aurliczek and Bustelli, the first master modeller at the Nymphenburg Porcelain Manufacture, created a first golden age for 18th-century porcelain art in Munich.

The palace's northern wing is occupied by dinosaurs and other highlights in the Earth's history. The **Museum Mensch und Natur** (Humans and Nature) uses slide shows, displays and models to explain evolution to adults and children. The "Spielerische Naturkunde" (Natural History through Play) department is very popular, giving young visitors the chance to test their knowledge. Recently, the "Gen-Welten" (Genetic Worlds) department was opened.

State coach in the Marstallmuseum

Flowers and Palm Trees

You'll also encounter nature at the northern end of Nymphenburger Park, but this time it's the living world of plants. In **Neuer Botanischer Garten** (New Botanical Gardens), greenhouses lure visitors to the jungle and the desert, while outdoor plantings present the range of indigenous plants. With their 15,000 specimens growing in an area of 20ha (50 acres), the Botanical Gardens comprise the most complete collection of plants and one of the most beautiful parks of its kind in Europe. They have an alpine garden and an arboretum, a fern gorge and a rose garden, and a herb and healing plant garden. The best time to see all this is in May and June, when the alpines and the rhododendron grove are in full floral splendour.

For Kids

The **Museum Mensch und Natur** (left) teaches playfully about nature, using interactive games. Colourful, shimmering **butterflies** flutter through the aquatic plant house in the Botanischer Garten, mainly from New Year to the end of March. **Guided tours for children** are held throughout the year, at irregular intervals. The **ice creams** in the Botanischer Garten Café are reputed to be out of this world!

TAKING A BREAK

Enjoy a coffee break at the **Schlosscafé im Palmenhaus** (in the former Orangery), seated under palm trees and a giant oil painting of Ludwig II – or outdoors in summer.

192 A2

Schloss Nymphenburg, Marstallmuseum, Porzellansammlung Bäuml
(089) 17 90 80 9–6 Tram No 17 Schloss Nymphenburg Expensive
www.schloesser.bayern.de

Museum Mensch und Natur
(089) 179 58 91 20 Tue–Sun 9–5
Inexpensive

Neuer Botanischer Garten
Menzinger Strasse 65 (089) 17 86 13 10
Nov–Jan 9–4:30; Feb–Mar, Oct 9–5; Apr, Sep 9–6; May–Aug 9–7; Greenhouses closed for lunch 11:45 –1 Tram No 17 Botanischer Garten
Inexpensive

Water-lily pond in the Botanical Gardens

NYMPHENBURG/BOTANISCHER GARTEN: INSIDE INFO

Top tips Take a **walk through the park**, past the Monopteros round temple to the cascade. The bustle of visitors in the palace is far away and here you can enjoy the statues of Greek and Roman gods in peace and quiet.

- The **Nymphenburger Schlosskonzerte** (www.hubertussaal.de) presents classical music in the recently renovated Hubertussaal.

Hidden gem At the **Erwin-von-Kreibig-Museum**, in the palace's southern round tower No 1, works by the eponymous Munich painter and graphic artist are on show – a tip for art enthusiasts.

At Your Leisure

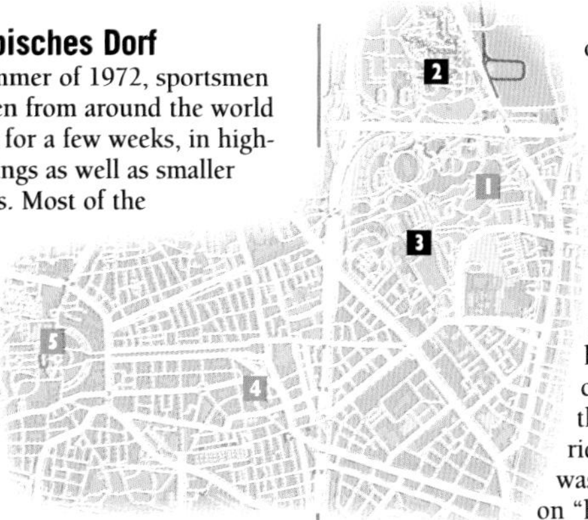

2 Olympisches Dorf

In the summer of 1972, sportsmen and women from around the world lived here for a few weeks, in high-rise buildings as well as smaller bungalows. Most of the Olympic village accommodation has long since been converted into privately owned apartments. However, the rooms of one of the high-rises as well as the bungalows have been used to alleviate the housing shortage for students. Today a stroll through the alleyways of the bungalow complex reveals the students' creativity. Many of the smaller houses are imaginatively painted: the Loch Ness Monster snakes across one façade and giraffes lift their heads out of the ivy on another house front. Render and paint may be peeling away everywhere, but perhaps this is just part of the slightly anarchic touch of the small settlement.

193 E4
Olympiazentrum

3 Ost-West-Friedenskirche

To the south-west of Olympiaberg, the droll Russian Orthodox church made from debris, such as sweet papers and tin cans, has achieved something of a cult status, just like its creator, the Russian hermit Father Timofej. Not only has Timofej lived here self-sufficiently for decades, since 1952, he also stood up to the state, when he built his hermitage and church. When the Olympic riding stadium was to be built on "his estate", he resisted the eviction order – helped by Munich citizens – and the stadium was built in far-away Riem instead! Timofej, whose age (rumoured to be in excess of 100 years) was the cause of much speculation, died in 2004, in an old people's home.

193 E3 Irregular opening times
Olympiazentrum

Olympisches Dorf, with the popular students' bungalows in the foreground

Brewery with tradition

Red-brick buildings are no longer state-of-the-art architecture. In the middle of the 19th century, however, when increasing mechanization of the brewing process forced the Augustiner brewery to move to Schwanthaler Höhe in Landsberger Strasse, the new complex of buildings was regarded as remarkable. The plant is still in operation today, the last remaining example of traditional Munich brewery architecture. And the noble beverage can be no fresher than that served in the bar of the Augustiner Bräuhaus (Landsberger Str. 19, tel: 089/50 70 47), where you can also enjoy a proper *brotzeit* at the long wooden tables.

6 Kindermuseum

The Children's Museum, situated in a side wing of the central station, aims to awaken children's curiosity, to surprise and to promote their active learning and understanding. The range of themes on offer for children and young people is wide-ranging. Thus children might be invited to blow giant soap bubbles – sticky and messy, but great fun – or to explore the miraculous world of chemistry, or to visit an exhibition dealing with a difficult subject, such as death, in a sensitive way.

196 C4 Arnulfstrasse 3 (089) 54 54 08 80 Tue–Fri 2–5:30, Sat–Sun and school holidays 11–5:30 Hauptbahnhof Moderate

7 Alter Botanischer Garten

Apart from the neo-classical portal on its eastern side, nothing remains of Munich's first botanical gardens, dating back to 1804. People still speak of the so-called crystal palace – an architectural miracle at the time, where the "First General Exhibition of German Industry in the year 1854" was held, although the glass and iron structure was completely destroyed by a fire in 1931. Today, the Old Botanical Gardens are a small oasis and a refuge from the bustle of the big city. In summer they are resplendent with flowers around the Neptune fountain, erected in 1937, which seems to be modelled on Michelangelo's *David*. The Park-Café (► 158), on the site of the former crystal palace, is a popular meeting point for night owls.

190 A4 Elisenstrasse Stachus

8 Zirkus Krone

Europe's largest circus is based in Marsstrasse, but the clowns, acrobats and lion tamers, together with all their trained animals, are on the road from April until November. During this time, the circus building becomes a concert hall. From January to March, the circus ring is again reserved for its stars. A statue of Charlie Rivel, who was probably the best known clown in the world, points the visitor

Carl Sembach Krone rebuilt Zirkus Krone after World War II

Bavaria's strongest woman: patron saint Bavaria with the lion

in the direction of the arena, which seats 3,000 people.

196 B5 Marsstrasse 43
(089) 545 80 00 Hackerbrücke
www.circus-krone.de

9 Bavaria

Did you ever wonder what a statue looks like on the inside? You can explore Ludwig von Schwanthaler's colossal bronze amazon for yourself, climbing over 121 steps right into her head. The mighty allegorical figure of Bavaria, weighing 78,000kg (86 US tons), wears an oak wreath and guards Theresienwiese with her sword, a lion at her side. Every year, many visitors climb up the stairs to the statue and inside the Bavarian patron saint to get an aerial overview of the Oktoberfest taking place below. Behind the statue is the large Doric hall of fame, built in 1834 by von Klenze, a temple-like memorial holding the busts of 95 pre-eminent Bavarian personalities.

196 B3 Theresienhöhe 16
(089) 29 06 71 Daily 9–6, during the Oktoberfest 9–8 Schwanthaler Höhe Inexpensive

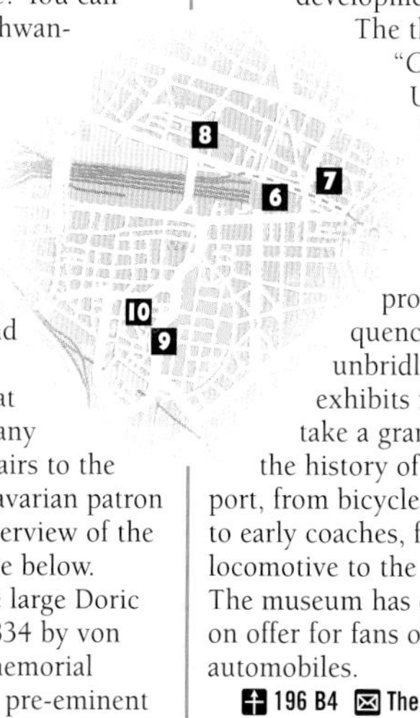

10 Deutsches Museum Verkehrszentrum

A branch of the Deutsches Museum, the Verkehrszentrum is dedicated to the subject of transport and mobility. The museum, based in three listed halls on the Theresienhöhe, focuses on technology, history and the future development of transport.

The theme of Hall I is "Chaos and Order in Urban Traffic"; Hall II deals with the subject of travel – from the wide range of vehicles in use to the problematic consequences caused by unbridled mobility. The exhibits in Hall III finally, take a grand sweep through the history of means of transport, from bicycles and motorcycles to early coaches, from the steam locomotive to the Transrapid. The museum has of course plenty on offer for fans of historical automobiles.

196 B4 Theresienhöhe 14a
(089) 217 95 29
Fri–Wed 9–5, Thu until 8
Schwanthaler Höhe Inexpensive

Where to... Eat and Drink

Prices
Prices given are for one person, excluding drinks.
€ under 12 euros **€€** 12–25 euros **€€€** over 25 euros

Restaurants

The Big Easy €€
The restaurant has the Southern USA as its theme and specializes in the local food. Relax in a pleasant atmosphere and try such specialities as bacon-wrapped dates with a red pepper jam or the Southern classic, jambalaya. On Thursday evenings there is live jazz music, ranging from mainstream to classic jazz, to accompany the spicy food. Sunday special is the Jazz Cooking Breakfast Brunch, when you can gorge yourself on oysters, muesli, pancakes and cake to the sound of a live jazz band, while junior brunchers enjoy the play corner.
193 D2 Frundsbergstrasse 46 (089) 15 89 02 53 Mon–Sat 5 pm–1 am, Sun 10 am–1 am Rotkreuzplatz

Broeding €€€
There is only one menu, changing every day, but it's top class. Freshness, creativity and style combine here to create a special treat. The six-course menu, served in a modern, minimalist interior, is accompanied by excellent Austrian wines – a delightful meal which you should set some time aside to fully enjoy. If you especially enjoyed one of the fine wines, you can buy a bottle as a souvenir from the attached wine shop or you can order it online, from www.broeding.de.
193 D1 Schulstrasse 9 (089) 16 42 38 Tue–Sat 7 pm–1 am Rotkreuzplatz

Löwengarten €–€€
This successful mixture of Bavarian tavern and sophisticated restaurant is a great place to visit at any time of year; there's a small beer garden in summer and at weekends an extensive brunch is served. The kitchen likes to play with different traditions, and so the German roast pork with cheese *spaetzle* is as successful as the spicy Thai curry or the all-American cheesecake. The food at the Löwengarten is good value and there are toys to keep the little ones amused.
193 D2 Volkartstrasse 32 (089) 16 13 73 Mon–Fri 11 am–1 am, Sat–Sun 10 am–1 am Rotkreuzplatz

Osteria Mugolone €€–€€€
Tom Wening serves up his own creations at this stylish and modern Italian hostelry, inspired by Mediterranean and Tuscan cuisine. The menu changes daily, and in his meals he only uses organic ingredients of the highest quality. The restaurant has regular displays of photographs and paintings, which are changed every two months. The Osteria is also recommended for its excellent service. Eating a meal in the small bright room is sheer pleasure. Make sure you reserve a table as it's always busy.
193 E1 Maillingerstrasse 12 (089) 12 73 98 36 Mon–Fri 11:30 am–3 pm, 6–midnight, Sat 6 pm–midnight Maillingerstrasse

Ruffini €–€€
The Ruffini, a "a self-governing business" with 25 shareholders, has been a classic eatery since 1978. Best quality is adhered to and the meat is strictly organic. The culinary focus is on Italy, with the

addition of specialities from around the world. The menu also features excellent vegetarian dishes. Finally, there is a lively cultural scene at the Ruffini, with wine-appreciation seminars, live music and readings. In summer you can eat on the pleasant terrace.

193 D2 ✉ Orffstrasse 22 ☎ (089) 16 11 60 ⏱ Tue–Sun 10 am–midnight 🚇 Rotkreuzplatz

Ysenegger €

More of a pub than a restaurant, Ysenegger boasts an international menu, ranging from the typically German *Allgäuer kässpätzle* (cheesy *spaetzle*) to chilli con carne and sea bass. The decor is dark wooden panelling, in the coffee-house style. The guests are a typical Neuhausen crowd: from students to business people. A tip for cocktail fans: on Mondays you get a double serving for the standard price.

193 D1 ✉ Ysenburgstrasse 3 ☎ (089) 16 27 91 ⏱ Daily 9 am–1 am 🚇 Rotkreuzplatz

Beer gardens

Augustinerkeller €–€€

Time passes quickly under the giant chestnut trees, some of which are over 100 years old. In this beer garden you can enjoy a Bavarian *brotzeit* from the "Schmankerlngasse" (alleyway of snacks) with a fresh Augustiner beer. On balmy summer evenings, up to 5,000 visitors eat and drink here. It's easy to forget the time and to miss your train from the nearby station. On cold or rainy days, substantial Bavarian dishes are served in the historic beer cellar.

196 B5 ✉ Arnulfstrasse 52 ☎ (089) 59 43 93 ⏱ Daily 10 am–1 am 🚋 Trams Nos 16, 17 Hopfenstrasse

Hirschgarten €

Where once aristocratic hunters chased after game, the fallow deer can today watch the up to 8,000 visitors from their game enclosure, free from any danger. Jar after jar of Augustiner beer and tasty Bavarian snacks are carried past. This beer garden is one of the largest and most popular in Munich, and in mid-July the Magdalenenfest, a small fun fair, takes place right next to it.

192 B1 ✉ Hirschgarten 1 ☎ (089) 17 25 91 ⏱ Daily 11:30 am–11:30 pm 🚌 Buses Nos 41, 42 Hirschgartenallee

Löwenbräukeller €–€€

You can't miss this giant inn with its small turret and the beer garden on Stiglmaierplatz. Waitresses serve typically substantial meals in the brewery salon, and perusing the menu is almost like taking a course in Bavarian for beginners. During the strong beer period, just before Lent, guests compete trying to lift a stone jar weighing 254kg (560lb).

196 C5 ✉ Nymphenburger Str. 3 ☎ (089) 52 60 21 ⏱ Daily 10 am–midnight 🚇 Stiglmaierplatz

Taxisgarten €

In good old-fashioned beer garden tradition you collect your Bavarian snacks yourself. Meat is butchered on the premises. Specialities include spare ribs and the green *obatzder* (mashed cheese with herbs and spices). You can enjoy your food and a cool beer in the shade of the tall ash and chestnut trees, and there's a playground for children.

192 C2 ✉ Taxisstrasse 12 ☎ (089) 55 68 27 ⏱ Daily 10 am–11:30 pm 🚇 Gern

Ice Cream Parlour

Sarcletti

The Italian Sarcletti family has made ice cream in Munich for four generations, and it's said to be the best. Peter Paul Sarcletti opened the first ice-cream parlour on the banks of the Isar as early as 1879. Unusual flavours include Mozart (nougat and marzipan) or Carapino (caramel with pine kernels).

193 D1 ✉ Nymphenburger Strasse 155 ☎ (089) 15 53 14 ⏱ Daily 8 am–11 pm 🚇 Rotkreuzplatz

Where to... Shop

Neuhausen and Nymphenburg are sophisticated shopping areas, both districts boasting a large selection of small but at times fairly expensive specialist shops.

If you've walked till you have holes in your shoes, head straight for **Move** (Nymphenburger Strasse 156a), a shoe shop selling the entire range of sporty footwear, in all fashionable colours and shapes – not to be worn when jogging of course, but simply as fashion statements. Punk and classics fans can browse through second-hand CDs and records at **PhonX** (Landshuter Allee 25). There is a world of dolls beyond Barbie, as is amply proven by **Das Puppenhaus** (Blutenburgstrasse 63) with its great selection of dolls, dolls' houses and dolls' equipment. Rustic carpets, made from wool and sisal, wooden furniture and accessories for the home can be found at **Vaeverie** (Blutenburgstrasse 82), which is committed to ecological living. The culinary delights of Tyrol and South Tyrol are crammed into the smallest shop at **Armin's Räucherkuchl** (Blutenburgstrasse 55). More wines, including the very finest – mainly from France and Italy – are available at **Vin-Wein-Vino** (Nördliche Auffahrtsallee 66); and the owner is more than happy to advise you too. A few houses along is **Flügels Spiel & Holzwerkstatt** (Nördliche Auffahrtsallee 62), where you can buy colourful wooden souvenirs and games. If you have 14,800 euros to spare, the **Porzellan Manufaktur Nymphenburg** (Nördliches Schlossrondell 8) will sell you a standing fountain. Alternatively, you could purchase a serving platter for a mere 29,500 euros...or a Bavarian lion, available from 29 euros! All the exclusive pieces are reproduced from historical models.

Where to be... Entertained

Discos, Clubs

Live concerts and DJ music with guitar-based rock, punk and ska are played at "Container-Stadt" in **Backstage** (Friedenheimer Brücke 7, tel: 089/126 61 00, www.backstage089.de, daily 7 pm–4 am).

An oldie among Munich's party venues is the **Nachtwerk** (Landsberger Strasse 185, tel: 089/578 38 00, www.nachtwerk.de, Tue, Fri–Sat from 11:30 pm). The former factory was converted into a dance club some 14 years ago.

Club culture in all its forms is celebrated at **Feierwerk** (Hansastrasse 39, tel: 089/72 48 80, www.feierwerk.de). DJs and live acts include the entire range of musical tastes, from indie and electro to drum 'n' bass, techno and Goa. But nothing much happens at Kranhalle, Hansa 39 and Orangehouse before 11:30 pm!

The **Park-Café** (Sophienstrasse 7, tel: 089/59 83 13, Wed, Fri–Sat 11 pm–4 am), located at the Stachus, hidden behind Alter Botanischer Garten, is a neo-classical building, with a very lively scene indoors. Here, young ladies and gentlemen, wearing top gear, dance until they drop – that's if the door attendant admitted them in the first place. The Blub-Partys on the first Saturday in the month are legendary – filled with giant soap bubbles and dreams.

Theatre

If you're not afraid of a little blood in the evening, visit the **Blutenburg-Theater** (Blutenburgstrasse 35, tel: 089/123 43 00, www.blutenburg-theater.de) for gruesome entertainment. Munich's crime theatre specializes in staging crime and detective plays.

Excursions

The three excursions will take you to the grand, romantic castles of the Bavarian rulers and to a museum dedicated to an unconventional artist. At the same time you can explore the beautiful countryside at the foothills of the Alps with their idyllic lakes and pleasant inns.

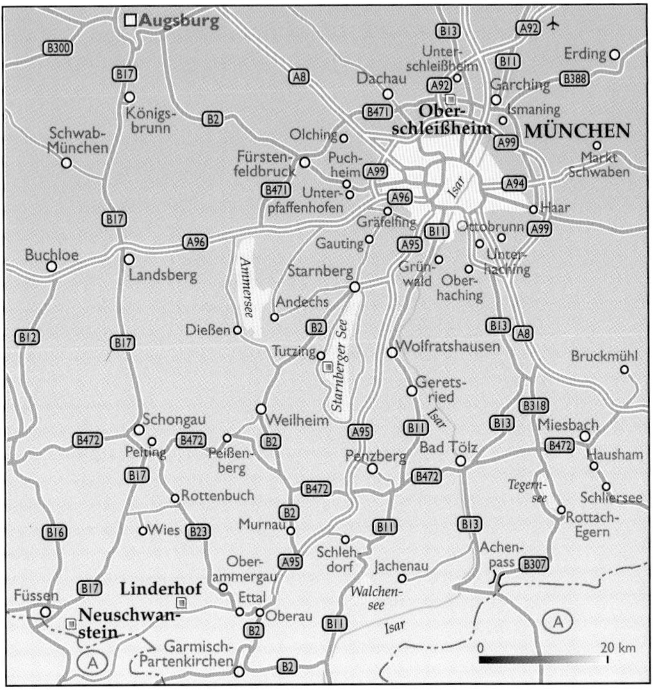

Starnberger See

Make sure you pick a sunny day for your excursion to this lovely lake, known as the "Bavarian ocean". It is in the sun that Starnberger See is at its most picturesque, resplendent against the mighty backdrop of the Alps.

For all Bavarian royalists, Starnberger See is a fateful place: it was here, or to be more precise near the commune of **Berg** on the northeastern banks of the lake, that on June 13, 1886, the much-loved King Ludwig II went into the waters and drowned under mysterious circumstances. A simple wooden cross in the lake and a neo-Romanesque votive chapel

Chivalry and romance: Schloss Possenhofen

Page 159: Schloss Linderhof

Left: A simple cross is a reminder of Bavaria's fairy-tale king

Idyllic Bavaria: Seeshaupt on Starnberger See

commemorate the unlucky monarch. Ludwig II's cousin and friend Elisabeth, known as "Sisi", the future empress of Austria, grew up opposite Berg, in Schloss Possenhofen on the lake's west bank, and spent many summers in residence at Feldafing nearby. The two young royals are said to have shared close moments on the offshore Roseninsel island.

Pack your swimwear

For Munich residents, the elongated lake, measuring 56sq km (22 sq miles), is a giant bathtub close to the city. Along its 46km (28mile) shoreline, three resorts vie for visitors with their sunbathing lawns, sausage stands, ice-cream sellers and bars: **Kempfenhausen** in the north and **Ambach** in the south-east as well as the delightfully atmospheric lawns of **Schlosspark Possenhofen**, where Empress Sisi took her tame stag for walks. There are of course many other bathing places along the lake's shores – locals can tell you where to find the most picturesque and secluded spot.

Following in Sisi's Footsteps

Take the regional road to Possenhofen, leading from Starnberg to Tutzing. **Schloss Possenhofen** is privately owned, but from the Schlosspark (Palace Park), which is open to the public, you can see the castle with its four corner towers. The tavern

in **Feldafing**, just south of the castle, is today called Golfhotel Kaiserin Elisabeth (Tutzinger Str. 2–6, D 82340 Feldafing, tel: 08157/930 90, fax 930 91 33, www.kaiserin-elisabeth.de). The empress spent her summers here, but if an overnight stay in the Sisi Suite is too costly for you, you can still take the time to enjoy a cup of coffee on the attractive hotel terrace.

Roseninsel

In 1848, King Maximilian of Bavaria bought a piece of land bordering the lake south of Feldafing and commissioned the garden architect Joseph von Lenné to create a castle park. The castle itself was never built; in its place, on the offshore Roseninsel (Rose Island), stands the small villa "Casino", amid fragrant rose gardens. Maximilian's son, King Ludwig II, loved this place and spent much of his time on the idyllic island. Find out for yourself what was so special about the spot by going from Schlosspark to the island in one of the traditional *plätten*, a flat punt steered with a pole by the bosun. Go in summer when the roses are in full bloom.

Museum der Phantasie

Lothar Günther Buchheim's museum is in Bernried, south of Tutzing. The author of the worldwide bestseller *Das Boot* (The Boat) is a rugged, difficult and at times rather gruff character. In his museum, however, which was finally built after decades of wrangling, a completely different, cheerful side of the artist

Buchheim's Museum, with its streamlined architecture, is impressive

and collector can be seen. His renowned and extensive collection of expressionist artworks is not the only highlight in the museum. You can also admire a wonderful exhibition of *verre églomisé* pictures (painting behind glass), superb collages of autumnal leaves made by Buchheim's wife Ditti, Nepalese stupas (domed places of worship) and African sculptures. Buchheim clearly did not want to follow the mainstream – his interest lay in the lesser explored avenues of art. And so you will find kitsch next to high art and the exotic next to the traditionally Bavarian. The museum opened in 2001, after taking nearly 30 years to complete. A suitable location was sought for a long time before the commune of Bernried was finally chosen. Architect Günter Behnisch

designed a light, modern building with clear lines, which perfectly blends into the shore scape of the lake, overgrown with reeds.

Buchheim's Expressionists

The main focus of the collection are the works of the artists' association "Die Brücke" (The Bridge, 1905–13), to which Ernst Ludwig Kirchner, Erich Heckel and Max Pechstein belonged as full members and Emil Nolde and Otto Mueller as temporary ones. Otto Dix, whom Buchheim counts as part of the second generation of Expressionists, is represented by a large collection of his works, and so is Lovis Corinth, a precursor of this art movement.

The museum by boat

Probably the nicest way to travel to the museum is on the museum ship *Phantasie*. It departs in May to October at 11:15 am, 1:30 and 3:45 pm from Starnberg (S-Bahn S 6 from Munich), chugging across the lake to Bernried in about an hour. From there a few minutes walk through Museumspark will take you to the entrance. A return ticket including admission to the museum costs 16 euros. Alternatively, you can take the scheduled ferry service from Starnberg to Bernried too.

Kloster Andechs

The Benedictine Abbey Andechs was founded in 1455, about 20km (12½ miles) west of Starnberg, and ever since the monks have brewed "Andechser Bier" here. So you could finish your excursion to Starnberger Lake, or to neighbouring Ammersee, in the Andechs brewery pub or in its pretty, shaded beer garden. However, before you relax over a beer, it's worth visiting the **Klosterkirche** (Abbey Church), with its sumptuous baroque and rococo stucco work.

Top: The church tower of Andechs Abbey

Above: A toast to the "holy mountain"

Museum der Phantasie
Am Hirschgarten 1, Bernried (08158) 99 70 60 Apr–Oct Tue–Sun 10–6; Nov–Mar Tue–Sun 10–5 S 6 Tutzing, then Bus No 9614 Buchheim-Museum Expensive www.buchheim-museum.de

Kloster Andechs und Bierstüberl
Bergstrasse 2, Andechs (08152) 37 62 61 Daily 10–8
S 6 Starnberg, then Buses Nos 951 or 956 Kloster Andechs; S 5 to Herrsching, then about 4km (2.5 miles) walk through the Kiental
www.kloster-andechs.de

Directions: about 20km (12½ miles) southwest of Munich; A 95 to Starnberg, then regional roads around the lake; S-Bahn S 6 from Munich to Starnberg, Possenhofen, Feldafing and Tutzing

Neuschwanstein and Linderhof

King Ludwig II chose the Bavarian foothills of the Alps as the site for his two fairy-tale castles. Schloss Neuschwanstein is one of Bavaria's, and perhaps the world's, best-known castles; Schloss Linderhof, less visited, is nevertheless a gem of garden architecture.

Perfect setting: the fairy-tale castle in front of the awe-inspiring Alpine backdrop

In solitary splendour on top of a rock, an alpine lake surrounded by dense woodland below, the romantic Schloss Hohenschwangau opposite, and everything framed by the majestic Ammergau mountains – King Ludwig II could not have picked a more picturesque setting for his **Schloss Neuschwanstein**. When the City of Munich upset the Wagner-obsessed king by refusing to finance the construction of a festival hall (➤ 28), a disappointed Ludwig withdrew in 1867 to his father's castle at Hohenschwangau where he promptly found solace in a new project. He would build the "Neue Burg" (New Castle), where the medieval world of myths from Richard Wagner's operas would be brought to life.

Climbing up to the castle

You'll need to be fit to make it up to Neuschwanstein: at first you will climb for about 30 minutes uphill (200m/656 feet in height) to get to the Schlosshof; once inside, you'll have climb a further 300 steps during the guided tour. A romantic ascent to the castle is by horse-drawn coach. The trip costs about 5 euros per person.

A tragic dreamer

On 12 June, 1886, in his bed chambers at Neuschwanstein, the king was handed the form which certified him legally insane. Ludwig II was forced to travel to Schloss Berg, together with his psychiatrist who had penned this declaration. The following day, both drowned in Starnberger See.

A Medieval Castle

The foundation stone for Neuschwanstein was laid on 5 September, 1869, but the castle was never completed. The plans were continually changed, and it took 15 years before Ludwig was at last able to move in; the king died two years later and construction of the castle was stopped. Neuschwanstein with its battlements and turrets looks like a copy of a Disneyland creation, but it was, in fact, the other way around: the fairy-tale castle in Disney's *Sleeping Beauty* was inspired by Neuschwanstein.

Of Heroes and Swans

As a child the young king was fascinated by the world of medieval myths and legends. He recognized his own ideals in the figures of mythical heroes such as Perceval, the Knight of the Grail, the knight Lohengrin and the poet Tannhäuser, and so he had Neuschwanstein furnished "in the authentic style of an old German knight's castle". Each room was dedicated to a different mythical figure and furnished accordingly. Thus his own **Wohnzimmer** (Living Chamber) is painted all over with scenes from the Lohengrin saga. Tannhäuser in the Hörselberg and other motifs from the same cycle of legends adorn the king's **Arbeitszimmer** (Study). Finally, the grand **Sängersaal** (Minstrels' Hall) is themed around the first part of the Lohengrin saga, Perceval and the Holy Grail. And since Ludwig II saw himself as king by the grace of God, he had the **Thronsaal** (Throne Chamber) decorated in the style of a Byzantine church. A throne was never set up in the chamber, but it was to have taken the place of the altar. Although the individual rooms vary greatly in style, the motif of the swan, a symbol of Christian purity in the eyes of the king, appears everywhere. After the king's death, the castle was named Neuschwanstein, due to the numerous paintings and sculptures of swans.

Linderhof: Ludwig's Refuge

The young king considered a number of different proposals for converting his father's hunting lodge in the Graswang Valley near Ettal into a showcase castle. He eventually decided to go for the smallest solution. Linderhof is more of a villa than a palace, surrounded by magnificent **gardens**. Here, Ludwig did not wish to perform official duties – but instead he wanted to immerse himself into his world of myths and legends. In a picturesque setting, a perfectly symmetrical baroque garden, playful cascades and fountains, as well as an English landscape garden, were created to help the king relax.

Versailles in Miniature

The neo-baroque palace was completed in 1878. Linderhof revels in the splendour of its baroque and rococo decorations. They're at their most magnificent in the **Spiegelsaal** (Hall of Mirrors), created by Jean de la Paix in 1874, where cut glass mirrors are framed in gold and blue. The dining room features **Tischlein deck dich**, a "self-setting table" as in the Grimm's fairy tale. It was laid by his servants on the ground floor and then pulled up to the king by a lift, leaving him undisturbed.

A Moorish Kiosk for a mild-mannered dreamer

Gardens and Kiosks

The royal garden architect Carl von Effner was responsible for the design of the gardens at Linderhof, which were completed in 1880, surrounding the small castle with stairs and water

Formal landscaping at Linderhof

Venus Grotto: here Ludwig II became Tannhäuser

basins, fountains and hedges. As early as 1876, craftsmen erected the **Maurischer Kiosk** (Moorish Kiosk), decorated with ornamental stucco work and crowned by a golden cupola. Inside it is adorned with colourful glass lamps, Moorish seating areas and a white marble fountain. Another allusion to Wagner's operas was Tannhäuser's **Venus Grotto**, an artificial cave with a lake on which Ludwig could row in a golden shell boat. The king also liked to spend his time at the **Marokkanisches Haus** (Moroccan House), dressed as an Oriental ruler and surrounded by servants in similar attire. The **Hundinghütte** finally carried the dreamy monarch off to the Wagner opera *Valkyrie*, from the Nibelungen cycle.

Admission tickets for Neuschwanstein can only be bought from the ticket booth at Hohenschwangau. On the ticket, the time is marked when the guided tour starts. To avoid long waiting times at the ticket booth, it is advisable to buy tickets in advance on the internet or to reserve them by fax.

Schloss Neuschwanstein
✉ Ticketcenter, Alpseestrasse 12, Hohenschwangau ☎ (08362) 93 08 30; fax (08362) 930 83 20 🕐 Apr–Sep 9–6, Ticket Office 8–5; Oct–Mar 10–4, Ticket Office 9–3 ✋ Expensive ? www.neuschwanstein.de, www.ticket-center-hohenschwangau.de

Schloss Linderhof
✉ Linderhof 12, Ettal ☎ (0882) 920 30; fax (0882) 92 03 11 🕐 Apr–Sep 9–6; Oct–Mar 10–4 ✋ Expensive ? www.linderhof.de

Directions Neuschwanstein: A 95 to Dreieck Starnberg, then B 2 to Weilheim, B 472 to Schongau and B 17 to Füssen and Hohenschwangau (about 110 km/68 miles); by railway to Füssen, then Bus No 9713 to Hohenschwangau

Directions Linderhof: A 95 to Dreieck Starnberg, then B 2 to Oberau, B 23 to Ettal, sign-posted from here (about 90km/56 miles); by railway to Oberammergau, then Bus No 9622 to Linderhof

From Neuschwanstein to Linderhof: The shortest route (about 50km/31 miles) is via Füssen, continuing along the other side of the Austrian border to Ettal

Schloss Schleissheim and Flugwerft

Oberschleissheim, to the north of Munich, has much to offer to visitors interested in culture or technology. The palace complex of Schleissheim, with its magnificent halls, collection of paintings and beautiful baroque gardens forms a unified work of art, combining architecture and nature. The Flugwerft next to it, once the birthplace of the Royal Bavarian Flying Corps, today invites the visitor on a fascinating journey in its historical and modern exhibition halls through the history of aviation and aircraft construction.

The reasons for building a castle at Schleissheim was not a need for ostentation but a longing for seclusion and peace. Duke Wilhelm V abdicated in favour of his son at the end of the 16th century. He had a simple hermitage built near the small village of Schleissheim, where he wished to devote his future days to contemplation and prayer. His son, Maximilian I, however, was of a rather different disposition. In 1617, he began transforming his father's hermitage into the splendid **Altes Schloss**, complete with Wirtschaftshof (Palace Kitchens) and Torturm (Gate Tower). Less than 80 years after its completion, his successor, the Blue Prince Elector, started the magnificent baroque palace complex of the Neues Schloss opposite. Much more spectacular, it puts the Altes Schloss into the shade.

A Bavarian Versailles

After his victory over the Turks at Belgrade in 1688, Max II Emanuel felt at the height of his absolutist powers, and he wanted to demonstrate this fact.

Christian symbolism

The Altes Schloss is home to the Ecumenical Collection of Gertrud Weinhold, comprising sculptures and paintings from around the world which have a link to Christian festivities. Among the exhibits, for example, are the depiction of the *Adoration by the Three Holy Kings* by the African Yoruba as well as a painting of St George by Christians in Ethiopia.

Grosse Galerie in the Neues Schloss

The first step was the construction, around 1690, by the Royal architect Enrico Zuccalli of the Hunting Lodge **Lustheim** on an artificial island, at the requisite distance from Altes Schloss. It had two apartments for the Elector Prince and his wife and a large central hall with a *trompe l'oeil* ceiling fresco. In 1702, Zuccalli started on the **Neues Schloss**, modelled on Versailles, and in 1719 Joseph Effner continued his work. Gradually, the baroque garden planned by Zuccalli started taking shape. Today it is one of only a few remaining baroque gardens in Germany preserved in their original form.

Fountains and symmetrical gardens in front of Neues Schloss Schleissheim

Paintings and Music

A balmy summer night, doors and windows of the festively lit castle are wide open, torches light the baroque garden where couples in elegant attire stroll...no, this is not a dream. The summer concerts in Schloss Schleissheim's Festsaal, performed by world-famous musicians (programme tel: 089/811 61 91, www.bellarte-muenchen.de) are among Munich's most exciting musical events. But even when there is no concert being performed you will be enchanted by the elegant and sumptuous, yet by no means over-ornate, halls and sweeping staircases at Schleissheim. And if you are interested in baroque paintings you will find here an important collection of the works of 17th-century Italian, Dutch and Flemish painters. Finally, don't forget to visit Lustheim, the Hunting Lodge, with its extensive exhibition of Meissen porcelain.

Zeppelins and Flying Machines

On sunny summer days you may sometimes see a zeppelin circling above Oberschleissheim. A canny entrepreneur offers flights over Munich, which start and end at the old airfield of the Royal Bavarian Flying Corps immediately next to the palace complex, in operation since 1912. Also based here is the aviation department of the Deutsches Museum (► 124).

Located in halls, some of which date back to 1919, while others are contemporary extensions, its exhibitions deal with the history of aviation and space travel. The exhibits range from early flying machines (such as Otto Lilienthal's "Normal Gliding Apparatus") via historical machines for civil and military aviation (such as a Heinkel HE 111) to the Starfighter and MIG. You can also watch from a gallery how planes are maintained and restored in a "glass workshop". And you are even allowed to climb into many of the planes, something that children find particularly exciting.

For Kids

- The **Werftladen** (shop) gets young – and older – children's hearts beating faster. On sale are all sorts of aeroplane models to make at home!
- The café-restaurant Pegasus inside the Flugwerft has a children's **play corner** where kids can romp around while their parents enjoy the delicious Mediterranean and Bavarian cooking.
- In summer, from the beer garden, you can **watch the starting and landing** of the zeppelin, the "Tante Ju" JU-52 (► 37) and the various sports planes that fly here.

Touch a plane at the Flugwerft

Schleissheim Palaces

Max-Emanuel-Platz 1, Oberschleissheim (089) 315 87 20
Neues Schloss, Schloss Lustheim Apr–Sep Tue–Sun 9–6, Oct–Mar 10–5; Altes Schloss Tue–Sun 10–5 Moderate www.schloesser.bayern.de

Flugwerft

Effnerstrasse 18, Oberschleissheim (089) 31 57 14
Daily 9–5 Moderate www.deutsches-museum.de

Directions: **12km (7.5 miles) north of the city centre; S 1 to Oberschleissheim**

Walks and Tours

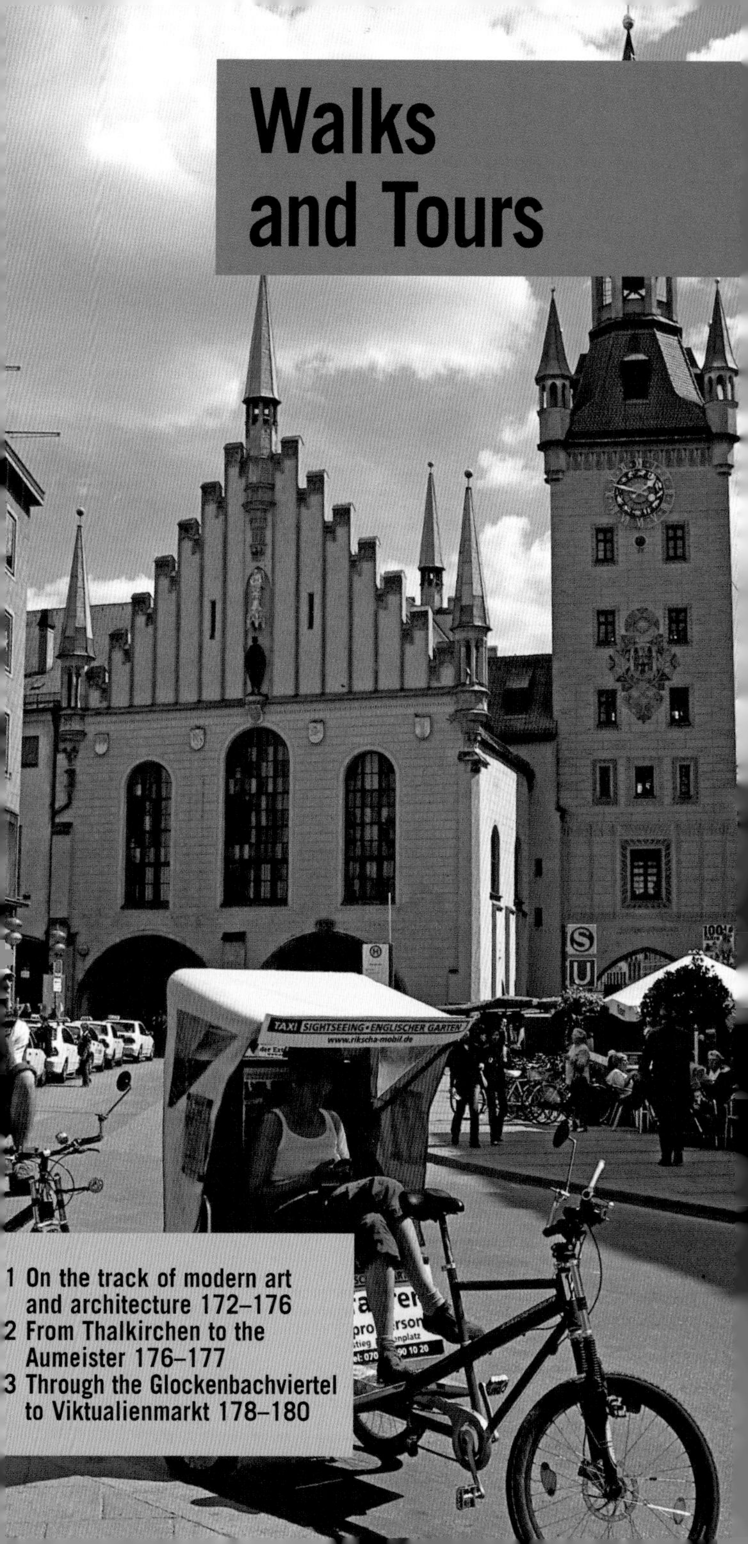

1 ON THE TRACK OF MODERN ART AND ARCHITECTURE

Rickshaw or Cycle Tour

DISTANCE: 18km (11 miles) **TIME:** 2.5–3 hours
START POINT: Marienplatz Ⓤ Marienplatz ✚ 191 D3
END POINT: Marienplatz

Munich has plenty to offer to friends of modern art and architecture: there are futuristically elegant shopping passages, transparent churches, abstract sculptures and daring high-rise towers. The highlights are scattered all over the city area so it's easiest to explore them by bicycle. And if you don't wish to tread the pedals yourself, you can always hire a rickshaw.

1–2

From **Marienplatz** cycle along Theatinerstrasse past the elegant shopping centre **Fünf Höfe** (Five Courtyards) to the old Greek Orthodox **Salvatorkirche** (1494) in the square of the same name. The school building next to the church, dating from 1887, with arcades on the ground floor, was modernized in 1995–97 by the architects Kiessler&Partner and transformed into the **Literaturhaus** (House of Literature).

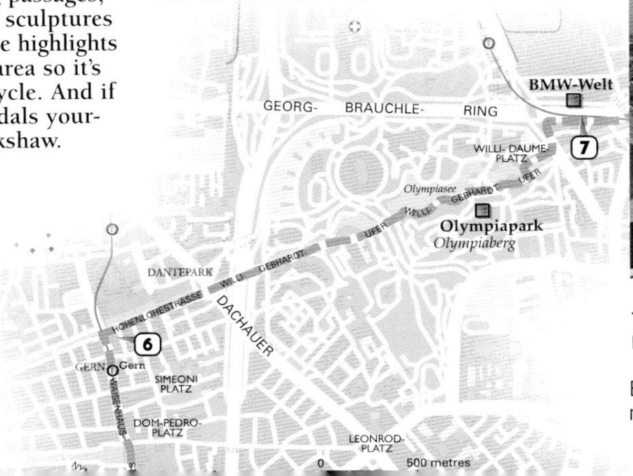

The start point of the rickshaw or cycle tour is Marienplatz in the Old Town

Everything revolves around books and the media here, and readings and discussions also take place at the attached Café Dukatz (► 89).

An installation by New York artist Jenny

Page 171: In front of Altes Rathaus

Holzer, with electronic reading columns and quotes on granite tables and crockery, celebrates the Bavarian poet Oskar Maria Graf.

2–3
Continuing along Jungfernturmstrasse beside the remains of the old Munich town wall you'll get to **Platz der Opfer des Nationalsozialismus** (Square of the Victims of National Socialism), once the Munich headquarters of the Gestapo, where in 1985 Andreas Sobeck erected a grey granite memorial to the victims of the Nazi tyranny, with an eternal flame.

3–4
The **Pinakothek der Moderne** (➤ 104) is itself an architectural work of art. At the main entrance in Barer Strasse stands *Buscando la Luz*, a sculpture by Eduardo Chillida. The imposing façade of the **Neue Pinakothek** (➤ 110) is lightened by the artificial lake in front of it. Note the sculptures: Georg Brenninger's *Kontinente* in the water basin, Marino Marini's *Miracolo* at Theresienstrasse and Henry Moore's *Reclining Woman* at the corner of Arcisstrasse.

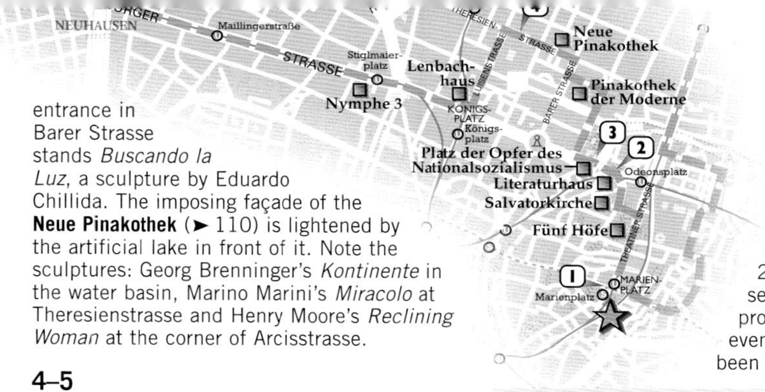

4–5
Crossing the neo-classical Königsplatz you'll get to the open-air exhibition space in front of the **Lenbachhaus** (➤ 100). Continually changing sculptures and installations are shown here – allow yourself to be surprised by the displays. A short way further along, on Nymphenburger Strasse, you'll pass the transparent glass façades of **Nymphe 3**, a modern office complex (Büro Betz) with an idyllic courtyard that invites you to take a break.

5–6
In the solid middle-class area of Neuhausen, the wood and glass cube of the **Herz-Jesu-Kirche** (➤ 147), dedicated in 2000, may seem like a provocation. But even sceptics have been won over by the

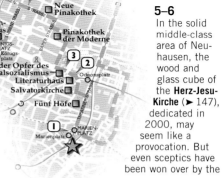

Memorial for the victims of National Socialism

Set aside some time to visit the shopping centre of the **Fünf Höfe** at the end of your tour. The cool elegance of the steel and glass architecture imbues these modern "hanging gardens" with a very special charm: green climbing plants clamber along a chain net that spans the courtyards. Use the opportunity for a relaxed window- or real shopping session or take a break for a visit to the **Hypo-Kunsthalle**, where past exhibitions have included Gauguin, Picasso, Monet, Magritte, Giacometti and Emil Nolde.

church's mood of transparency and solemnity. Old and new are combined in the **Haus der Architektur** (House of Architecture, architects Drescher/Kubina) in Waisenhausstrasse. This building, almost translucent thanks to its glass walls, has interesting exhibitions and events based on architecture.

6–7

Continue along Hohenlohestrasse and Willi-Gebhardt-Ufer, through the green spaces of **Olympiapark** (➤ 144), opened in 1972, noted for its famous tented roof. On the other side of Mittlerer Ring, the cylinder-shaped BMW building dominates the cityscape. In front of it, a cloud-shaped **BMW-Welt** "experience centre" will be built to the designs of the Viennese architects Coop Himmelb(l)au by 2007.

7–8

Continue for a short distance on the cycle path parallel to the busy Mittlerer Ring road which eventually disappears into a tunnel. The Petuelpark above leads to the **"Münchner Tor"**, consisting of the 85-m (279-ft) high tower of the Munich Re (architects Allmann/Sattler/Wappner) and the two **Highlight Munich Business Towers** (architects Murphy/Jahn), 113-m (371-ft) and 126-m (413-ft) high respectively, whose much admired steel and glass silhouettes are linked by four bridges. Behind it, a new district is being developed, **Parkstadt Schwabing**, integrating private and social housing and business space.

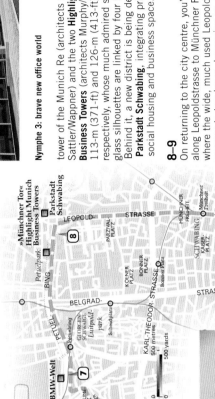

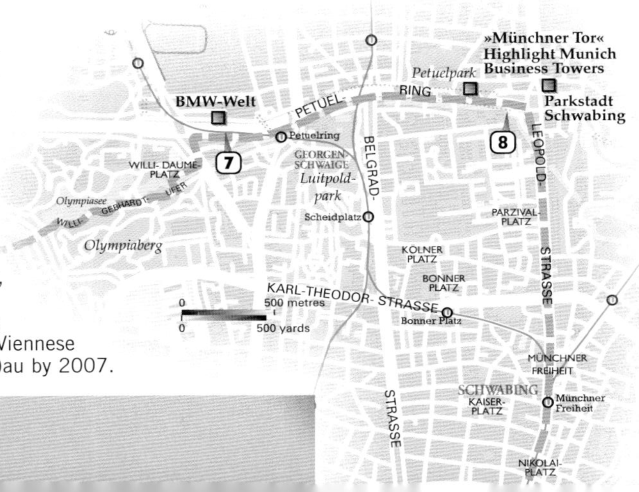

Nymphe 3: brave new office world

8–9

On returning to the city centre, you'll cycle along Leopoldstrasse to Münchner Freiheit, where the wide, much used Leopoldstrasse narrows to two lanes, becoming an attractive boulevard. On the left-hand side, at the corner of Giselastrasse, the shiny figure of Jonathan

The BMW building on Mittler Ring

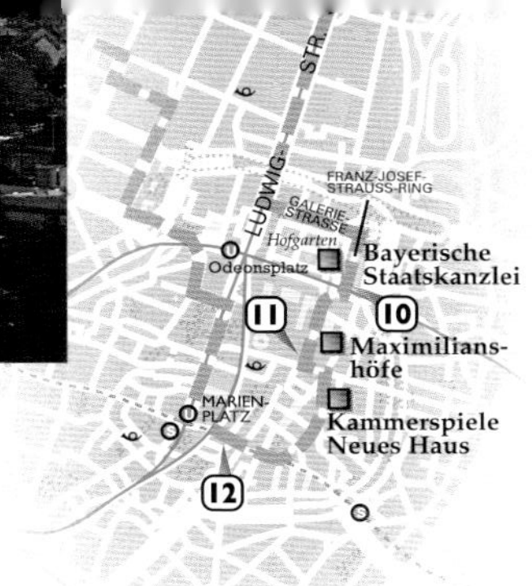

Borofsky's 17-m (56-ft) high sculpture of the ***Walking Man*** can be glimpsed between the tall poplar trees in front of the Munich Re computer centre, built in 1995.

9–10

Via Ludwigstrasse and Galeriestrasse the tour will take you to the monumental **Bayerische Staats-kanzlei** (Bavarian State Chancellery, ➤ 87), an architectural carbuncle. Two imposing steel and glass office wings extend either side of the former Army Museum on Franz-Josef-Strauss-Ring.

Taking a Break

Half way up the Olympic Mountain, the **Olympia-Alm** beer gardens (only opened during the summer months) are a great place to stop for a cool glass of beer and a Bavarian *brotzeit*.

10–11

The attempt to combine historical structures with innovative modern designs was much more successful in the buildings of the former royal stables at the Residenz (➤ 76). The highlight here is the **Maximilianshöfe** (➤ 86) complex, designed by architects Gewers Kühn: futuristic architecture is discreetly concealed behind an ancient façade.

11–12

Because of continuing modernization work, the Münchner Kammerspiele (➤ 94) have had to decamp to various alternative stages, including the **Neues Haus**, opened in 2000. With its studio stage and rehearsal rooms, it is now considered, along with the Kammer-spiele, as an innovative theatre building, satisfying the most up-to-date demands.

Way to go

You can do this tour by bicycle (bicycle rental ➤ 36) or by rickshaw. The stopping place for rickshaws is at Marienplatz (price: 42 euros per hour for a maximum of two passengers, ➤ 37).

Hypo-Kunsthalle
191 D4 Theatinerstrasse 8 (089) 22 44 12
10–8 Marienplatz, Odeonsplatz
Expensive www.hypo-kunsthalle.de

Haus der Architektur
192 C2 Waisenhausstrasse 4 (089) 13 98 80
Irregular Rotkreuzplatz Moderate

2 FROM THALKIRCHEN TO THE AUMEISTER

Cycle Tour

DISTANCE: 12.5km (7¾ miles) (bicycle rental ➤ 36) **TIME:** 3 hours
START POINT: Thalkirchner Platz 196, south of the B1 Thalkirchen (Zoo)
END POINT: Aumeister 195 F5 Studentenstadt

Munich is the only city in Europe where you can cycle beside a mountain stream. You'd best set aside a whole day for this enchanting tour along the river, which the Celts called Isaria, "the raging one". Many shingle beaches, beer gardens, children's playgrounds and interesting sights along the stream will invite you to take a break. And in summer make sure you don't forget your swimming trunks, towel and sun protection!

In-line skaters

The greater part of the tour is on metalled roads, the rest is on firm paths. You'll have to watch out for in-line skaters, however, when you turn off towards the beach.

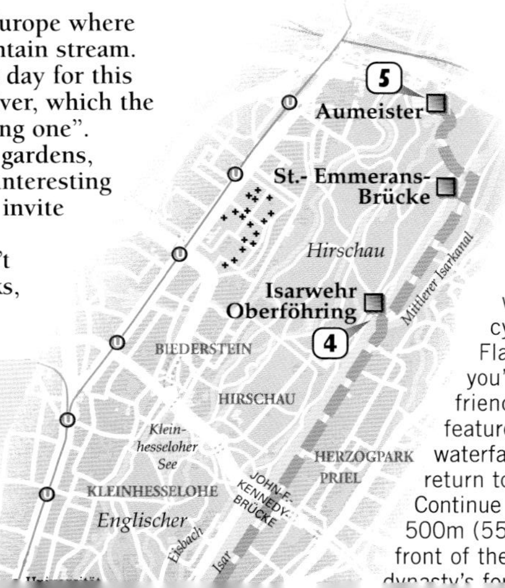

1–2

From **Thalkirchner Platz** cross over the Thalkirchner Bridge to the Isar's east bank and follow the river northwards. As you cycle along the Flauchersteg, you'll pass child-friendly "water features" and gushing waterfalls before you return to the west bank. Continue for just another 500m (550 yds), and in front of the Wittelsbach dynasty's former Hunting Lodge you'll encounter the first temptation: the **Zum Flaucher** beer garden. Resist and continue to the Brudermühlbrücke Bridge, the Mittlerer Ring river crossing. Cross over to return to the

The raging Isar

In the year 2000, work began to renaturalize the Isar which had been forced into a narrow river bed. The first successes can be seen between Flaucher and Reichenbachbrücke: the river seeks its own path, flooding and branching and laying bare new shingle beaches.

Munich's most attractive cycling route

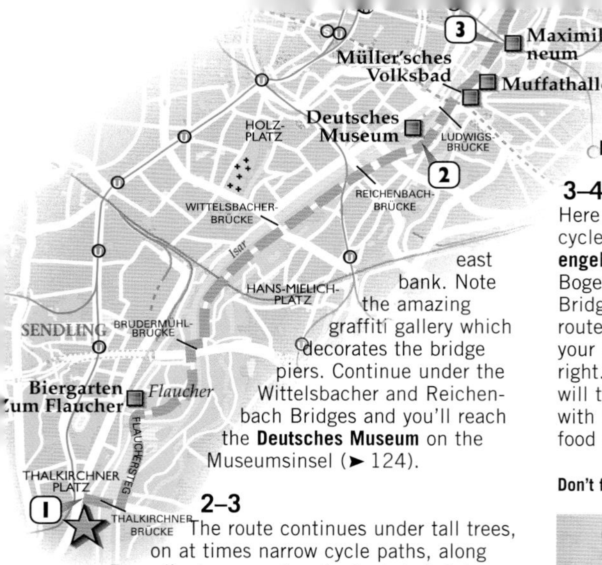

east bank. Note the amazing graffiti gallery which decorates the bridge piers. Continue under the Wittelsbacher and Reichenbach Bridges and you'll reach the **Deutsches Museum** on the Museumsinsel (➤ 124).

2–3

The route continues under tall trees, on at times narrow cycle paths, along Zeppelinstrasse and under Ludwigsbrücke. The scent of fresh herbs wafts across as you pass the windows of **Müller'sches Volksbad** (➤ 130), and shortly after, at the **Muffathalle** (➤ 137), you'll reach the next beer garden. Opposite, the white waters of the Isar Canal gush down the weir into the old river bed. A short ascent followed by a brief steep descent (16%), and you'll pass along underneath the **Maximilianeum** (➤ 131).

3–4

Here the Isar flows calmly and slowly. You'll cycle through parks, passing the **Friedensengel** (Angel of Peace, ➤ 131). Elegant Bogenhausen begins north of the Max-Joseph-Bridge. For the next 2.5km (1½ miles), the route is framed by the wide, sluggish Isar on your left and by attractive mansions on your right. At the **Isar Weir Oberföhring**, a detour will take you to the Wirtshaus im Grün Tal, with a pretty beer garden, where both the food quality and the prices are high.

Don't forget to take a break

4–5

You'll need to push your bicycle across the first part of the Isar weir (cycling is forbidden). Keep on the right to continue along the path on the east bank, through peaceful countryside. Along the Isar, shingle beaches and BBQ areas invite you to stop and grill your own food and swim, but swimming is forbidden. Cross the river again on the wooden **St Emmerans Bridge** and continue on the wide path in a northwesterly direction until you've reached the end point: the **Aumeister** beer gardens.

Taking a Break

Biergarten Zum Flaucher, Isarauen 8, tel: (089) 723 26 77, 10–midnight. **Wirtshaus im Grün Tal**, Grüntal 15, tel: (089) 998 41 10, 11 am–1 am. **Biergarten Aumeister**, Sondermeierstrasse 1, tel: (089) 32 52 24, Mon–Sat 10–11 pm, Sun 9:30 am–11 pm.

3 THROUGH THE GLOCKENBACH-VIERTEL TO VIKTUALIENMARKT

Walk

DISTANCE: 3km (2 miles) **TIME:** 1.5–2 hours
START POINT: Sendlinger-Tor-Platz 190 B1 Sendlinger Tor
END POINT: Viktualienmarkt 191 D2 Marienplatz

After the transformation of Schwabing and Haidhausen, new housing developments are beginning to spring up in the former industrial – and more recently gay – district of Glockenbachviertel. The walk starts in a cemetery, but then it takes you through one of Munich's liveliest areas, past beautifully restored houses, funky pubs, unusual shops and avantgarde galleries right to the Viktualienmarkt.

1–2

Facing the old city gate on **Sendlinger-Tor-Platz**, walk right along Blumenstrasse and after a few steps turn right into Pestalozzistrasse. Walk southwards along this road to Stephansplatz with its plain 17th-century **Stephanskirche**. Next to it is the **Alter Südlicher Friedhof** (the Old Southern Cemetery), originally a burial ground for paupers which later became a cemetery for celebrities. There have been no burials here since 1944. As is typical in Germany, the cemetery is a green oasis of peace in the bustling city, and therefore it's hardly surprising that people go for walks or spend their lunch hours here.

2–3

Next to the entrance is an orientation board, which tells you who lies buried where. Take the central path through the cemetery, to the tomb of the German romantic painter Carl Spitzweg. On the way, you will pass the grave of the architect Friedrich Bürklein, who built Maximilianstrasse (➤ 86) but

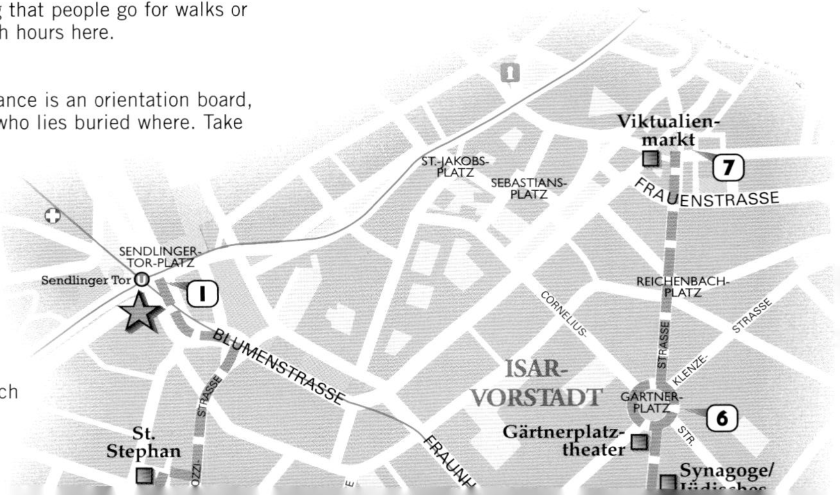

was driven insane by the king's ever-changing demands. The final resting places of architects Leo von Klenze and Friedrich von Gärtner and of the sculptor Ludwig von Schwanthaler, who created the Bavaria statue, are in the arcaded new square in the cemetery. Take your time strolling around; you'll discover beautiful tombstones, including some from the Jugendstil period. Leave at the passage between the old and the new cemetery, turning left at the bridge to cross the Westermühlbach stream.

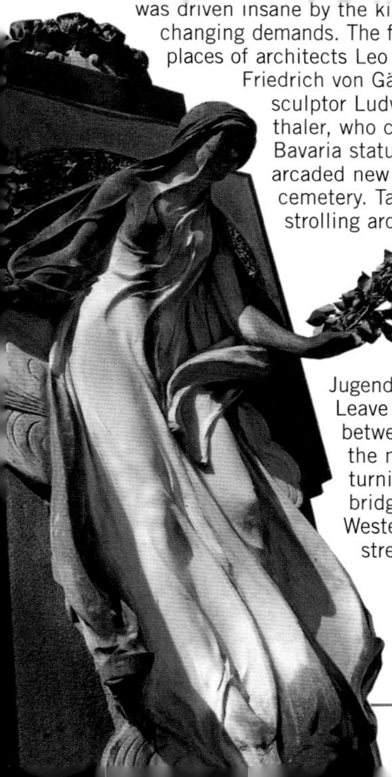

Art deco memorial on the Südfriedhof

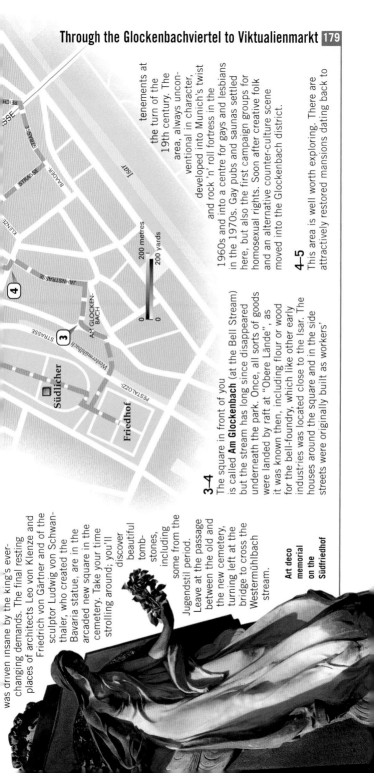

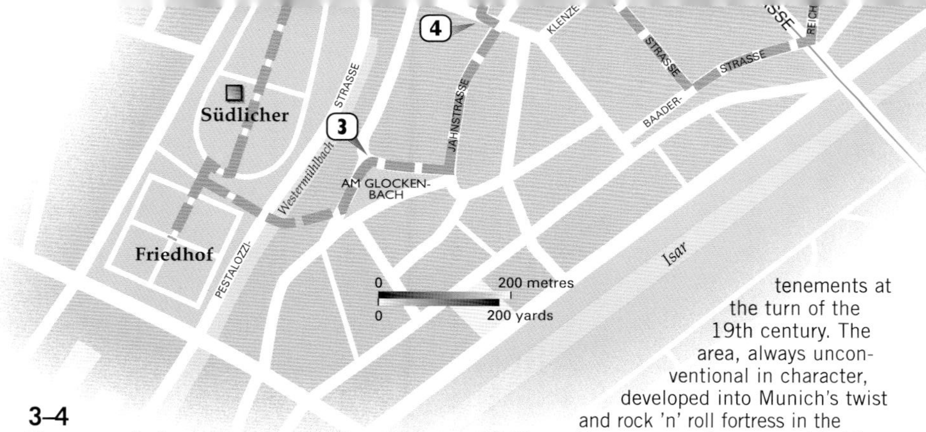

3–4

The square in front of you is called **Am Glockenbach** (at the Bell Stream) but the stream has long since disappeared underneath the park. Once, all sorts of goods were landed by raft at "Obere Lände", as it was known then, including flour or wood for the bell-foundry, which like other early industries was located close to the Isar. The houses around the square and in the side streets were originally built as workers' tenements at the turn of the 19th century. The area, always unconventional in character, developed into Munich's twist and rock 'n' roll fortress in the 1960s and into a centre for gays and lesbians in the 1970s. Gay pubs and saunas settled here, but also the first campaign groups for homosexual rights. Soon after creative folk and an alternative counter-culture scene moved into the Glockenbach district.

4–5

This area is well worth exploring. There are attractively restored mansions dating back to the early 1900s and in between some houses that have seen better days; but best of all there are numerous pubs, bars, shops and art galleries in Jahnstrasse, Hans-Sachs-Strasse or the side streets. Look for street gear at Siebter Himmel, for an espresso at Faun, make your own paper at Selberschön, admire photographic art at Kleinformat or indulge in hot chocolate at Götterspeise. In the Glockenbach district people are very outgoing. You can see it in the passers-by: "I'm here to have some fun", is the general motto of the Glockenbach crowd.

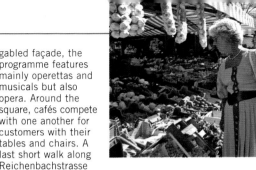

Glockenbachviertel: tasteful and alternative

5–6

Turn right into Ickstattstrasse and continue until you reach Baaderstrasse where you keep on the left until you reach the Isar. Cross Fraunhoferstrasse to get to Reichenbachstrasse which leads straight to the Gärtnerplatz. Here you'll find antiques and more recent furniture from the 1950s, retro clothes and patisseries such as the Crème, which sells probably the best croissants in the city. Just before reaching Gärtnerplatz you will pass the house of the Israeli cultural community with a **synagogue** and the **Jüdisches Museum** (Jewish Museum). Until the days when Hitler seized power, the area around Gärtnerplatz was inhabited by Jewish craftsmen.

6–7

Take a look at the **Gärtnerplatztheater** in the round Gärtnerplatz. Ludwig II dedicated it in 1865; behind the beautiful, late-neo-classical gabled façade, the programme features mainly operettas and musicals but also opera. Around the square, cafés compete with one another for customers with their tables and chairs. A last short walk along Reichenbachstrasse will take you directly to the **Viktualienmarkt** (➤ 52). At one of the market stalls, in a genuine Bavarian ambience over a *brotzeit*, you can recover from the alternative excitements of the Glockenbach and Gärtnerplatz districts.

A great selection at Viktualienmarkt

Taking a Break

Crème (Reichenbachstrasse 27) serves an aromatic cup of coffee, a comforting hot chocolate and delicious pastries. If your mood is for something typically Bavarian, take a break immediately after the cemetery, at **Rumpler** (Baumstrasse 21). Eat your fill of roast pork with crackling or roast pork with onions either in the comfortable inn or in the beer garden. And at the end point, in the Viktualienmarkt, you will find a vast selection of different "Schmankerln" (Bavarian snacks).

When to go

Don't set off too early. Life in the Glockenbach district does not really get into full swing until the late afternoon. The mornings are quiet.

Jüdisches Museum

197 E3 · Reichenbachstrasse 27 · 20 00 96 93
Tue 2–6, Wed 10–noon, 2–6, Thu 2–8 · Moderate

Practicalities

GETTING ADVANCE INFORMATION

Websites
- www.muenchen-tourist.de
- www.muenchen.de
- www.muenchen-nightlife.de

In Germany
Fremdenverkehrsamt München
80313 München
☎ (089) 233 03 00

In the UK
German National Tourist Office
PO Box 2695
London W1A 3TN
☎ 020 7317 0908

BEFORE YOU GO

WHAT YOU NEED

● Required
○ Suggested
▲ Not required

	UK	USA	Canada	Australia	Ireland	France	Netherlands	Spain
Passport/National Identity Card	●	●	●	●	●	●	●	●
Visa	▲	▲	▲	▲	▲	▲	▲	▲
Onward or Return Ticket	▲	▲	▲	▲	▲	▲	▲	▲
Health Inoculations (tetanus and polio)	▲	▲	▲	▲	▲	▲	▲	▲
Health Documentation (➤ 186, Health)	●	●	●	●	●	●	●	●
Travel Insurance (➤ 186)	○	○	○	○	○	○	○	○
Driving Licence (national)	●	●	●	●	●	●	●	●
Third Party Car Insurance Certificate	●	n/a	n/a	n/a	●	●	●	●
Car Registration Document	●	n/a	n/a	n/a	●	●	●	●

WHEN TO GO

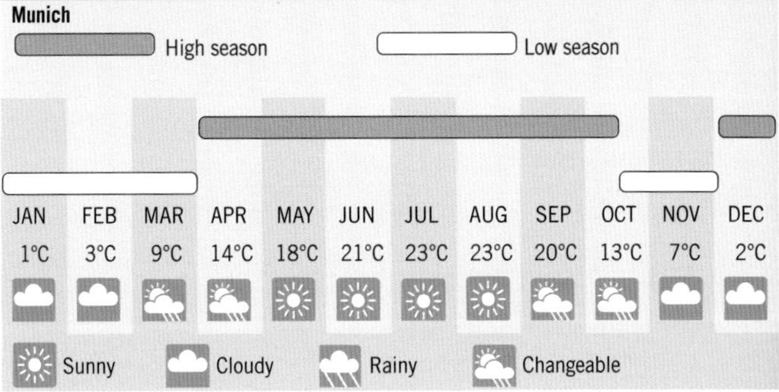

The temperatures indicated are the average **daytime temperatures** in the respective months. **The most pleasant time to visit** Munich is from May to October, which is when you will find tables and chairs set up outside the street cafés, and sun worshippers stretching out in Englischer Garten and on the banks of the Isar. But the city also has plenty to attract visitors when it is covered under a blanket of snow, and in December there are Christmas markets on almost all of the larger city squares. So Munich, or "Italy's most northerly city", is in fact a good place to visit all year round.

In the USA
German National Tourist Office
52nd floor
122 East 42nd Street
New York NY 10168-0072
☎ (001 212) 661 72 00

In Australia
German National Tourist Office
PO Box 1461
Sydney South
NSW 2001
☎ (00 61 2) 8296 0488

In Canada
German National Tourist Office
Suite 1410
480 University Avenue
Toronto, Ontario M5G 1V2
☎ (001) 416 968-1685

GETTING THERE

By Plane After Frankfurt, the airport at **Munich-Erding**, also known as **Airport Franz Josef Strauss**, is Germany's second largest international aviation hub, handling departures to many countries. Domestic flights with the large airlines are relatively expensive but more and more "no-frills airline" crowd onto the market, offering inexpensive fares to and from European destinations, especially to the cities. Ask your airline or at your travel agents, or make use of the flights on offer on the internet.

By Train Munich can be reached from all directions by IC, ICE, EuroCity and InterRegio trains. The central station is **Hauptbahnhof**, in the heart of the city. In addition, the eastern part of the inner city is served by some long-distance trains stopping at Ostbahnhof, and the western part by trains stopping at Bahnhof München-Pasing. The **motorail train** to northern Germany and southern European countries is loaded in Ostbahnhof.

By Car Munich is well connected to other German cities by autobahn (motorway) – you can reach Nuremberg via the A9, Passau via the A94, Salzburg via the A8, Garmisch-Partenkirchen via the A95, Lindau via the A96 and Stuttgart via the A8. A motorway ring road, not yet completed, will take eastbound, northbound and westbound traffic from the Salzburg motorway around Munich to the Stuttgart motorway; the onward connection to the Lindau motorway is under construction. Whether the ring road will be closed as a full circle by connecting the motorways to Lindau and Salzburg in the southwest of the city is still being debated.

TIME

Munich is in the Central European time zone, i.e. one hour ahead of Greenwich Mean Time. At the end of March clocks are adjusted one hour forwards for summer time (GMT =1), until the end of October.

CURRENCY AND FOREIGN EXCHANGE

Currency Germany is one of the European countries to use a single currency, the **euro (€)**. The official abbreviation for the euro is EUR. Euro notes are available in the following denominations: 5, 10, 20, 50, 100, 200 and 500; coins to the value of 1, 2 and 5 euro cents (bronze-coloured), 10, 20 and 50 euro cents (gold-coloured), and the 1 and 2 coins are available.
An **exchange rate calculator** is available on the internet: www.oanda.com.

Exchange Exchange bureaux can be found in the main railways stations and airports. **Travellers' cheques** can be cashed at all bank branches which are plentiful throughout the city. All transactions are subject to a commission charge. Outside of bank opening hours, **ATMs** (Geldautomat) are available in many locations.

Credit cards are accepted in almost all hotels, restaurants and shops. VISA and MasterCard with four-digit PINs can be used at most ATMs.

TIME DIFFERENCES

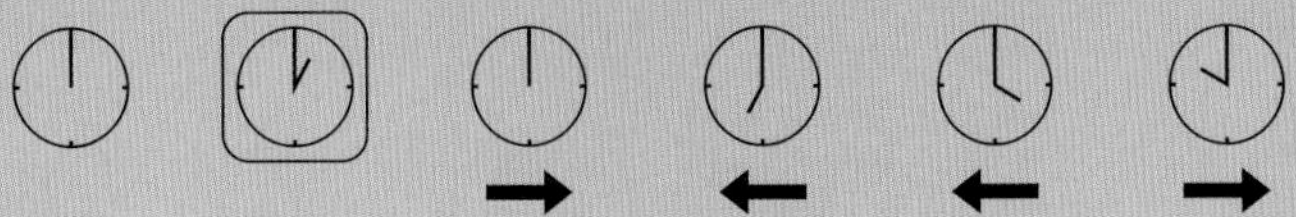

GMT	Munich	Spain	New York	Los Angeles	Sydney
12 noon	1 pm	1 pm	7 am	4 am	10 pm

WHEN YOU ARE THERE

CLOTHING SIZES

UK	Germany	USA	
36	46	36	Suits
38	48	38	Suits
40	50	40	Suits
42	52	42	Suits
44	54	44	Suits
46	56	46	Suits
7	41	8	Shoes
7.5	42	8.5	Shoes
8.5	43	9.5	Shoes
9.5	44	10.5	Shoes
10.5	45	11.5	Shoes
11	46	12	Shoes
14.5	37	14.5	Shirts
15	38	15	Shirts
15.5	39/40	15.5	Shirts
16	41	16	Shirts
16.5	42	16.5	Shirts
17	43	17	Shirts
8	36	6	Clothes
10	38	8	Clothes
12	40	10	Clothes
14	42	12	Clothes
16	44	14	Clothes
18	46	16	Clothes
4.5	36	6	Shoes
5	37	6.5	Shoes
5.5	38	7	Shoes
6	39	7.5	Shoes
6.5	40	8	Shoes
7	41	8.5	Shoes

NATIONAL HOLIDAYS

1 Jan	New Year's Day
6 Jan	Three Kings' Day
Mar/Apr	Good Friday, Easter Sunday and Monday
1 May	Labour Day
May/Jun	Ascension Day
May/Jun	Whit Sunday and Monday
May/Jun	Corpus Christi
15 Aug	Assumption (in Catholic areas)
3 Oct	Reunification Day
1 Nov	All Saints' Day
25, 26 Dec	Christmas

OPENING HOURS

○ Shops ● Post Offices
● Offices ● Museums/Monuments
● Banks ● Pharmacies (Apotheke)

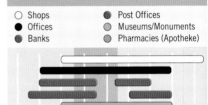

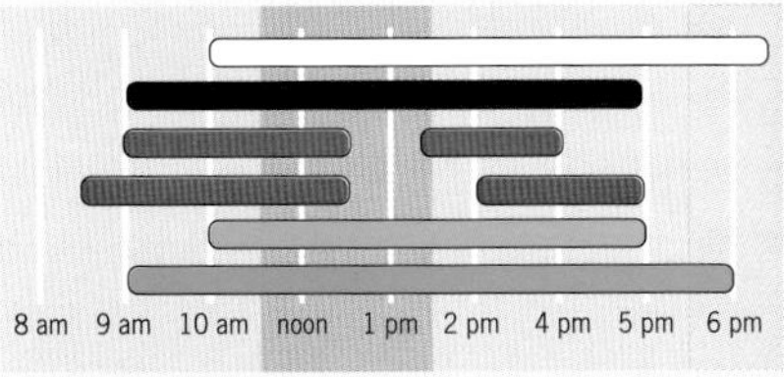

☐ Morning ☐ Midday ☐ Evening

Shops Most shops are open Monday to Friday 10–8 and on Saturday 9–6, some until 8 pm. Shops in the stations and at the airport, which offer supplies for visitors and a wide range of other goods, are also open on Sundays.

Banks Banks and savings banks (Sparkasse) are generally open from Monday to Friday from 8:30 am or 9 am and close at 3:30 pm or 4 pm, on Thursdays at 6 pm. They also close for about an hour at lunchtime (usually 12:30 pm–1:30 pm).

Museums Almost all Munich museums are open Tuesday to Sunday from 10 am until 5 pm. Some museums have longer opening hours on Thursdays, and most are closed on Mondays.

EMERGENCY 110

POLICE 110

FIRE (and ambulance) 112

POISONING 192 40

PERSONAL SAFETY

Munich is considered to be Germany's second safest city after Stuttgart, and tourists are not usually confronted by violence. Small-scale criminal activity is mostly limited to pickpocketing in busy shopping and sightseeing areas (such as Marienplatz, the pedestrianized areas in the centre, or the station).

- Visitors to the Oktoberfest are advised to take extra care, as it attracts not only fun-seeking revellers but also pickpockets from around the world.
- Late at night it is safer to avoid certain areas in the Englischer Garten, for example the surroundings of the Monopteros temple, as drug dealers may be active there.

Police assistance:
110 from any phone

TELEPHONES

Public telephones in Munich are grey and pink open booths (plus a few old-style yellow closed booths). Almost all require a *Telefonkarte* (telephone card), available at post offices, stationery shops and newsagents. For overseas calls, after the country code, omit the "0" from the area code.

International Dialling Codes
Dial 00 followed by

UK:	**44**
Ireland:	**353**
USA/Canada	**1**
Australia	**61**

POST

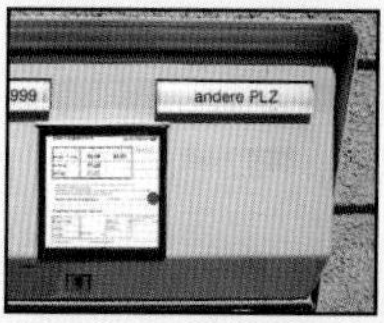

There are post offices in every district in Munich. The post office at Bahnhofplatz 1 is open from Monday to Friday 7:30 am until 8 pm and on Saturday 9 am until 4 pm; it is closed on Sunday. The post office in the airport is open daily from 7:30 am until 9 pm. Post office branches have also been set up in selected stationery shops, where stamps may be bought and letters, small packages and parcels can be sent. Poste restante (general delivery) mail, however, can only be collected from a post office.

ELECTRICITY

The power supply in Germany is 220 volts. The sockets accept two round-pin plugs. Travellers from outside continental Europe should use an adaptor.

TIPS/GRATUITIES

It is common practice to round up restaurant, drinks and taxi bills generously. Five per cent is a good general rule.

Hotel porters	1–2 euros
Chambermaids	1–2 euros
Tour guides	at own discretion
Lavatory attendants	30 cents

EMBASSIES AND CONSULATES

UK	US Consulate	Australia	Canada
☎ (089) 211090	☎ (089) 28 88	☎ (030) 88 00 88-0	☎ (089) 2199 570

HEALTH

Insurance: Special travel health insurance is recommended, particularly for visitors from non-EU countries. Nationals of EU countries can obtain medical treatment at reduced cost with a form E111 or a European insurance card (from 2006).
Doctors: Doctors and specialist consultants are listed in the yellow pages of the telephone directory. The medical emergency service (Ärztlicher Bereitschaftsdienst) can be reached on tel: (0180) 519 12 12.

Dental Services: Dental treatment for non-German visitors can be expensive. Patients are given a bill, which they must claim on their health insurance. The dental emergency service (Zahnärztlicher Bereitschaftsdienst) can be reached on tel: (089) 723 30 93 (weekends and holidays only).

Weather: Sensitive travellers could suffer from the foehn winds in Munich, which may cause headaches and irritability.

Drugs: There are many pharmacies (Apotheke) selling prescription and non-prescription medicines. Outside normal shop opening hours, an emergency service (Apothekennotdienst) operates; addresses are posted in all pharmacy windows.

Safe Water: Munich's tap water can safely be drunk because the boreholes for the supply are all based in the foothills of the Alps.

CONCESSIONS

Concessions (discounts) are generally granted to German citizens and visitors who are unemployed, welfare recipients, soldiers, trainees, students, disabled or retired, on presentation of the appropriate documentation. Children and groups of school children usually receive concessions. Children and young people also pay reduced fares on **public transport**.

The tourist information offices sell several versions of the **München Welcome Card**, valid for varying lengths of time; holders of the card benefit from free public transport as well as reduced admission prices to many sights and museums.

TRAVELLING WITH A DISABILITY

The airport is entirely accessible to wheelchairs but, of the stations, only Hauptbahnhof is free from barriers. Many car parks have lifts or ramps for disabled access. The majority of U-Bahn and S-Bahn stations also have wheelchair access. Detailed information is available in a tourist office leaflet, *München für Touristen mit Handicap (Munich for Disabled Visitors).* Most tram lines have special wheelchair-assisted doors. Vehicles with facilities for visitors with disabilities are easily identifiable.

CHILDREN

Children are welcome at most hotels and restaurants. Check www.muenchen.de on the internet for special children's performances or programmes by clicking on the menu heading "Pomki.de".

LAVATORIES

Public toilets are rarely found above ground in Munich. Most are underground, in the stations of the public transport services.

LOST PROPERTY

Städtisches Fundbüro): Ötztalerstrasse 17, tel: (089) 233 00, Mon–Thu 8–noon, Fri 7–noon, Tue also 2–6:30 pm.

MUNICH PLACE NAMES

For ease of use this guide uses "ss" instead f *ß* in all cases. You may however find the correct German spelling on street signs, for example in "Straße".

The following German terms have been used throughout:
U-Bahn underground railway (subway)
S-Bahn overground (often overhead) local and regional railway

SURVIVAL PHRASES

Yes/no **Ja/nein**
Good morning **Guten Morgen**
Good afternoon **Guten Tag**
Good evening **Guten Abend**
Goodbye **Auf Wiedersehen**
How are you? **Wie geht es Ihnen?**
You're welcome **Bitte schön**
Please **Bitte**
Thank you **Danke**
Excuse me **Entschuldigung**
I'm sorry **Es tut mir Leid**
Do you have ...? **Haben Sie...?**
I'd like ... **Ich möchte ...**
How much is that? **Was kostet das?**
I don't understand **Ich verstehe nicht**
Do you speak English? **Sprechen Sie Englisch?**
Open **Geöffnet** Closed **Geschlossen**
Push/pull **Drücken/Ziehen**
Women's lavatory **Damen**
Men's lavatory **Herren**

DAYS OF THE WEEK

Monday **Montag**
Tuesday **Dienstag**
Wednesday **Mittwoch**
Thursday **Donnerstag**
Friday **Freitag**
Saturday **Samstag**
Sunday **Sonntag**

OTHER USEFUL WORDS & PHRASES

Yesterday **Gestern**
Today **Heute**
Tomorrow **Morgen**
Could you call a doctor please? **Könnten Sie bitte einen Arzt rufen?**
Do you have a vacant room? **Haben Sie ein Zimmer frei?**
- with bath/shower **mit Bad/Dusche**
Single room **Das Einzelzimmer**
Double room **Das Doppelzimmer**
One/two nights Eins/Zwei Nächte
How much per night? **Was kostet es pro Nacht?**

DIRECTIONS & GETTING AROUND

Where is...? **Wo ist...?**
- the train/bus station **der Bahnhof/Busbahnhof**
- the bank **die Bank**
– the nearest toilets **die nächsten Toiletten**
Turn left/right **Biegen Sie links ab/rechts ab**
Go straight on **Gehen Sie geradeaus**
Here/there **Hier/da**
North **Nord**
East **Ost**
South **Süd**
West **West**

NUMBERS

1 **eins**
2 **zwei**
3 **drei**
4 **vier**
5 **fünf**
6 **sechs**
7 **sieben**
8 **acht**
9 **neun**
10 **zehn**
11 **elf**
12 **zwölf**
13 **dreizehn**
14 **vierzehn**
15 **fünfzehn**
16 **sechzehn**
17 **siebzehn**
18 **achtzehn**
19 **neunzehn**
20 **zwanzig**
21 **einundzwanzig**
22 **zweiundzwanzig**
30 **dreissig**
31 **einunddreissig**
32 **zweiunddreissig**
40 **vierzig**
50 **fünfzig**
60 **sechzig**
70 **siebzig**
80 **achtzig**
90 **neunzig**
100 **hundert**
101 **einhunderteins**
102 **einhundertzwei**
200 **zweihundert**
300 **dreihundert**
400 **vierhundert**
500 **fünfhundert**
600 **sechshundert**
700 **siebenhundert**
800 **achthundert**
900 **neunhundert**
1,000 **tausend**

EATING OUT

A table for ..., please **Einen Tisch für ... bitte**
We have/haven't booked **Wir haben/haben nicht reserviert**
I'd like to reserve a table for ... people at ... **Ich möchte einen Tisch für ... Personen um ... reservieren**
I am a vegetarian **Ich bin Vegetarier/in**
May I see the menu, please? **die Speisekarte bitte?**
Is there a dish of the day, please? **Gibt es ein Tagesgericht?**
We'd like something to drink **Wir möchten etwas zu trinken**
Do you have a wine list in English? **Haben Sie eine Weinkarte auf Englisch?**
This is not what I ordered **das habe ich nicht bestellt**
Could we sit there? **Können wir dort sitzen?**
When do you open/close? **Wann machen Sie auf/zu?**
The food is cold **das Essen ist kalt**
The food was excellent **das Essen war ausgezeichnet**

Can I have the bill, please? **Wir möchten zahlen, bitte**
Is service included? **Ist das mit Bedienung?**

Breakfast **das Frühstück**
Lunch **das Mittagessen**
Dinner **das Abendessen**

Starters **die Vorspeise**
Main course **das Hauptgericht**
Desserts **die Nachspeisen**

Fish dishes **Fischgerichte**
Meat dishes **Fleischgerichte**
Fruit **Obst**
Vegetables **Gemüse**
Dish of the day **das Tagesgericht**
Wine list **die Weinkarte**

Salt **das Salz**
Pepper **der Pfeffer**

Knife **das Messer**
Fork **die Gabel**
Spoon **der Löffel**

Waiter **der Kellner**
Waitress **die Kellnerin**

MENU A–Z

Äpfel Apples
Apfelsaft Apple juice
Apfelsinen Oranges
Aufschnitt Sliced cold meat
Austern Oysters
Belegte Brote Sandwiches
Birnen Pears
Blumenkohl Cauliflower
Brathähnchen Roast chicken
Bratwurst Fried sausage
Brokkoli Broccoli
Brötchen Bread roll
Creme Cream
Eintopf Casserole
Eisbein Knuckle of pork
Ente Duck
Erbsen Peas
Erdbeeren Strawberries
Fasan Pheasant
Fenchel Fennel
Flunder Flounder
Forelle Trout
Frühstücksspeck Grilled bacon
Gans Goose
Gekochtes Ei Boiled egg
Gulasch Goulash
Grüne Bohnen Green beans
Heilbutt Halibut
Hering Herring
Himbeeren Raspberries
Honig Honey
Hummer Lobster
Kabeljau Cod
Kaffee Coffee
Kalbsleber Calf's liver
Karotten Carrots
Kartoffeln Potatoes
Käse Cheese
Käsekuchen Cheesecake
Kasseler Smoked pork loin
Kirschen Cherries
Krabben Shrimps
Kohl Cabbage
Konfitüre Preserves
Kopfsalat Lettuce
Lachs Salmon
Lammbraten Roast lamb
Lauch Leeks
Mais Sweet corn
Milch Milk
Obsttorte Fruit tart
Obstsalat Fruit salad
Orangensaft Orange juice
Paprika Pepper
Pfirsiche Peaches
Pflaumen Plums
Pilze Mushrooms
Rinderbraten Roast beef
Rotkohl Red cabbage
Rührei Scrambled egg
Schinken Ham
Scholle Plaice
Schokoladentorte Chocolate cake
Schweinebraten Roast pork
Schweinekotelett Pork chop
Seezunge Sole
Spargel Asparagus
Spiegelei Fried egg
Spinat Spinach
Suppen Soups
Tee Tea
Tomaten Tomatoes
Vanillesauce Custard
Wiener Schnitzel Veal escalope
Weintrauben Grapes
Wild Game
Zucchini Courgettes
Zwiebeln Onions

Streetplan

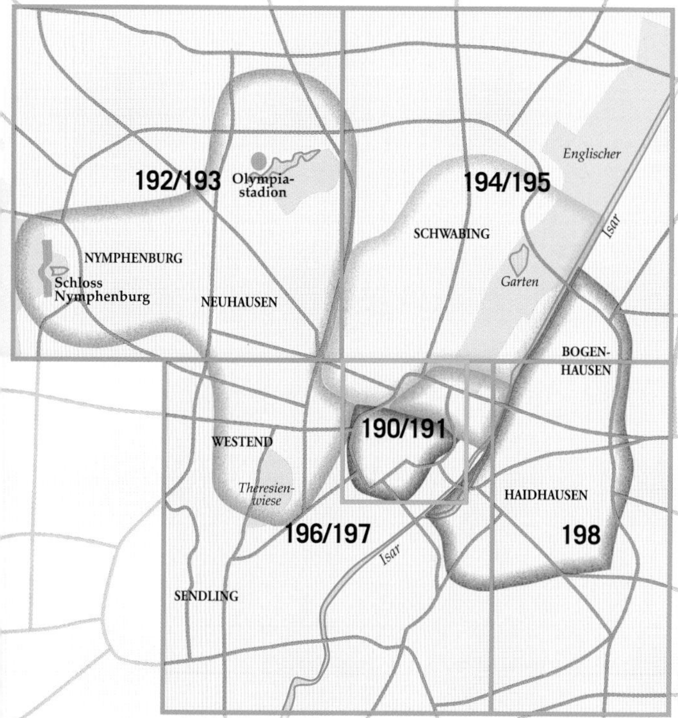

To identify the regions, see the map on the inside of the front cover

Legend

Main road	Park
Other road	Important building
Tunnel	Featured place of interest
Pedestrianised way	U-Bahn station
Rail line	S-Bahn (local rail) station
U-Bahn (underground) line	

190/191 — 0, 100, 200, 300, 400 metres; 0, 100, 200, 300, 400 yards

192–198 — 0, 250, 500, 750, 1000 metres; 0, 250, 500, 750, 1000 yards

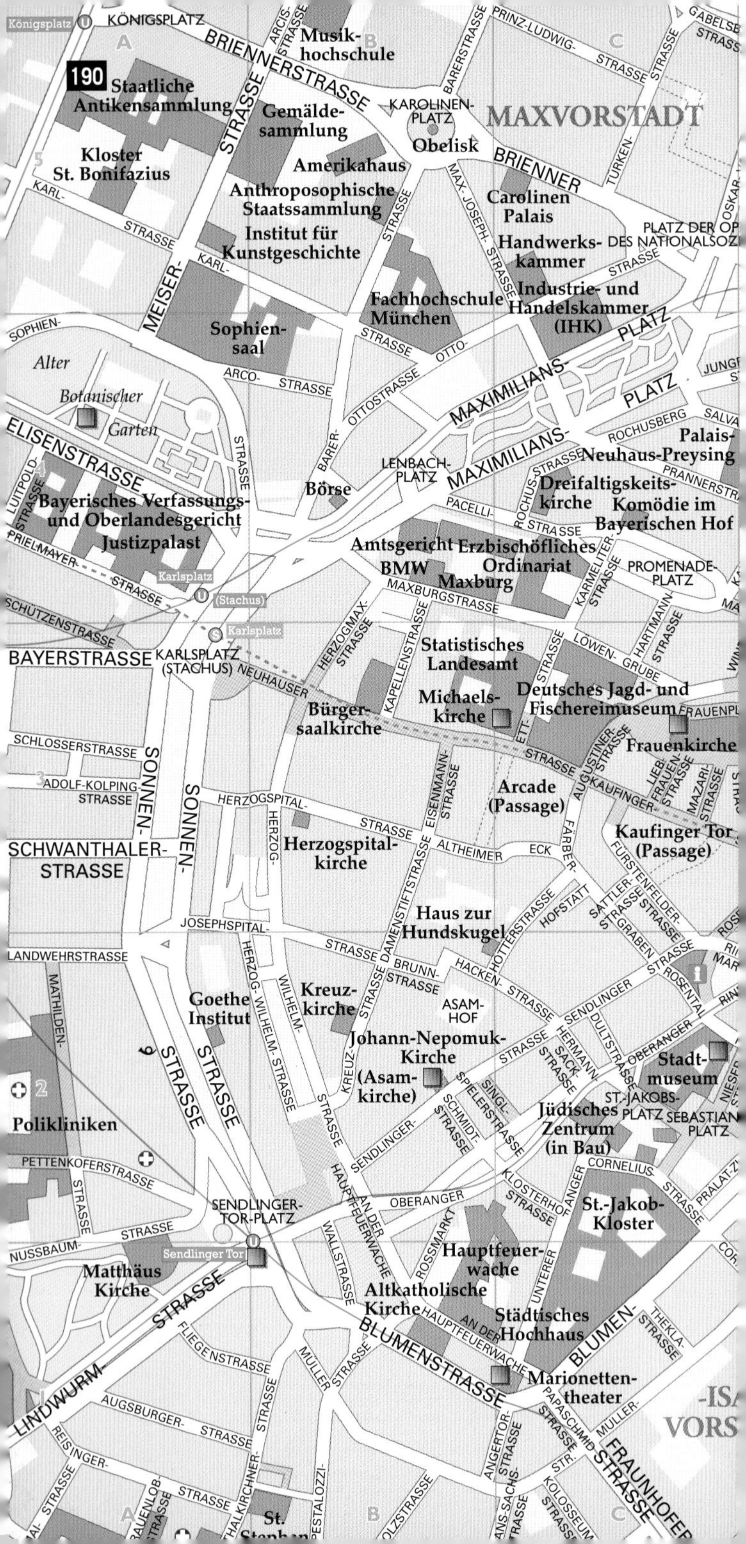
Königsplatz
KÖNIGSPLATZ
Musik-
hochschule
BRIENNERSTRASSE
Staatliche
Antikensammlung
Gemälde-
sammlung
KAROLINEN-
PLATZ
MAXVORSTADT
Obelisk
Kloster
St. Bonifazius
Amerikahaus
BRIENNER
Anthroposophische
Staatssammlung
Carolinen
Palais
Institut für
Kunstgeschichte
Handwerks-
kammer
PLATZ DER OP
DES NATIONALSOZ
MEISER-
Fachhochschule
München
Industrie- und
Handelskammer
(IHK)
Sophien-
saal
Alter
Botanischer
Garten
ARCO-
OTTOSTRASSE
MAXIMILIANS-
PLATZ
ELISENSTRASSE
LENBACH-
PLATZ
Börse
Palais-
Neuhaus-Preysing
Dreifaltigkeits-
kirche
Komödie im
Bayerischen Hof
Bayerisches Verfassungs-
und Oberlandesgericht
Justizpalast
PRIELMAYER-
STRASSE
Amtsgericht
BMW
Erzbischöfliches
Ordinariat
Maxburg
PROMENADE-
PLATZ
Karlsplatz
(Stachus)
SCHÜTZENSTRASSE
MAXBURGSTRASSE
BAYERSTRASSE
KARLSPLATZ
(STACHUS)
NEUHAUSER
Statistisches
Landesamt
Michaels-
kirche
Deutsches Jagd- und
Fischereimuseum
Bürger-
saalkirche
Frauenkirche
SCHLOSSERSTRASSE
SONNEN-
ADOLF-KOLPING-
STRASSE
HERZOGSPITAL-
Arcade
(Passage)
Kaufinger Tor
(Passage)
SCHWANTHALER-
STRASSE
Herzogspital-
kirche
ALTHEIMER
ECK
JOSEPHSPITAL-
Haus zur
Hundskugel
LANDWEHRSTRASSE
Goethe
Institut
Kreuz-
kirche
ASAM-
HOF
Johann-Nepomuk-
Kirche
(Asam-
kirche)
Stadt-
museum
Polikliniken
Jüdisches
Zentrum
(in Bau)
ST.-JAKOBS-
PLATZ
SEBASTIAN
PLATZ
PETTENKOFERSTRASSE
SENDLINGER-
TOR-PLATZ
OBERANGER
St.-Jakob-
Kloster
NUSSBAUM-
Sendlinger Tor
Matthäus
Kirche
Hauptfeuer-
wache
Altkatholische
Kirche
Städtisches
Hochhaus
BLUMENSTRASSE
LINDWURM-
STRASSE
Marionetten-
theater
AUGSBURGER-
STRASSE
FRAUNHOFER
STRASSE
VORS
St.
Stephan

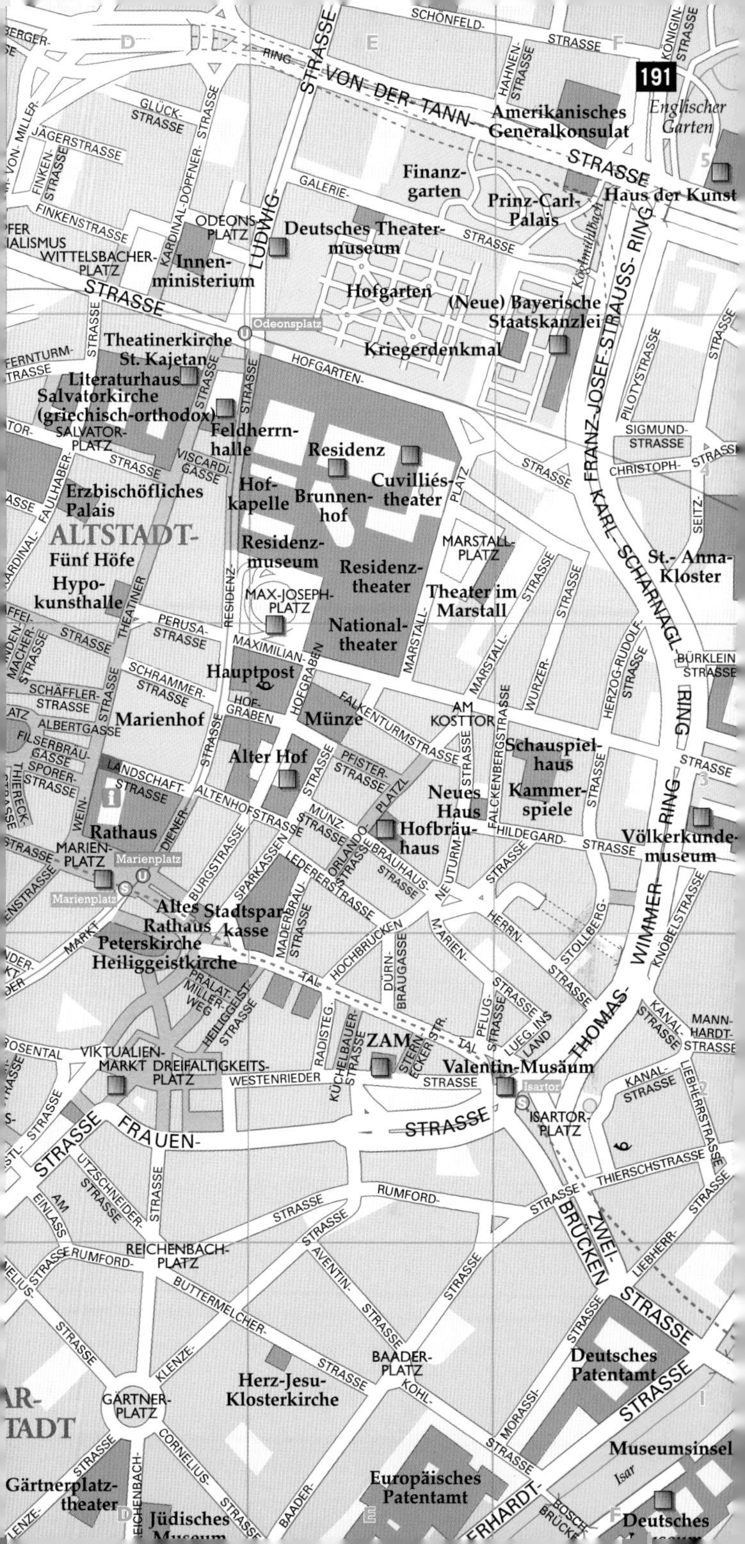
Amerikanisches Generalkonsulat
Englischer Garten
Haus der Kunst
Finanzgarten
Prinz-Carl-Palais
Deutsches Theatermuseum
Hofgarten
(Neue) Bayerische Staatskanzlei
Kriegerdenkmal
Odeonsplatz
Innenministerium
Theatinerkirche St. Kajetan
Literaturhaus
Salvatorkirche (griechisch-orthodox)
Feldherrnhalle
Residenz
Cuvilliés-theater
Hofkapelle
Brunnenhof
Erzbischöfliches Palais
ALTSTADT-
Fünf Höfe
Hypo-kunsthalle
Residenzmuseum
Residenztheater
Theater im Marstall
Max-Joseph-Platz
Nationaltheater
St.-Anna-Kloster
Hauptpost
Marienhof
Münze
Alter Hof
Schauspielhaus
Kammerspiele
Neues Haus
Hofbräuhaus
Völkerkundemuseum
Rathaus
Marienplatz
Altes Rathaus
Stadtsparkasse
Peterskirche
Heiliggeistkirche
Viktualienmarkt
Dreifaltigkeitsplatz
ZAM
Valentin-Musäum
Isartor
Isartorplatz
Reichenbachplatz
Baaderplatz
Herz-Jesu-Klosterkirche
Gärtnerplatz
Deutsches Patentamt
Museumsinsel
Isar
Europäisches Patentamt
Gärtnerplatztheater
Jüdisches Museum
Deutsches Museum
Von-der-Tann-Strasse
Schönfeldstrasse
Ludwigstrasse
Galeriestrasse
Hofgartenstrasse
Franz-Josef-Strauss-Ring
Karl-Scharnagl-Ring
Thomas-Wimmer-Ring
Maximilianstrasse
Frauenstrasse
Rumfordstrasse
Zweibrückenstrasse
Tal
Westenriederstrasse
Thierschstrasse
Sparkassenstrasse
Ledererstrasse
Falkenturmstrasse
Marstallplatz
Sigmundstrasse
Christophstrasse
Bürkleinstrasse
Hildegardstrasse
Kanalstrasse
Liebherrstrasse
Mannhardtstrasse
Knöbelstrasse
Herrnstrasse
Stollbergstrasse
Buttermelcherstrasse
Klenzestrasse
Corneliusstrasse
Reichenbachstrasse
Baaderstrasse
Kohlstrasse
Erhardtstrasse
Morassistrasse
Aventinstrasse
Utzschneiderstrasse
Am Einlass
Residenzstrasse
Theatinerstrasse
Perusastrasse
Schrammerstrasse
Hofgraben
Burgstrasse
Dienerstrasse
Weinstrasse
Landschaftstrasse
Altenhofstrasse
Pfisterstrasse
Platzl
Münzstrasse
Orlandostrasse
Bräuhausstrasse
Neuturmstrasse
Falckenbergstrasse
Am Kosttor
Wurzerstrasse
Herzog-Rudolf-Strasse
Seitzstrasse
Pilotystrasse
Kardinal-Döpfner-Strasse
Jägerstrasse
Finkenstrasse
Glückstrasse
Wittelsbacherplatz
Odeonsplatz
Salvatorplatz
Viscardigasse
Schäfflerstrasse
Albertgasse
Filserbräugasse
Sporerstrasse
Maderbräustrasse
Hochbrückenstrasse
Dürnbräugasse
Radlsteg
Küchelbauerstrasse
Sterneckerstr.
Marienstrasse
Pflugstrasse
Lueg ins Land
Prälat-Miller-Weg
Heiliggeiststrasse
Rosental
Bosch-Brücke
Köglmühlbach

192
A
B
C
MAX-
BORN-
STRASSE
WILDERMUTH-
STRASSE
EGGMÜHLER-
STRASSE
WICHERTSTRASSE
DONAUSTAUFERSTRASSE
DACHAUER
STRASSE
HAYLER-
STRASSE
SAARLOUISER STRASSE
ROTH-
OH-
LAUER
RATH-
HAN-
NOVER
STRASSE
EININGER-
STRASSE
HOLLEDAUER
STRASSE
JAKOB-HAGEN-BUCHER-
STRASSE
GÖRLITZER STRASSE
DRESDNER
LEIPZIGER
NAUMBURGER
STRASSE
GERASTRASSE
FODERMAYR-
STRASSE
TRIEB-
STRASSE
ANDERNACHER
STRASSE
DOBMANN-
STRASSE
WEISSENBÖCK
STRASSE
EHRENBREITSTEINER
STRASSE
BINGENER
Olympia-
Einkaufszentrum
SCHAWAIGE-
STRASSE
GEBER-
ZUR GRÜNEN EICHE
PUCHHEIMER
STRASSE
BENZ-
STRASSE
MEMMINGER
PLATZ
Moosach
SIEGMUND-SCHACKY-
STRASSE
PELKOVEN-
ST.-MARTINS-
PLATZ
PLAUENER
SEYDLITZ-
MOOSACH
SCHARN-
HORST
SCHOPFER-
PLATZ
DESSAUER
BUNZLAUER STRASSE
DACHAUER
FRANZ-FIHL-
STRASSE
QUEDLINBURGER STRASSE
HARDENBERG-
SEYDLITZ-
PLATZ
FELDMOCHINGER-
MEGGENDORFER
HANAUER
GNEISENAU
GUBE-
STRASSE
KARLINGERSTRASSE
GARTNER-
KARL-LIPP-STRASSE
NANGA-PARBAT-STRASSE
TREITSCHKESTRASSE
Georg-Brauchle-Ring
HANS-BUNTE-
STRASSE
ROTHSTRASSE
ERNST-
NETZER-
GLEISSMÜLLER
WELZENBACHSTRASSE
GEORG-BRAUCHLE-
RING
FEICHTMAYR-
STRASSE
DARMSTÄDTER STRASSE
WARSCHAUER
STRASSE
BAUBERGER
GAGGENAY-
HUGO-TROENDLE-
TEMPLE-
STRASSE
AM
KAPUZINER-
HÖLZL
WEISHAUPT-
SIMMERLEIN-
PLATZ
St. Mauritius
RIGAER
HANAUERS TRASSE
EMMY-
NOETHERSTRASSE
SICKINGER
STRASSE
IRMA-WENKE-
STRASSE
Westfriedhof
KAPUZINERHÖLZL
FRANZ-MADER-STRASSE
Ludwig-Jall-Halle
Post-Sportpark
NEDERLINGER STRASSE
Westfriedhof
Aussegnungshalle
HOMER-
STRASSE
IN DEN
AM
KIRSCHEN
NEDERLING
BALDUR-
STRASSE
DANTE-
HANE-
NEDERLINGER
LECHSTRASSE
REINMAR-
PLATZ
Dantebad
WINTRICH-
NACHTIGALSTRASSE
WERTACH-
PLATZ
Biedersteiner Kanal
HOHENLOHE-
Dritter Orden
Nymphenburg
Kapelle
TASCHNER-
STRASSE
FUSTSTRASSE
SADELER-
TAXIS-
Botanische
Staatssammlung
VOLPINI-
STUBER-
STAENGL
NEDERLINGER
PLATZ
WAISEN-
NÜRNBERGER
Palmenhaus
Allerheiligste
Dreifaltigkeits-Kirche
Friedhof
VON-GOEBEL-
PLATZ
MENZINGER
LUDWIG-
FERDINAND-PLATZ
CANALETTO-
DEMOLL-
BÖCKLIN-
KLUG-
GERNER-
KRAIZERSTRASSE
Gern
GERN
Neuer
Botanischer
Garten
ARMI-
Nymphenburger
MAREESSTRASSE
BAUMLSTR.
DALL-
KUGLMÜLLER-
ZAMBONINI-
FRAAS-STRASSE
GUTENBERG-
BANDEL-
STRASSE
SIMEONI-
Museum
Mensch und Natur
Magdalenen-
kapelle
NÖRDLICHES
SCHLOSSRONDELL
TIZIAN-
PLATZ
TIZIAN-
MALSEN-
STR.
DOM
ST.-GALL
Kapelle
Fontäne
NÖRDLICHE
AUFFAHRTS-
Schloßkanal
Hubertus-
brunnen
Schloss
Nymphenburg
NYMPHENBURG
SÜDLICHES
SCHLOSSRONDELL
Christ-
könig
DULLINGER-
MARIA-
MONTEN-
STRASSE
RENATA-
WINTHIR-
NYMPHENBURGER STRASSE
Porzellansammlung
Krankenhaus der
Barmherzigen Brüder
Neuapostolische
Kirche
Herz-Jesu-
Kirche
Amalienburg
Marstall-
museum
ROMAN-
STRASSE
ROMAN-
PLATZ
AIBLINGER
STRASSE
Brunnenhaus
HIRSCHGARTEN-
GASSNERSTRASSE
ARNULF-
FERDINAND-
HUBERTUS-
FLÜGGENSTR.
LACHNER-
JAGD-
VOLKART
ROTKREUZ
PLATZ
ZUCCALI-
LAIMER STRASSE
NIBELUNGEN-
RICHILDENSTRASSE
LIER-
FRICKASTRASSE
TROJANOSTRASSE
BOLIVARSTR.
OFTERDINGENSTRASSE
GUDRUN-
KEMNATENSTRASSE
KRIEMHILDENSTRASSE
DIETRICH-
WENDL-
RENATA-
196
WALHALLA-
ALLEE
STEUBEN-
PLATZ
KARL-SCHURZ-STRASSE
HERTHA-
SIEGRUNESTRASSE
KÖNIG-
BAUER-
SCHLUDER-
SCHÄRINGER
PLATZ
Hirschgarten
DE-LA-PAZ-
GINHARDTSTRASSE
SEDLMAYR-
WINFRIED-
Briefzentrum
HIRSCHBERG
St.
Clemens

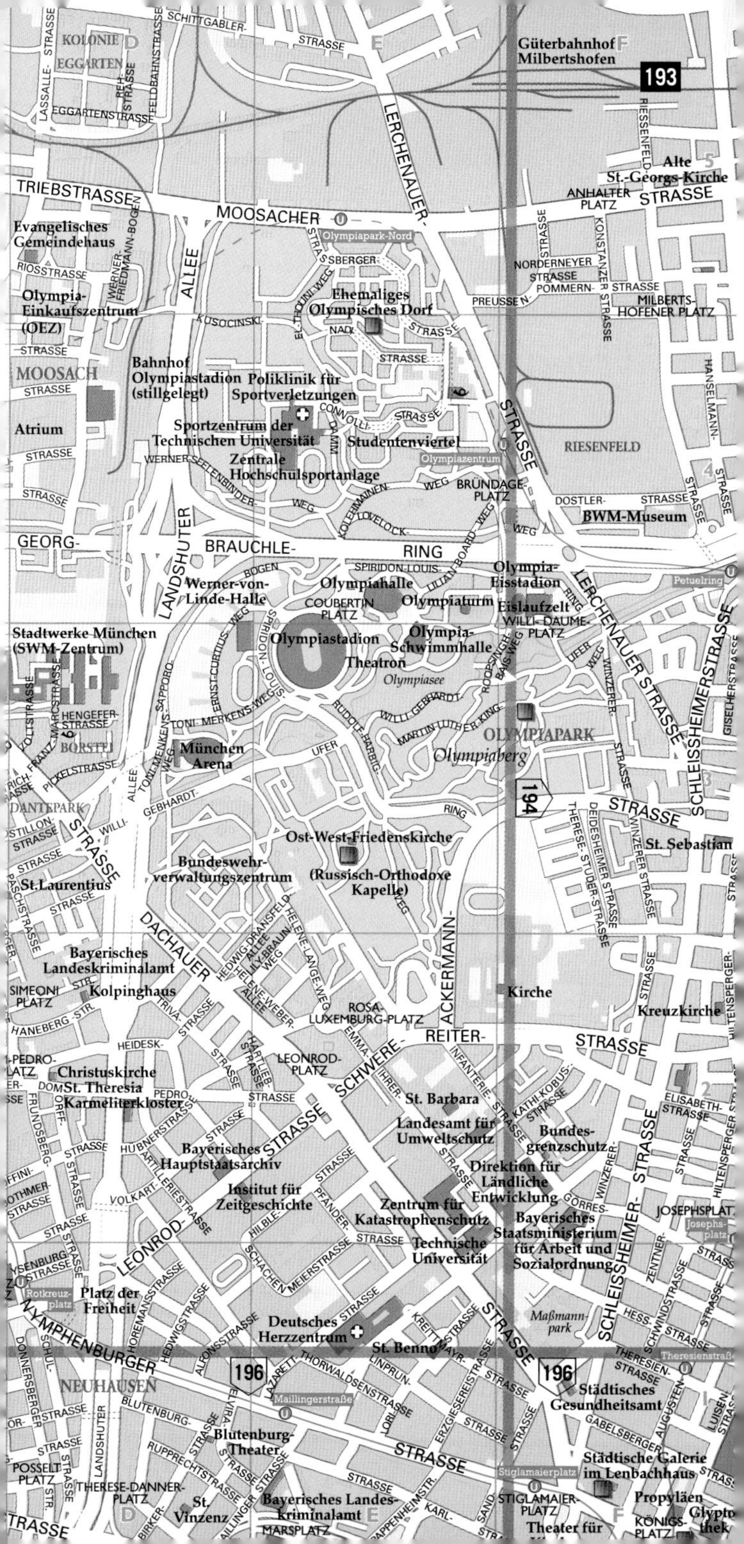
193
194
196
Güterbahnhof Milbertshofen
Kolonie Eggarten
Schittgabler-Strasse
Lassalle-Strasse
Reh-Strasse
Feldbahnstrasse
Eggartenstrasse
Lerchenauer-Strasse
Riessenfeld-
Alte St.-Georgs-Kirche
Triebstrasse
Moosacher Strasse
Anhalter Platz
Olympiapark-Nord
Evangelisches Gemeindehaus
Riosstrasse
Werner-Friedmann-Bogen
Allee
Strassberger-Strasse
Norderneyer Strasse
Pommern-Strasse
Konstanzer Strasse
Milbertshofener Platz
Preussen-
Olympia-Einkaufszentrum (OEZ)
Kusocinski-
El-Touni-Weg
Ehemaliges Olympisches Dorf
Nadi-Strasse
Moosach
Bahnhof Olympiastadion (stillgelegt)
Poliklinik für Sportverletzungen
Hanselmann-
Atrium
Connollistrasse
Damm
Sportzentrum der Technischen Universität
Studentenviertel
Riesenfeld
Werner-Seelenbinder-Weg
Zentrale Hochschulsportanlage
Olympiazentrum
Kolehmainen-Weg
Bründage-Platz
Dostler-Strasse
BWM-Museum
Lovelock-Weg
Georg-Brauchle-Ring
Landshuter Allee
Spiridon-Louis-
Lilian-Board-Weg
Olympia-Eisstadion
Petuelring
Werner-von-Linde-Halle
Olympiahalle
Olympiaturm
Eislaufzelt
Coubertin Platz
Willi-Daume-Platz
Stadtwerke München (SWM-Zentrum)
Olympiastadion
Olympia-Schwimmhalle
Theatron
Olympiasee
Ernst-Curtius-Weg
Sapporo-
Rodpsingh-Bais-Weg
Ufer-Weg
Winzerer-Strasse
Lerchenauer Strasse
Schleissheimerstrasse
Gieselherstrasse
Voltstrasse
Hengeferstrasse
Marcstrasse
Toni-Merkens-Weg
Willi-Gebhardt-
Rudolf-Harbig-
Martin-Luther-King-
Olympiapark
Olympiaberg
Borstei
München Arena
Franz-
Pickelstrasse
Ufer
Dantepark
Gebhardt-
Ring
Strasse
St. Sebastian
Deidesheimer Strasse
Therese-Studer-Strasse
Winzerer Strasse
Ost-West-Friedenskirche (Russisch-Orthodoxe Kapelle)
Bundeswehrverwaltungszentrum
St. Laurentius
Dachauer
Hedwig-Dransfeld-Allee
Lily-Braun-Weg
Helene-Lange-Weg
Helene-Weber-Allee
Ackermann-
Bayerisches Landeskriminalamt
Simeoni Platz
Kolpinghaus
Kirche
Kreuzkirche
Hiltensperger-
Haneberg-Str.
Triva-Strasse
Rosa-Luxemburg-Platz
Reiter-Strasse
Heideck-Strasse
Hartlieb-Strasse
Leonrod-Platz
Emma-Ihrer-
Infanterie-Strasse
Kathi-Kobus-Strasse
Christuskirche
St. Theresia
Karmeliterkloster
Dom-Pedro-Platz
Orff-
Frundsberg-
Schwere-Reiter-Strasse
St. Barbara
Landesamt für Umweltschutz
Bundesgrenzschutz
Elisabeth-Strasse
Hübnerstrasse
Artilleriestrasse
Bayerisches Hauptstaatsarchiv
Direktion für Ländliche Entwicklung
Institut für Zeitgeschichte
Volkart-
Hilble-
Pfänder-
Zentrum für Katastrophenschutz
Gorres-
Bayerisches Staatsministerium für Arbeit und Sozialordnung
Technische Universität
Josephsplatz
Leonrod-
Schachenmeierstrasse
Zentner-
Schwindstrasse
Rotkreuzplatz
Platz der Freiheit
Horemansstrasse
Maßmannpark
Hess-Strasse
Nymphenburger
Deutsches Herzzentrum
St. Benno
Kreittmayr-Strasse
Lazarett-
Thorwaldsenstrasse
Linprun-
Theresienstraße
Theresien-Strasse
Hedwigstrasse
Alfonsstrasse
Neuhausen
Maillingerstraße
Städtisches Gesundheitsamt
Augusten-
Luisen-
Blutenburg-Strasse
Elvira-
Erzgiessereistrasse
Lori-
Landshuter
Donnersberger
Gabelsberger-
Blutenburg-Theater
Rupprechtstrasse
Strasse
Posselt Platz
Therese-Danner-Platz
St. Vinzenz
Bayerisches Landeskriminalamt
Marsplatz
Stiglmaierplatz
Städtische Galerie im Lenbachhaus
Stiglmaier-Platz
Propyläen
Glyptothek
Pappenheimstr.
Karl-
Sand-
Königsplatz
Theater für

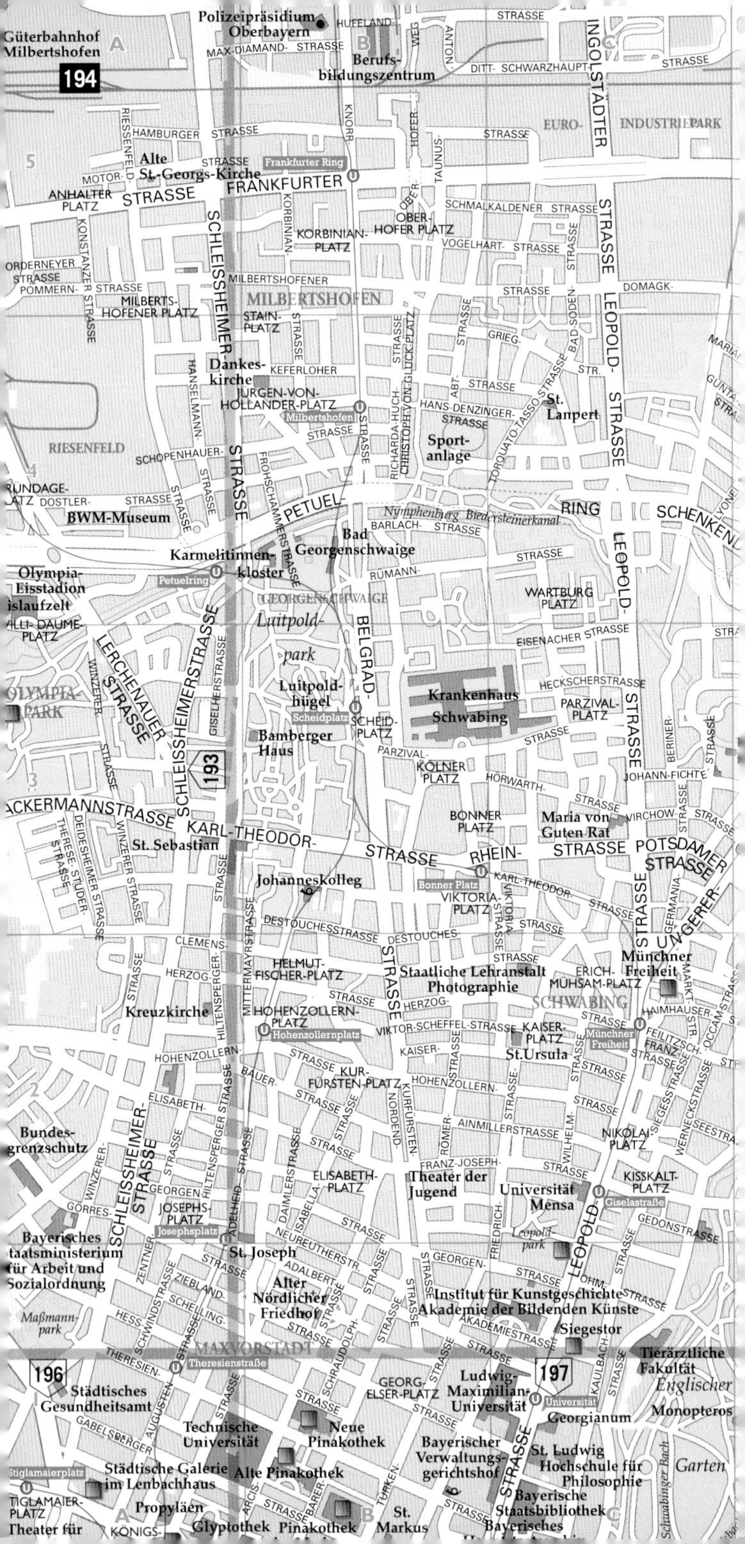

Güterbahnhof Milbertshofen
194
Polizeipräsidium Oberbayern
Berufsbildungszentrum
Ingolstädter Strasse
Euro-Industriepark
Alte St.-Georgs-Kirche
Frankfurter Ring
Anhalter Platz
Korbinianplatz
Oberhofer Platz
Milbertshofen
Milberts-hofener Platz
Stainplatz
Dankeskirche
Jürgen-von-Hollander-Platz
Milbertshofen
Riesenfeld
Sportanlage
St. Lanpert
Leopoldstrasse
BWM-Museum
Petuelring
Ring
Schenkendorfstrasse
Nymphenburg Biedersteinerkanal
Karmelitinnenkloster
Bad Georgenschwaige
Olympia-Eisstadion
Eislaufzelt
Willi-Daume-Platz
Georgenschwaige
Luitpoldpark
Wartburgplatz
Olympiapark
Lerchenauer Strasse
Schleissheimerstrasse
Luitpoldhügel
Scheidplatz
Krankenhaus Schwabing
Parzivalplatz
Bamberger Haus
193
Kölner Platz
Ackermannstrasse
Karl-Theodor-Strasse
St. Sebastian
Bonner Platz
Maria von Guten Rat
Potsdamer Strasse
Johanneskolleg
Viktoriaplatz
Destouchesstrasse
Münchner Freiheit
Helmut-Fischer-Platz
Staatliche Lehranstalt Photographie
Erich-Mühsam-Platz
Schwabing
Kreuzkirche
Hohenzollernplatz
Kaiserplatz
St.Ursula
Kurfürstenplatz
Bundesgrenzschutz
Nikolaiplatz
Elisabethplatz
Theater der Jugend
Universität Mensa
Kisskaltplatz
Giselastraße
Josephsplatz
Bayerisches Staatsministerium für Arbeit und Sozialordnung
St. Joseph
Leopoldpark
Alter Nördlicher Friedhof
Institut für Kunstgeschichte
Akademie der Bildenden Künste
Siegestor
Maßmannpark
Maxvorstadt
Theresienstraße
Tierärztliche Fakultät
196
Städtisches Gesundheitsamt
Georg-Elser-Platz
Ludwig-Maximilian-Universität
197
Universität
Englischer Garten
Georgianum
Monopteros
Technische Universität
Neue Pinakothek
Bayerischer Verwaltungsgerichtshof
St. Ludwig
Hochschule für Philosophie
Stiglmaierplatz
Städtische Galerie im Lenbachhaus
Alte Pinakothek
Bayerische Staatsbibliothek
Propyläen
Glyptothek
Pinakothek
St. Markus
Theater für

195
198
D
E
F
5
4
3
2
Freimann
FREIMANN
St Nikolaus
Gewerbepark
Samariterkirche
LOTTE-BRANZ-STRASSE
LINDBERGH-STRASSE
ALLEE
VÖLCKERSTRASSE
GEORG-WOPFNER-STRASSE
MAX-VALIER-STRASSE
SITULISTRASSE
FREISINGER
FLORIANSMÜHLSTRASSE
LANDSTRASSE
GROHPLATZ
UNTER DER LINDE
LEINTHALER-STRASSE
LIBELLENSTRASSE
Garchinger Mühlbach
MEIER-STRASSE
LILIENTHAL-
RING
FÖHRINGER RING
AUTOBAHN MÜNCHEN-NÜRNBERG
AUMEISTER WEG
SONDERMEIER-STRASSE
Schwabinger Bach
Max-Planck-Institut
Alabamahalle
DOMAGK-
WILHELM-WAGENFELD-STRASSE
Studentenstadt
Neuer Israelischer Friedhof
UNGERER-STRASSE
GRASMEIER-STRASSE
WILLGRAFSTRASSE
HERMANN-VOGEL-STRASSE
STUDENTENSTADT
Dankeskirche
SCHLODERER-PLATZ
MARCHGRABENPLATZ
Nikodemuskirche
Allerheiligenkirche
Alte Heide
GRUNECKER-STRASSE
GARCHINGER-STRASSE
OSKAR-SCHLEMMER-STRASSE
GROPIUS-
WALTER-
FRÖTTMANINGER-STRASSE
CRAILSHEIM-STRASSE
RÖHMEDER-STRASSE
Schwabinger Bach
Obersöggemeisterbach
Nordfriedhof
ALTE HEIDE
Allerheiligenkirche (orthodox)
Aussegnungshalle
Sportanlage
Hirschau
Isarkanal
THEODOR-DOMBART-STRASSE
Nordfriedhof
NIEBUHR-
KARL-AMOLDWEG
Ungererbad
Unterer Wehrbach
Mittlerer
MITTLERE-ISAR-
St. Lorenz
Schwarze Lacke
ISAR-RING
Dietlindenstraße
BIEDERSTEIN
SCHWEDENSTRASSE
Schwabinger Bach
Oberer Wehrbach
EMST-PENZOLDT-WEG
Reitbach
Stauwehr
MAUERKIRCHER-
GRÜNTAL
KLEMENTINENSTRASSE
BIEDERSTEINERSTRASSE
Freizeitpark Biederstein
DIETLINDENSTRASSE
OSTERWALD
HIRSCHAU
ALLEE
RÜMELINSTRASSE
BURGERSTRASSE
Brunnbach
LEITE
BAYREUTHER STRASSE
HAUSHOFERSTRASSE
BRUNNBACH-
WAHNFRIED
BIEDERSTEINER-
KEFERSTRASSE
St. Sylvester
Kleinhesseloher See
Seehaus
GYSSLING
Eisbach
OPITZ-STRASSE
ADALBERT-STIFTER-STRASSE
TITURELSTRASSE
ALLEE
HERZOGPARK
HEINRICH-MANN-
PRIEL
KLEINHESSELOHE
ODIN-STRASSE
Krankenhaus Bogenhausen
JOHN-F.-KENNEDY-BRÜCKE
PIENZENAUER
MAUERKIRCHER-
FLEMING-
RÜDLIEB-
ORTHNIT-
ASGARD-
NORMANNENPLATZ
NORMANNENSTRASSE
TEUTONENSTRASSE
Englischer
Rumfordhalle
IFFLANDSTRASSE
ISAR-
Herzog-Albrecht-Anlage
OBERFÖHRINGER-RING
ENGLSCHALKINGER STR
Arabellapark
Chinesischer Turm
Eisbach
Isar
ALLEE
EFFNERPLATZ
Staatsministerium für Landesentwicklung und Umweltfragen
ROSENKAVALIERPLATZ
Arabellahaus
ARABELLASTRASSE
ARABELLAPARK
Institut der Universität
Monopteros
Garten
ILLIRSCHAUER STRASSE
THOMAS-MANN-
MAUERKIRCHER-
HERKOMERPLATZ
GEBELE-STRASSE
AMBERGER-STRASSE
DENNINGER STRASSE
MAX-JOSEPH-BRÜCKE
OETTINGEN-
KUFSTEINER PLATZ
Bundesfinanzhof
Österreichisches Generalkons.
Bogenhauser Kirchplatz
St. Georg
WEHRLE-
Dreieinigkeitskirche
Herling Blut
WIDDERSTRASSE
Richard-Strauss-Straße
KIRCHPLATZ
Neuapostolische
DONAUSTR
REGENSBURGER PLATZ
Denninger Anger

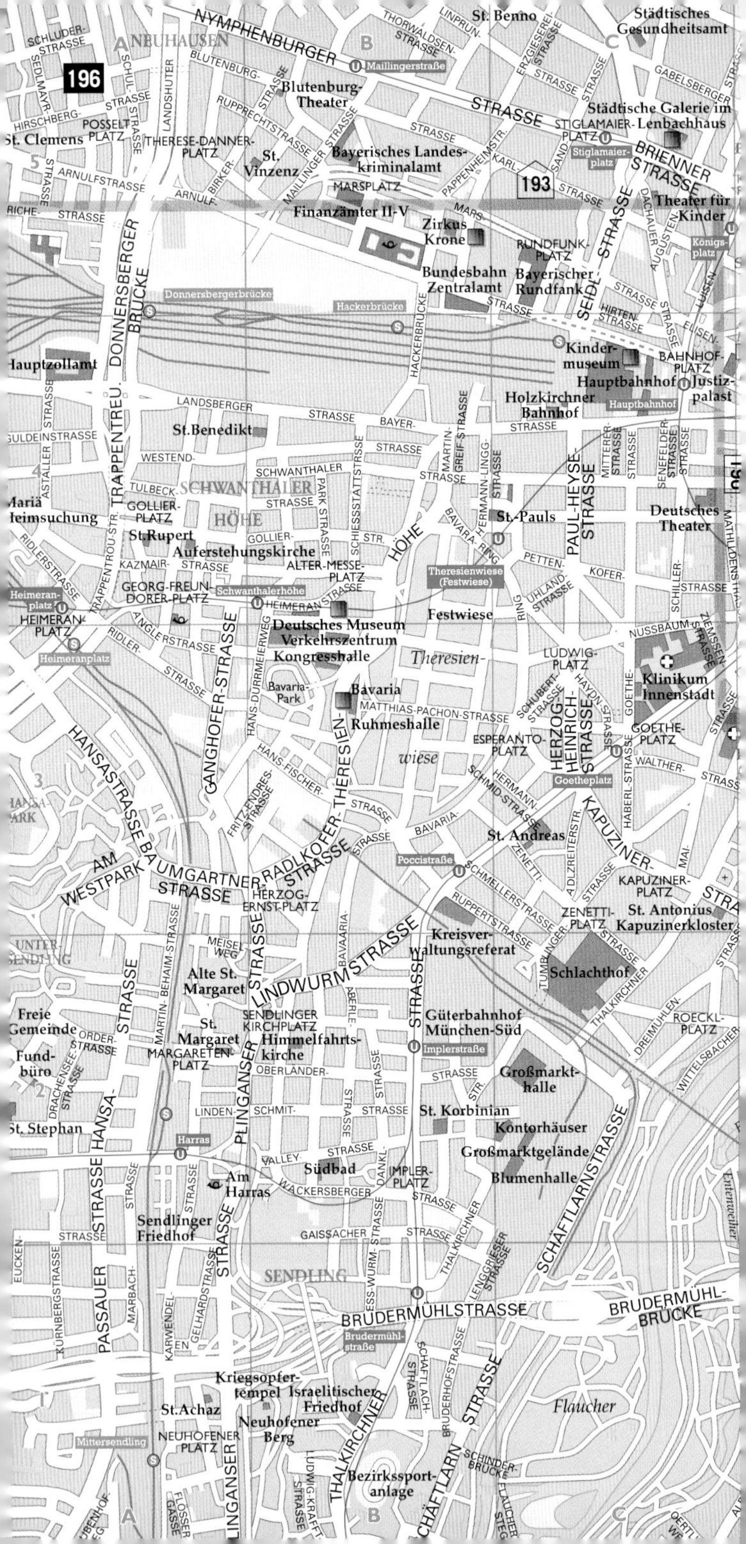
196
NEUHAUSEN
NYMPHENBURGER STRASSE
Maillingerstraße
St. Benno
Städtisches Gesundheitsamt
SCHLUDER-STRASSE
SEDLMAYR-STRASSE
SCHUL-STRASSE
LANDSHUTER
BLUTENBURG-STRASSE
Blutenburg-Theater
THORWALDSEN-STRASSE
LINPRUN-STRASSE
ERZGIESSEREI-STRASSE
GABELSBERGER
Städtische Galerie im Lenbachhaus
HIRSCHBERG-STRASSE
POSSELT-PLATZ
St. Clemens
THERESE-DANNER-PLATZ
RUPPRECHTSTRASSE
MAILLINGER STRASSE
St. Vinzenz
Bayerisches Landeskriminalamt
MARSPLATZ
PAPPENHEIMSTR.
KARL-STRASSE
STIGLAMAIER-PLATZ
Stiglamaier-platz
BRIENNER STRASSE
193
ARNULFSTRASSE
BIRKER-
ARNULF-
Finanzämter II-V
MARS-
Zirkus Krone
DACHAUER
AUGUSTEN-
Theater für Kinder
Königsplatz
DONNERSBERGER BRÜCKE
Donnersbergerbrücke
Hackerbrücke
HACKERBRÜCKE
Bundesbahn Zentralamt
RUNDFUNK-PLATZ
Bayerischer Rundfunk
SEIDL-STRASSE
HIRTEN-STRASSE
LUISEN-
ELISEN-
Kindermuseum
BAHNHOF-PLATZ
Hauptbahnhof
Justizpalast
Hauptzollamt
TRAPPENTREU-
LANDSBERGER STRASSE
BAYER-STRASSE
Holzkirchner Bahnhof
MARTIN-GREIF-STRASSE
St.Benedikt
GULDEINSTRASSE
ASTALLER STRASSE
WESTEND-
SCHWANTHALER STRASSE
SCHWANTHALER HÖHE
TULBECK-
GOLLIER-PLATZ
GOLLIER-
PARK STRASSE
SCHIESSSTÄTTSTR.
HERMANN-LINGG-STRASSE
MITTERER-STRASSE
SENEFELDER-STRASSE
PAUL-HEYSE-STRASSE
Mariä Heimsuchung
St.Rupert
Auferstehungskirche
HÖHE
BAVARIA-RING
St.-Pauls
Deutsches Theater
MATHILDENSTRASSE
RIDLERSTRASSE
KAZMAIR-STRASSE
ALTER-MESSE-PLATZ
PETTEN-KOFER-
SCHILLER-STRASSE
Theresienwiese (Festwiese)
Heimeranplatz
HEIMERANPLATZ
GEORG-FREUNDORFER-PLATZ
Schwanthalerhöhe
HEIMERANSTRASSE
Festwiese
RING
UHLAND-STRASSE
NUSSBAUM-STRASSE
ZIEMSSEN-STRASSE
ANGLERSTRASSE
RIDLER-STRASSE
Deutsches Museum Verkehrszentrum
Kongresshalle
Theresien-
LUDWIG-PLATZ
Klinikum Innenstadt
Bavaria-Park
Bavaria
HANS-DURRMEIERWEG
GANGHOFER-STRASSE
MATTHIAS-PACHON-STRASSE
Ruhmeshalle
SCHUBERT-STRASSE
HAYDN-STRASSE
GOETHE-
GOETHE-PLATZ
ESPERANTO-PLATZ
wiese
HERZOG-HEINRICH-STRASSE
WALTHER-STRASSE
HANSASTRASSE
HANS-FISCHER-STRASSE
THERESIEN-
HERMANN-SCHMID-STRASSE
Goetheplatz
HANSA-PARK
FRITZ-ENDRES-STRASSE
BAVARIA-STRASSE
KAPUZINER-STRASSE
HABERL-STRASSE
ADLZREITERSTR.
ZENETTI-
St. Andreas
MAI-
AM WESTPARK
BAUMGARTNER-STRASSE
RADLKOFER-STRASSE
Poccistraße
SCHMELLERSTRASSE
KAPUZINER-PLATZ
HERZOG-ERNST-PLATZ
RUPPERTSTRASSE
ZENETTI-PLATZ
St. Antonius Kapuzinerkloster
UNTER-SENDLING
MEISEL-WEG
BAVARIARING
Kreisverwaltungsreferat
TUMBLINGER-STRASSE
LINDWURMSTRASSE
Schlachthof
MARTIN-BEHAIM-STRASSE
Alte St. Margaret
THALKIRCHNER
DREIMÜHLEN-
ROECKL-PLATZ
Freie Gemeinde
SENDLINGER KIRCHPLATZ
ABERLE-
Güterbahnhof München-Süd
ORDER-STRASSE
St. Margaret
Himmelfahrtskirche
MARGARETEN-PLATZ
Implerstraße
WITTELSBACHER
Fundbüro
DRACHENSEE-STRASSE
OBERLÄNDER-
Großmarkthalle
LINDEN-
SCHMIT-
STRASSE
St. Korbinian
St. Stephan
HANSA-STRASSE
PLINGANSER STRASSE
Kontorhäuser
Harras
VALLEY-
Südbad
Großmarktgelände
IMPLER-PLATZ
Blumenhalle
Am Harras
WACKERSBERGER
DANKL-
SCHÄFTLARNSTRASSE
Entenbacher
Sendlinger Friedhof
GAISSACHER
THALKIRCHNER
LENGGRIESER STRASSE
EUCKEN-
PASSAUER STRASSE
NÜRNBERGSTRASSE
MARBACH-
GELHARDSTRASSE
SENDLING
ESS-WURM-STRASSE
BRUDERMÜHLSTRASSE
BRUDERMÜHL-BRÜCKE
KARWENDEL-
Brudermühlstraße
SCHÄFTLACH-STRASSE
BRUDERHOFSTRASSE
Kriegsopfertempel
Israelitischer Friedhof
St.Achaz
Neuhofener Berg
Flaucher
Mittersendling
NEUHOFENER PLATZ
PLINGANSER STRASSE
THALKIRCHNER
SCHÄFTLARN STRASSE
SCHINDER-BRÜCKE
LUDWIG-KRAFFT-STRASSE
Bezirkssportanlage
FLOSSER GASSE
FLAUCHER STEG

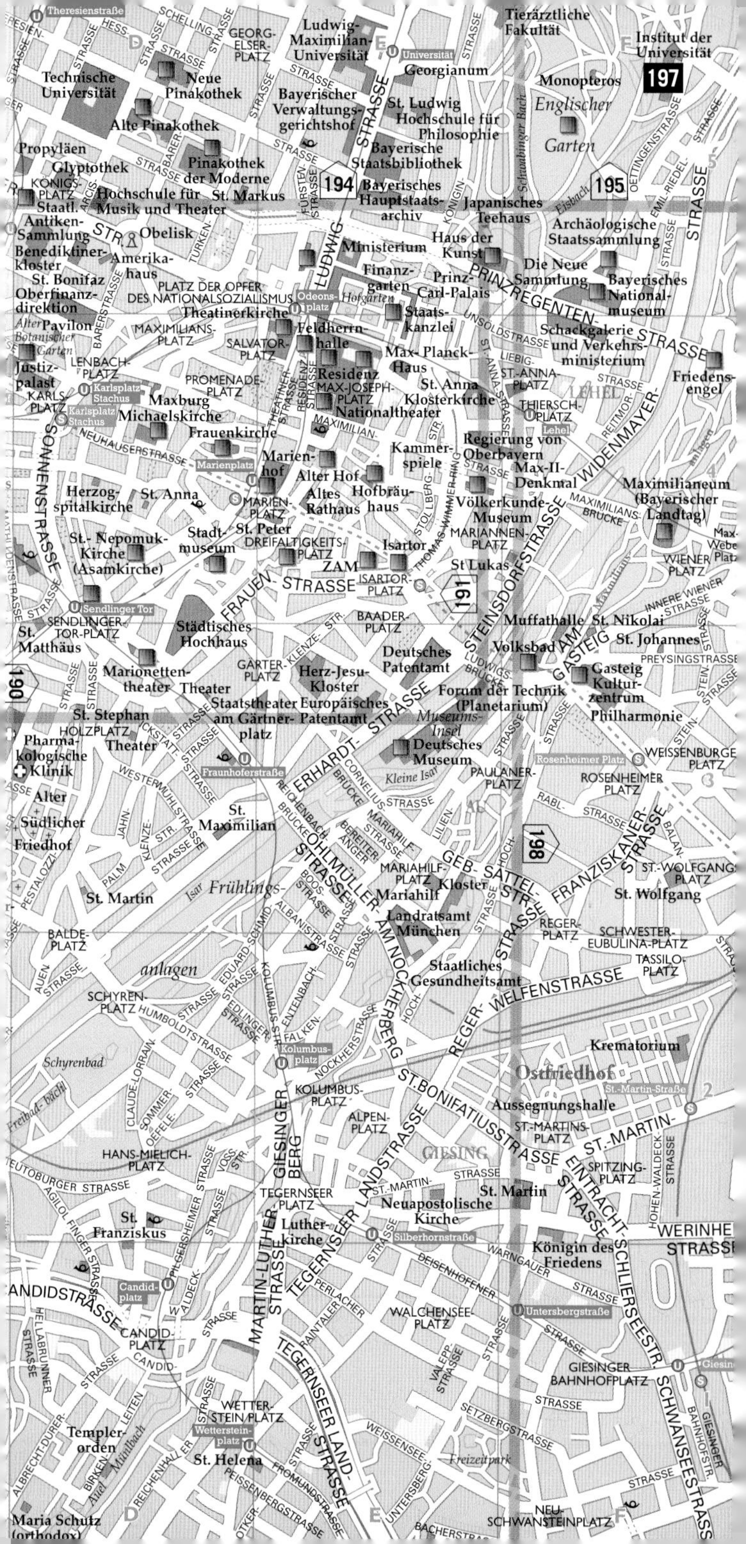
197
194
195
191
190
198
Theresienstraße
Technische Universität
Neue Pinakothek
Alte Pinakothek
Pinakothek der Moderne
Propyläen
Glyptothek
Königsplatz
Staatl. Antiken-Sammlung
Hochschule für Musik und Theater
St. Markus
Georg-Elser-Platz
Ludwig-Maximilian-Universität
Universität
Georgianum
St. Ludwig
Hochschule für Philosophie
Bayerischer Verwaltungsgerichtshof
Bayerische Staatsbibliothek
Bayerisches Hauptstaatsarchiv
Tierärztliche Fakultät
Institut der Universität
Monopteros
Englischer Garten
Japanisches Teehaus
Archäologische Staatssammlung
Obelisk
Benediktinerkloster
St. Bonifaz
Amerikahaus
Oberfinanzdirektion
Platz der Opfer des Nationalsozialismus
Ministerium
Haus der Kunst
Die Neue Sammlung
Bayerisches Nationalmuseum
Finanzgarten
Prinz-Carl-Palais
Odeonsplatz
Hofgarten
Theatinerkirche
Staatskanzlei
Prinzregentenstrasse
Schackgalerie und Verkehrsministerium
Alter Botanischer Garten
Pavilon
Maximiliansplatz
Salvatorplatz
Feldherrnhalle
Residenz
Max-Planck-Haus
Justizpalast
Lenbachplatz
Karlsplatz Stachus
Promenadeplatz
Max-Joseph-Platz
Nationaltheater
St. Anna Klosterkirche
St.-Anna-Platz
Lehel
Thierschplatz
Friedensengel
Maxburg
Michaelskirche
Frauenkirche
Marienplatz
Marienhof
Kammerspiele
Regierung von Oberbayern
Max-II-Denkmal
Widenmayerstrasse
Sonnenstrasse
Herzogspitalkirche
St. Anna
Alter Hof
Altes Rathaus
Hofbräuhaus
Völkerkunde-Museum
Maximilianeum (Bayerischer Landtag)
Maximiliansbrücke
St.-Nepomuk-Kirche (Asamkirche)
Stadtmuseum
St. Peter
Dreifaltigkeitsplatz
Isartor
ZAM
Mariannenplatz
St Lukas
Wiener Platz
Sendlinger Tor
Frauenstrasse
Isartorplatz
Steinsdorfstrasse
Sendlinger-Tor-Platz
St. Matthäus
Städtisches Hochhaus
Baaderplatz
Muffathalle
St. Nikolai
St. Johannes
Innere Wiener Strasse
Deutsches Patentamt
Volksbad
Am Gasteig
Preysingstrasse
Marionettentheater
Theater
Gärtnerplatz
Herz-Jesu-Kloster
Ludwigsbrücke
Forum der Technik (Planetarium)
Gasteig Kulturzentrum
Philharmonie
Staatstheater am Gärtnerplatz
Europäisches Patentamt
Museumsinsel
St. Stephan
Holzplatz
Theater
Erhardtstrasse
Deutsches Museum
Pharmakologische Klinik
Fraunhoferstraße
Rosenheimer Platz
Weissenburger Platz
Kleine Isar
Paulanerplatz
Alter Südlicher Friedhof
St. Maximilian
Corneliusstrasse
Mariahilfstrasse
Ohlmüllerstrasse
Mariahilfplatz
Mariahilf
Kloster
Gebsattelstr.
Franziskanerstrasse
St.-Wolfgangs-Platz
St. Wolfgang
St. Martin
Isar
Frühlingsanlagen
Am Nockherberg
Landratsamt München
Regerplatz
Schwester-Eubulina-Platz
Baldeplatz
Tassiloplatz
Staatliches Gesundheitsamt
Welfenstrasse
Regerstrasse
Schyrenplatz
Humboldtstrasse
Krematorium
Schyrenbad
Kolumbusplatz
Ostfriedhof
St.-Martin-Straße
Kolumbusplatz
Aussegnungshalle
St.-Martins-Platz
St. Bonifatiusstrasse
St.-Martin-Strasse
Alpenplatz
Giesing
Hans-Mielich-Platz
Spitzingplatz
Teutoburger Strasse
Tegernseer Platz
Tegernseer Landstrasse
Giesinger Berg
Martin-Luther-Strasse
St. Martin
Eintrachtstrasse
St. Franziskus
Lutherkirche
Neuapostolische Kirche
Silberhornstraße
Königin des Friedens
Werinherstrasse
Candidstrasse
Candidplatz
Walchenseeplatz
Untersbergstraße
Schlierseestr.
Giesinger Bahnhofplatz
Schwanseestrasse
Wettersteinplatz
Templerorden
St. Helena
Setzbergstrasse
Freizeitpark
Maria Schutz (orthodox)
Neuschwansteinplatz
Auer Mühlbach

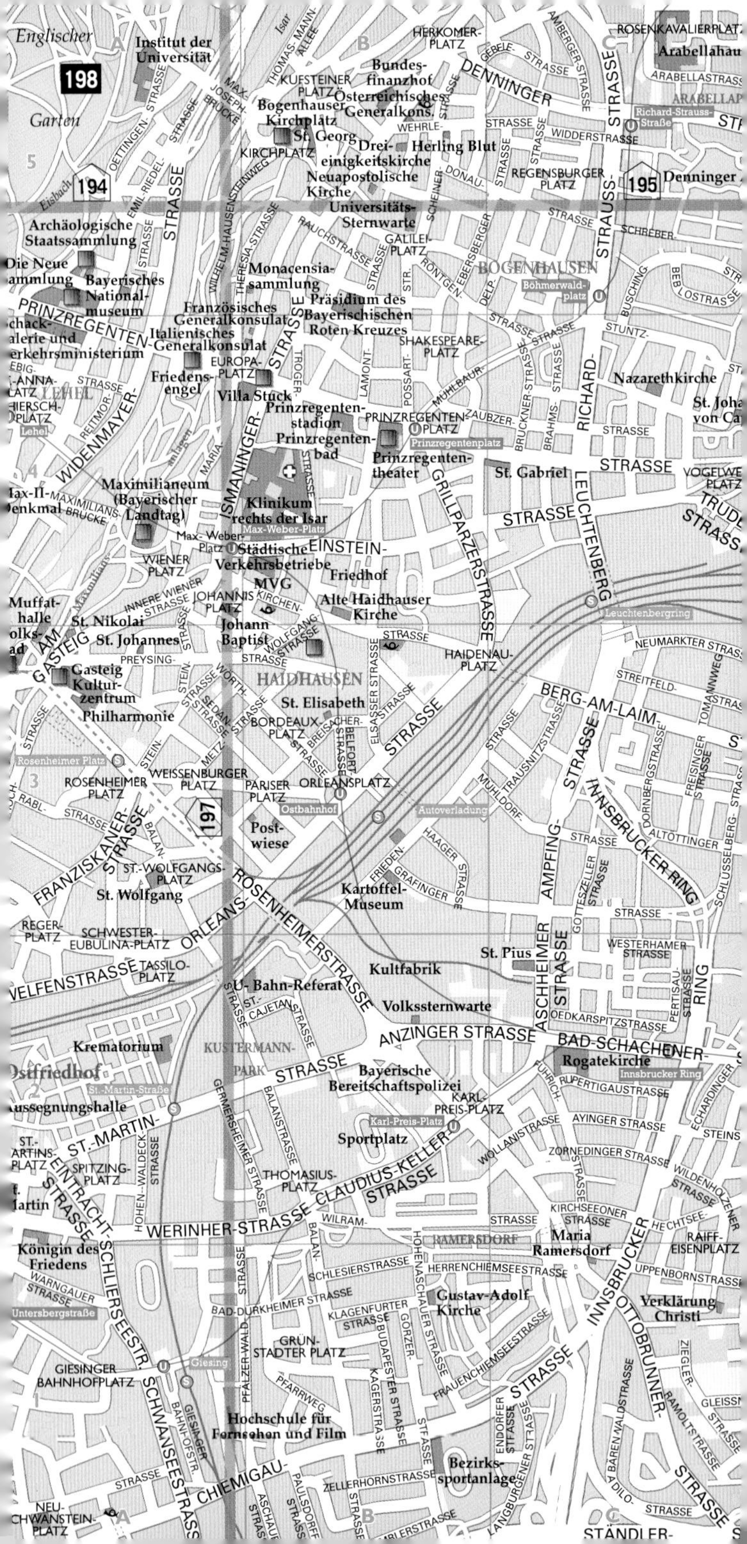

Englischer
Garten
198
194
195
197
5
4
3
2
1
A
B
C
Institut der Universität
Isar
Eisbach
OETTINGEN-STRASSE
EMIL-RIEDEL-STRASSE
MAX-JOSEPH-BRÜCKE
THOMAS-MANN-ALLEE
KUFSTEINER PLATZ
HERKOMER-PLATZ
Bundesfinanzhof
Österreichisches Generalkons.
Bogenhauser Kirchplatz
St. Georg
KIRCHPLATZ
Drei-einigkeitskirche
Herling Blut
WEHRLE-
DENNINGER STRASSE
GEBELE-STRASSE
AMBERGER-STRASSE
ROSENKAVALIERPLATZ
Arabellahaus
ARABELLASTRASSE
Richard-Strauss-Straße
WIDDERSTRASSE
REGENSBURGER PLATZ
Denninger
Neuapostolische Kirche
Universitäts-Sternwarte
WILHELM-HAUSENSTEIN-WEG
THERESIA-STRASSE
RAUCHSTRASSE
GALILEI-PLATZ
SCHREBER-
Archäologische Staatssammlung
Die Neue Sammlung
Bayerisches National-museum
Monacensia-sammlung
Präsidium des Bayerischischen Roten Kreuzes
RÖNTGEN-
EBERSBERGER
BOGENHAUSEN
Böhmerwald-platz
BEBLOSTRASSE
BUSCHING
PRINZREGENTEN-STRASSE
Französisches Generalkonsulat
Italienisches Generalkonsulat
Schackgalerie und Verkehrsministerium
SHAKESPEARE-PLATZ
STUNTZ-
EUROPA-PLATZ
Friedensengel
Villa Stuck
Prinzregentenstadion
Prinzregentenbad
TROGER-
LAMONT-
POSSART-
MÜHLBAUR-
BRUCKNER-STRASSE
BRAHMS-
Nazarethkirche
LEHEL
Lehel
REITMOR-
PRINZREGENTEN-PLATZ
Prinzregentenplatz
ZAUBZER-
Prinzregenten-theater
RICHARD-STRAUSS-STRASSE
St. Johannes von Capistran
WIDENMAYER-STRASSE
ISMANINGER-STRASSE
MARIA-
Maximilianeum (Bayerischer Landtag)
Max-II-Denkmal
MAXIMILIANS-BRÜCKE
Klinikum rechts der Isar
St. Gabriel
STRASSE
VOGELWEIDPLATZ
TRUDERINGER STRASSE
GRILLPARZERSTRASSE
LEUCHTENBERG
Max-Weber-Platz
Städtische Verkehrsbetriebe
MVG
EINSTEIN-STRASSE
Friedhof
WIENER PLATZ
INNERE WIENER STRASSE
JOHANNIS PLATZ
KIRCHEN-
Alte Haidhauser Kirche
Leuchtenbergring
Muffat-halle
St. Nikolai
St. Johannes
Johann Baptist
WOLFGANG-STRASSE
HAIDENAU-PLATZ
NEUMARKTER STRASSE
AM GASTEIG
PREYSING-
Gasteig Kulturzentrum Philharmonie
HAIDHAUSEN
St. Elisabeth
STREITFELD-
TOMANNWEG
BERG-AM-LAIM-STRASSE
SEDAN-STRASSE
WÖRTH-
BORDEAUX-PLATZ
BREISACHER-
BELFORT-STRASSE
ELSASSER STRASSE
Rosenheimer Platz
ROSENHEIMER PLATZ
WEISSENBURGER PLATZ
PARISER PLATZ
ORLEANSPLATZ
Ostbahnhof
Autoverladung
TRAUSNITZSTRASSE
MÜHLDORF-
INNSBRUCKER RING
DORNBERGSTRASSE
FREISINGER STRASSE
ALTÖTTINGER
SCHLÜSSELBERG-STRASSE
RABL-
FRANZISKANER-STRASSE
BALAN-
Post-wiese
HAAGER STRASSE
FRIEDEN-
GRAFINGER STRASSE
AMPFING-STRASSE
GOTTESZELLER STRASSE
ST.-WOLFGANGS-PLATZ
St. Wolfgang
ORLEANS-
ROSENHEIMERSTRASSE
Kartoffel-Museum
REGER-PLATZ
SCHWESTER-EUBULINA-PLATZ
WESTERHAMER STRASSE
WELFENSTRASSE
TASSILO-PLATZ
St. Pius
Kultfabrik
ASCHHEIMER STRASSE
PERTISAU-STRASSE
RING
U-Bahn-Referat
ST.-CAJETAN-STRASSE
Volkssternwarte
OEDKARSPITZSTRASSE
Krematorium
KUSTERMANN-PARK
ANZINGER STRASSE
BAD-SCHACHENER-STRASSE
Rogatekirche
Innsbrucker Ring
Ostfriedhof
St.-Martin-Straße
Aussegnungshalle
Bayerische Bereitschaftspolizei
KARL-PREIS-PLATZ
Karl-Preis-Platz
FÜHRICH-
RUPERTIGAUSTRASSE
ECHARDINGER
AYINGER STRASSE
STEINSEE
ST.-MARTIN-
ST.-MARTINS-PLATZ
SPITZING-PLATZ
HOHEN-WALDECK-STRASSE
GERMERSHEIMER STRASSE
BALANSTRASSE
Sportplatz
CLAUDIUS-KELLER-STRASSE
WOLLANISTRASSE
ZORNEDINGER STRASSE
WILDENHOLZENER STRASSE
St. Martin
EINTRACHT-
THOMASIUS-PLATZ
KIRCHSEEONER STRASSE
HECHTSEE-
RAIFF-EISENPLATZ
Königin des Friedens
WERINHER-STRASSE
WILRAM-
RAMERSDORF
Maria Ramersdorf
WARNGAUER STRASSE
Untersbergstraße
SCHLIERSEESTR.
SCHLESIERSTRASSE
HERRENCHIEMSEESTRASSE
UPPENBORNSTRASSE
BAD-DÜRKHEIMER STRASSE
KLAGENFURTER STRASSE
Gustav-Adolf Kirche
Verklärung Christi
INNSBRUCKER
OTTOBRUNNER-STRASSE
GRÜN-STADTER PLATZ
GORZER-
FRAUENCHIEMSEESTRASSE
BUDAPESTER STRASSE
HOHENASCHAUER STRASSE
Giesing
GIESINGER BAHNHOFPLATZ
PFÄLZER-WALD-STRASSE
PFARRWEG
KAGERSTRASSE
ENDORFER STRASSE
LANGBURGENER STRASSE
BÄRENWALDSTRASSE
ZIEGLER-
RAMOLTSTRASSE
GLEISSENTAL
SCHWANSEESTRASSE
GIESINGER BAHNHOFSTR.
Hochschule für Fernsehen und Film
Bezirkssportanlage
ZELLERHORNSTRASSE
CHIEMGAU-
ASCHAUER
PAULSDORFF
NEU-SCHWANSTEIN-PLATZ
ADILO-
STÄNDLER-

Streetplan Index

Index

Picture credits

Abbreviations for terms appearing below: (t) top; (b) bottom; (l) left; (r) right; (m) middle

Front cover: (t) T. Stankiewicz, (m) HB Verlag, (b) W. Dieterich

AKG: 20tl, 20tm, 20tr, 20bl, 20bm, 20br, 20m background, 21t, 21m, 21b, 102; R. Binder, München: 6/7b; W. Dieterich, Stuttgart: 2I, 2II, 3II, 5, 9ml, 11b, 30/31, 33, 50bl, 51t, 56b, 109b, 131t, 139, 140/141 background, 153, 176/177; R. Freyer, Freiburg: 2III, 3V, 15r, 28t, 47, 50mr, 55, 57b, 75t, 98b, 99b, 107m, 108b, 111t, 123t, 131b, 181; G. Jung, Ottobrunn: 3III, 6ml, 8tl, 9tr, 10ml, 10br, 11m, 12b, 14m, 16mr, 17b, 18, 19t, 19m, 22mr, 22bl, 23tr, 23b, 24t, 24m, 24b, 26mr, 28b, 28/29, 31tr, 53m, 53br, 61b, 65, 74bl, 76tl, 79, 85tr, 86, 87t, 87b, 97t, 99mr, 105t, 124/125, 126b, 126/127, 128, 129, 142b, 144, 145t, 145m, 146t, 150b, 154, 159, 160bl, 160/161, 161t, 162, 164/165, 166t, 166b, 167, 172; F. Köthe, München: 3IV, 7mr, 10tr, 22tl, 22tr, 27b, 48/49, 50tl, 53t, 54tl, 59t, 60l, 60r, 63m, 74tl, 75m, 76m, 77b, 81, 82, 83, 85tl, 126t, 147, 149, 169t, 170, 171, 179, 180l; La Terra Magica, München: (Manfred Kühn) 168/169 (Günter Lenz) 8mr, 9br, 13 background, 13mlt, 13mlb, 13tr, 13mtr, 13mbr, 14/15 background, 14bl, 15m, 16/17 background, 16t, 17m, 26ml, 52t, 54b, 56/57, 88, 100tl, 100bl, 109m, 124tl, 142t, 143t, 163t, 163m, 173, 174, 177, 185t, 185mr, 185ml; C. Naundorf, Paris: 2IV, 2V, 11t, 12ml, 13br, 25b, 27tl, 49t, 52b, 56ml, 58t, 61t, 64t, 71, 76bl, 77t, 95, 98m, 101tr, 111m, 122m, 125t, 130t, 150/151, 152m, 180r; T. Stankiewicz, München: 3I, 6tl, 7tl, 8bm, 12tl, 12mr, 14/15m, 16bl, 17tl, 19b, 22/23 background, 27m, 50/51, 51br, 54tr, 56tl, 59br, 63t, 64b, 72/73b, 73t, 78, 80, 84tl, 84/85, 97b, 99ml, 100/101, 104, 105m, 119, 123b, 132t, 132b, 143b, 146b, 152t, 155, 174/175; Hanna Wagner, Wörth: 8bl, 25tl, 25tr, 30b, 74mr, 75b, 99t, 107b, 108t, 120, 125b, 130b, 148; T.P. Widmann, Regensburg: 31br, 58b, 62b, 102b, 103t, 106, 110, 151

SPIRAL GUIDE

Questionnaire

Dear Traveller
Your comments, opinions and recommendations are very important to us. So please help us to improve our travel guides by taking a few minutes to complete this simple questionnaire.

You do not need a stamp (unless posted outside the UK). If you do not want to remove this page from your guide, then photocopy it or write your answers on a plain sheet of paper.

***Send to:* The Editor, Spiral Guides, AA World Travel Guides, FREEPOST SCE 4598, Basingstoke RG21 4GY.**

Your recommendations...

We always encourage readers' recommendations for restaurants, night-life or shopping – if your recommendation is used in the next edition of the guide, we will send you a FREE AA Spiral Guide of your choice. Please state below the establishment name, location and your reasons for recommending it.

____

____

____

____

____

Please send me AA Spiral ______________________________
(see list of titles inside the back cover)

About this guide...

Which title did you buy?

______________________________ AA Spiral

Where did you buy it? ______________________________

When? mm/ y y

Why did you choose an AA Spiral Guide? ______________________________

____

____

____

____

Did this guide meet your expectations?

Exceeded ☐ Met all ☐ Met most ☐ Fell below ☐

Please give your reasons ______________________________

____

____

____

____

continued on next page...

Were there any aspects of this guide that you particularly liked?

____

____

____

____

____

Is there anything we could have done better?

____

____

____

____

About you…

Name (Mr/Mrs/Ms) ______________________________

Address ______________________________

____

______________________ **Postcode** ______________

Daytime tel no ______________________ **email** ______________

Please *only* give us your email address and mobile phone number if you wish to hear from us about other products and services from the AA and partners by email or text or mms.

Which age group are you in?

Under 25 ☐ **25–34** ☐ **35–44** ☐ **45–54** ☐ **55–64** ☐ **65+** ☐

How many trips do you make a year?

Less than one ☐ **One** ☐ **Two** ☐ **Three or more** ☐

Are you an AA member? Yes ☐ **No** ☐

About your trip…

When did you book? mm/ y y **When did you travel?** mm/ y y

How long did you stay? ______________________________

Was it for business or leisure? ______________________________

Did you buy any other travel guides for your trip? ☐ **Yes** ☐ **No**

If yes, which ones? ______________________________

____

Thank you for taking the time to complete this questionnaire. Please send it to us as soon as possible, and remember, you do not need a stamp (unless posted outside the UK).